THE MARRIAG

The

WOMEN IN CULTURE AND SOCIETY
A SERIES EDITED BY CATHARINE R. STIMPSON

THE UNIVERSITY
OF CHICAGO PRESS

CHICAGO AND
LONDON

Marriage Exchange

PROPERTY, SOCIAL PLACE, AND GENDER IN CITIES OF
THE LOW COUNTRIES, 1300–1550

Martha C. Howell

MARTHA C. HOWELL is professor of history at Columbia University. She is the author of *Women, Production, and Patriarchy in Late Medieval Cities* (1986), also published by the University of Chicago Press.

The University of Chicago Press, Chicago 60637
The University of Chicago Press, Ltd., London
© 1998 by Martha C. Howell
All rights reserved. Published 1998
Printed in the United States of America
07 06 05 04 03 02 01 00 99 98   1 2 3 4 5

ISBN: 0-226-35515-2 (cloth)
ISBN: 0-226-35516-0 (paper)

Library of Congress Cataloging-in-Publication Data

Howell, Martha C.
    The marriage exchange : property, social place, and gender in
cities of the Low Countries, 1300–1550 / Martha C. Howell.
        p.   cm.—(Women in culture and society)
    Includes bibliographical references and index.
    ISBN 0-226-35515-2 (cloth : alk. paper).—ISBN 0-226-35516-0
(pbk. : alk. paper)
    1. Marital property—Flanders—History.   2. Husband and wife—
Flanders—History.   3. Marital property—France—Douai—History.
4. Husband and wife—France—Douai—History.   5. Law, Medieval.
I. Title.   II. Series.
KJC1162.H69   1998
346.44′280166—dc21   97-37905
                                                                                        CIP

CONTENTS

Today, few tourists sign up for trips to Douai, an industrial city in northern France. Historians know better. For Douai was once a powerhouse, a producer of textiles and a pioneering commercial center. It also created and then preserved an extraordinary municipal archive. Martha Howell, the distinguished historian, has explored this rich deposit of parchment and paper. The result is *The Marriage Exchange*, an important account of the evolution of the modern society and capitalism.

In 1300, Douai was one of the largest cities in the southern Low Countries, with a population of between 15,000 and 20,000. Then, between 1300 and 1550, it went through profound changes. To be sure, it never ceased to live by and for the market. If the assets of traditional Europe were in land, those of Douai were in urban real estate, inventories, tools, equipment, clothing, and cash. Nevertheless, the Douai of 1300 was not the Douai of 1550. Economically, prefiguring the American Rust Belt, it lost its dominant manufacturing position. If the city was to survive, it had to develop new industries, among them the grain trade. Politically, wars and other upheavals constricted its autonomy. Demographically, diseases such as the plague of the fourteenth century decimated its population. The survivors married, remarried, and remarried again.

Howell's first great achievement is to place changes in Douai's legal system in this historical context. She focuses on marital property law as the crucial nexus of law, economic goods, family, and gender. Howell argues that the law is not simply a way in which a powerful class enforces its interests. Nor is it a neat mirror image of a society that tells us what life actually meant to its people. Rather, the law embodies a "social logic" or "a social imaginary" to which people aspire and which they eventually establish, often after a struggle, through private acts and social practices.

Once people construct the law, the law in turn constructs their sense of social possibility.

Because wealth shifted constantly in form and value for the market-driven Douaisiens, they had to think more carefully than most Europeans about its control during their lives and its dispensation after their death. Marital and inheritance laws were their instruments. Slowly, unsystematically, often living with contradictions and hybridity, Douaisiens moved from a system of unwritten customs to one of written contracts. This meant much more than a shift from one technology of literacy to another. The former system worked for a household economy that needed the productive capacities of both husband and wife. Property, Douaisiens thought, properly went to a surviving spouse. The latter system worked for an economy more concerned with preserving than acquiring wealth, with stabilizing what people owned in unstable times. Property, the Douaisiens now thought, properly went to children, the surviving descendants of a male-identified line.

Howell's next great achievement is to unravel the connections among gender and these two legal systems. The systems overlapped in their assumptions that the household ought to be a nuclear unit consisting of husband, wife, children, and servants; that ties between parents and children ought to be strong; and that distinctions ought to exist between men and women, among them the distinction that men dominated women. However, the legal systems differed in their constructions of femininity. If customs projected women as creators of wealth, written contracts projected them as carriers of wealth. Marriage was seen no longer as a productive economic unit but as an affectionate, passionate union. Women were less actors in the market than creatures of the heart.

To her notable scholarship, Howell adds a strong and attractive faith in individual human beings as willful persons. I mean this in a double sense. First, both women and men wrote wills, and about half of Howell's sample of testators were women. Although a will is a formal document that must follow certain generic requirements, it is also a quasi-autobiographical act. In dictating what should happen to one's property after death, a will implicitly reveals one's values in life. Second, human beings exercise will. As much as her evidence permits, Howell shows people making choices within their circumstances, leaving, for example, featherbeds to two nephews but a "best bed" to a godson. In doing so, people break loose from the constrictions of both gender roles and law. These escapes can alarm others and disrupt social order. Indeed, Howell suggests that some Douaisien laws of marital property were meant to curb women's potential willfulness. Nevertheless, disruptions happen, and societies must respond to them, no matter how begrudgingly.

In 1986, Howell's *Women, Production, and Patriarchy in Late Medieval Cities* was published. Together, her two books illuminate the origins of modern societies and economies. Howell consciously and conscientiously limits their scope to Western Europe. However, as capitalism goes global so riotously and exuberantly, its Western European history has international significance. The archive of Douai echoes more widely than the Douaisiens might ever have imagined as they figured out their marriage contracts and last wills and testaments.

Catharine R. Stimpson

I have accumulated many debts in writing this book, and it is a pleasure to acknowledge the help I have received and to thank those who helped.

A fellowship from the Fulbright-Hays Foundation launched this project; leaves supported by a fellowship from the ACLS and by Columbia University allowed me to complete it. My work in Douai's municipal archive was expertly and kindly assisted by the municipal archivist, Mlle. Monique Mestayer, and her successor, Mon. Vincent Doom. My many stays in Douai were made infinitely more productive and pleasant by the assistant municipal archivist, Mme. Anick de Gouy. Dr. Robert Jacob, whose prior work on medieval Douai's marital property law was indispensable to my own, was unfailingly generous.

Scholars at the Rijksuniversiteit te Gent in nearby Belgium made it possible for me to undertake and complete my research in Douai. Professor dr. Walter Prevenier and his colleagues, Drs. Marc Boone and Thérèse de Hemptinne, not only provided indispensable logistical and technical support. They, along with many colleagues throughout the greater Low Countries, also offered me numerous opportunities, in various settings, to discuss my research with scholars who worked with similar materials. Few American historians entering European archives have been blessed with such support.

I was as well supported at home. Colleagues throughout North America, some of whom worked on subjects very different from mine, carefully read parts of the manuscript at various stages of production and gave wise counsel that inevitably forced me to be both clearer and more adventuresome. I would particularly like to thank Caroline Bynum, Ann Douglass, Atina Grossmann, Natalie Kampen, Barbara Hanawalt, Sarah Hanley, Barbara Harris, and Judith Walkowitz. Three colleagues at Columbia—Elizabeth Blackmar, Elaine Combs-Schilling, and Jean Howard—intervened at especially critical points in this book's history, by reading the manuscript in its entirety, making me see what I wanted to do, and helping me find a way to do it.

I am grateful as well to my editors at the University of Chicago Press. Catharine Stimpson asked for this book a long time ago, patiently waited the many years it took to finish it, and quickly acted once she had received it. Susan Bielstein intelligently guided it through the review and production process. To them, and to the anonymous readers they selected, my thanks.

Finally, I would like to thank Ned Whitney, my husband. His help did not come in the form of advice about the manuscript or assistance with its preparation. But his support for the project was constant, palpable, and essential. In our particular marriage exchange, I have done very well indeed.

NOTE ON MONEY, DATES, AND NAMES

Money

The value of the many coins that circulated in the Low Countries in this period was highly unstable. Simple wear was enough to force mild devaluations at regular intervals. Hence, the mint price for bullion (the number of coins a customer would receive for a mark of bullion) had to be raised periodically just to keep the intrinsic value of old and new coins commensurate. A more important cause of devaluation was political: this was the easiest way for a prince to raise revenue. When the currency was devalued, subjects brought their currency in to be reminted into the new, less valuable coins, and the prince took a mint fee. Essentially a tax on those who had money, debasement (unlike direct taxation) did not require the approval of any parliamentary bodies, as the right of coinage belonged unequivocally to the prince. In the twelfth and thirteenth centuries, rulers had made bargains to keep the currency strong in exchange for tax concessions. During the Hundred Years War, however, the Burgundian, English, and French kings in France all took advantage of the revenue potential of debasements. The French gros tournois was minted at 60 gros per mark of silver in 1336, but at 240 gros per mark in 1342 and at 480 gros per mark in 1355. The Burgundian and English kings also used debasement in this age, but less radically. From 1360 to 1417, currencies remained strong, but the final phase of the war was marked by rampant debasement. Because of debasement, and fear of debasement, exchange rates in Europe could be extremely volatile, changing radically from week to week or even day to day.

Not only was money minted in both gold and silver, which as commodities had a changing relationship to each other, but in a given area multiple coinages circulated. Hence, notional standards of value were developed—the moneys of account. In general, the moneys of account were originally based on actual coins, but as the bullion content of various coins was altered and the exchange values of gold and silver fluctuated, the market relationships diverged from the now fixed notional standards of the money of account. When payment was made, it was done according to current market relationships, but not necessarily with the coin of account. Indeed, moneys of account could persist even after the coin upon which they were based no longer circulated. From 1433 to 1444 the Burgundian receiver-general had to use eleven different moneys of account, some of which were based on coins that no longer circulated.

The money of account in Douai was the livre parisis monnaie de flandre (m.d.f.), which until at least 1259 mimicked the French livre parisis, after which it had been copied; afterward, the value of the Flemish livre parisis diverged. (In this book, the term *livre parisis*—or just *livre*—always means livre parisis monnaie de flandre unless otherwise noted.) By the latter half of the fourteenth century, the livre parisis m.d.f. was no longer minted, but it remained a money of account based on a fixed relationship to the Flemish gros. That coin began life as a derivative of the French gros tournois but gained a distinctive form under Louis de Nevers (1322–46). When the livre parisis m.d.f. became simply a money of account, the relationship was fixed at 1 gros = 1 sous parisis m.d.f. or 1 livre gros = 12 livres parisis m.d.f. The franc was originally a French gold coin, worth one livre tournois of silver, which continued to be known as the franc after the coin had ceased circulation. The franc was fixed in 1390 at 33 sous parisis m.d.f. or 33 gros. In 1433, the gros was fixed with relationship to all the other currencies of the Burgundian Netherlands.

As a result of trade links and military payments, many foreign currencies (and local copies) circulated in the Low Countries. The textile trade with England brought quite a few sterlings, or English pennies. In addition, there was native minting of the esterlin, which had the same silver content as the British penny. The gold noble was an English coin worth one-third of a pound sterling. The gold écu, which Philip VI of France began minting in 1337, flowed into the Low Countries as Philip paid his military allies. (In later incarnations, it existed as the courrone or écu à la courrone.) Florentine florins and Venetian ducats circulated as well and served as the principal standard of value for international trade. From 1370 on, the number of Flemish gros (and thus livre parisis m.d.f.) to the stable Venetian ducat increased steadily. In 1370 the ducat was worth about 32 gros, but in 1485 it was worth 74 gros. As late as 1354, the florin had been worth only 20 gros. This inflation should be taken into account when evaluating the values of various goods cited in this book.[1]

Dates

All dates have been changed to accord with the Gregorian calendar.

Names

All parts of proper names have been rendered with initial caps (thus, Marie Du Bosquiel and Jacques D'Auby).

Spelling follows the document itself, and names have not been standardized to accord with modern spellings. Variant spellings have been retained when quoting directly from a document (thus, "Marie Le Grand" and "Maroie Le Grande"), but the version appearing first or most commonly in the documents has been consistently used when referring to the individual in question.

1. For more detailed discussion, see Peter Spufford, *Handbook of Medieval Exchange* (London: Royal Historical Society, 1986); A. van Nieuwenhuysen, *Les finances du duc de Bourgogne, Philippe Le Hardi (1384–1404): Economie et politique* (Brussels: Editions de l'Université de Bruxelles, 1984).

Le Libert v. Rohard

In July 1434, Franchoise Rohard, the prosperous widow of a Douaisien butcher, was sued by three of her stepchildren for property left by her late husband, Jehan Le Libert.[1] Both Rohard and the plaintiffs, three of the five children born of Le Libert's first wife, were residents of Douai, one of the great commercial and industrial centers of medieval Flanders. The city had long been a major European producer of luxury woolens and was well established as a grain staple, a hub through which wheat, oats, rye, and barley from Picardy and Artois flowed northeast, to Ghent, Bruges, and Antwerp. In the mid–fifteenth century, when this case occurred, the city's economy was no longer as ebullient as it had once been, but it was still the home of a prosperous citizenry, a jewel in the crown of its present sovereign, the Duke of Burgundy.

Franchoise Rohard had married Le Libert more than thirty-two years earlier, when he was a newly widowed father of five. When the suit was brought, she was probably in her mid-fifties, the husband she had outlived had been perhaps twenty years her senior, and the eldest of her step-children was probably less than a decade younger than she. Rohard had reared her stepchildren, the youngest of whom was surely only a baby when Rohard first took responsibility for them, and she had borne at least two children of her own during her marriage to Le Libert. Rohard, like Le Libert, was from a family of butchers, and the two families had close ties to one another; two of her sisters had married Le Libert men, and both of them were also butchers, as were at least two of Le Libert's three sons.

---

1. AMD, FF 289, fols. 19–19v, 31v, and 134–37 (July 1434–February 1435).

This was, then, a suit between intimates, people closely bound to one another by shared experiences, shared property, shared affections. The three stepchildren were suing Rohard for property they may also have long shared with her, but the children clearly considered the property theirs alone, assets due them by virtue of lineal kinship. At issue were a one-fifth share in two houses and 100 francs (enough to buy another good-sized residence), which Le Libert had pledged to his five children in a document written thirty-two years earlier, in May 1402, just before his marriage to Rohard.[2] The three stepchildren thought the gift had been made to them absolutely, that it was to be divided among them, as theirs forever. One stepchild, Marie Le Libert, did not join the suit, for she had given up her one-fifth share of the real estate and the 100 francs at her own marriage eighteen years earlier, in 1416, in exchange for other property.[3] The fifth child, Wattelet, had died shortly before his father, and it was his share that was at issue in the suit. Wattelet's father had claimed it as his own when his son had died, and his father's widow, Franchoise Rohard, had in turn claimed it as hers.

In response to her stepchildren's deposition, Franchoise Rohard conceded that her late husband had made the gift to the children, but she argued that when Wattelet died "by the use and custom of the city and échevinage of Douai the part and portion in the two houses and the cash that was Wattelet's returned to his father" and that "all the goods, movables, chattels, and real property that was his [Le Libert's] belongs to me as his heir."[4] Douai's aldermen, or échevins as they were called, who judged all such matters in the city, found for the widow. They thus upheld the custom to which Franchoise Rohard had made her appeal: "It is our judgment that the defendant, as heir and representative of her deceased husband, owns the fifth part of the two houses with land and the aforesaid 100 francs as her own property."[5]

Le Libert v. Rohard is just one of thousands of disputes about marital property left by late medieval Douaisiens, a time when the city had per-

---

2. The document recording the gift has been lost; the marriage contract is catalogued as AMD, FF 600/1258 (29 May 1402).

3. AMD, FF 606/1628 (20 January 1416): marriage contract between Marie Le Libert and Jehan A Laudeluye.

4. AMD, FF 289, fols. 136 and 136v.

5. "Nous disson par jugement et . . . dites . . . le dite defenderesse come heritier et ayans cause de son dit feu mary a et doit avoir a son dite le quinte partie ces ii maisons et heritages et ces cent frans devans dis a joir come de se propre cose." (AMD, FF 289, fol. 137).

haps fifteen to twenty thousand residents, making it one of the largest in the southern Low Countries, then Europe's most densely urbanized region. The case turns on a technical question concerning succession that, as we shall see, had its specific origin in an unresolved tension between traditional customary law and new legal convention in Douai. By the end of the Middle Ages, the tension had been largely resolved, for by then old custom—the custom to which Rohard had made her successful appeal—had been all but overthrown. The dispute marks more, however, than just a moment in legal history. It marks a more profound shift as well, for this was a time when Douaisiens were reformulating the gender and social relations imbedded in marriage, and this legal dispute, like others in the Douaisien archive, were episodes in their struggle.

The archive Douaisiens created in their transition from one marital property and inheritance regime to another exposes what such legal texts so often conceal—the social and gender history that lies at the heart of the legal change. The legal reformation in Douai, in fact the very impulse to intervene in established custom, was born in and fueled by instabilities in the socioeconomic system of the period. This was the age of Europe's great commercial revolution, an age when new kinds of wealth were being created and when a new class of people, whose sociopolitical status was tied to this new wealth, were claiming space in the European landscape. The two and one-half centuries on which this book focuses were also a time of uncertainty, a time of occasional crisis brought on by disease, warfare, and economic downturns and of almost unrelenting pressure on the city's central industry, the drapery.

These uncertainties set the context for Douai's legal reform, but the argument of this book is that the reform was not a direct response to any single event in this local history, or even to a particular set of events. Instead, I have sought to place the Douaisien legal history in a larger history, one shared by many urban people throughout Europe in this age. For them, as for Douaisiens, marriage was the principal vehicle for the transfer of property between generations and the chief nexus for the formation of enduring social bonds. Marital property law was also for them the main site for the institutionalization of relations between women and men, a powerful legislator of gender norms. They too were struggling to manage wealth and social order in the face of unsettling socioeconomic conditions, brought on by commerce and the instabilities that in those days attended a life spent in trade.

Thus, the rich sources Douaisien left in their long legal reformation provide rare, even unparalleled, access to how marital property relations constructed and reconstructed the social and gender order in such commercial centers. They reveal how law sought to link people to property, and to each other through property, and they reveal as well how tortured those links could become when property had so many meanings and such uncertain value. They powerfully expose the way that gender itself—the roles and identities embedded in the terms *wife*, *widow*, and *mother* (or *husband*, *widower*, and *father*)—was constructed by property and laws of property. And they reveal how unstable those constructions were. Finally, they allow us to glimpse the ways that the cultural meanings attached to property and gender in this age were—and were not—representations of a social world where wealth changed form and value with such speed and where women such as Franchoise Rohard took active part in these transformations.

The Sources and the Legal Problem

To enter this social world through the records left in Douai, we must begin with the legal and institutional system that produced the records. The documents surrounding this case—the judicial hearing itself, the marriage contract between Le Libert and Rohard as well as those of their children and other kin, the wills they wrote, and the agreements they left that record piecemeal transfers of property *inter vivos*—are part of a huge archive in Douai similarly recording the personal financial affairs of propertied Douaisiens. From the period before 1500 alone, it contains more than five thousand marriage contracts and mutual donations, almost an equal number of wills, more than thirty thousand *contrats divers* (principally, records of sales and quitclaims), and thousands of court cases that record disputes about inheritance, succession, and marital property rights.[6] Although these are surely only a fraction of such documents that were actually written in late medieval Douai, they constitute an extraordinary collection, one probably unmatched anywhere else in the late medieval urban North.

Historians have known of these treasures since at least 1913, when Georges Espinas published his *La vie urbaine de Douai au moyen âge*, the

---

6. All but a small number of these documents are held in the Douaisien municipal archive, AMD, series FF; see the bibliography for details.

classic account of politics, economy, and social life in this period. The study is illustrated by two volumes of documents drawn from this collection, along with selected records from the administrative archive, and Espinas's many other publications about medieval Douai and the region depend on these and similar sources.[7] Since Espinas's day, however, social and cultural historians have rarely returned to the documents recording private financial affairs in Douai, principally because they are very difficult to use in any but the anecdotal way Espinas employed them.[8] The records exist as *chirographes* (separate parchments recording individual acts), as entries in registers, or as folio sheets in bound volumes. Until very recently, none of the document series was indexed and no volumes had any but the most rudimentary section headings, which were usually organized by the dates when the aldermen sat, seldom by subject or name. Over a decade ago, however, the city's archivist completed a comprehensive index and register of the marriage documents in chirographe in this collection—some five thousand contracts and mutual donations—finally making possible systematic study of this small but important portion of the archive.

Legal historians have made the best use of the marriage records, for these documents provide rare insight into the city's marital property law, an unusual version of a regional legal system that itself diverged in interesting ways from the norms elsewhere in northern Europe.[9] As we shall see, these scholars have provided the essential frame for interpreting the marriage documents in Douai, and they can also help us make sense of the voluminous collections of contrats divers, wills, and court cases regarding

---

7. George Espinas, *La vie urbaine de Douai au moyen-âge*, 4 vols. (Paris: A. Picard et fils, 1913). Espinas's major works on Douai also include *Les finances de la commune de Douai des origines au XVe siècle*, 2 vols. (Paris: A. Picard et fils, 1902), and *Les origines du capitalisme*, 4 vols. (Lille: E. Raoust, 1933–49), as well as numerous articles and edited source collections.

8. In recent years, scholars have begun, however, to mine these records more systematically. Jean Charles Desquiens has recently defended a doctoral thesis analyzing a long run of these documents for certain factual information contained in them: "Douai, topographie et société de 1224 à 1374, d'après un fonds d'archives particulier ou 'Du parchemin à l'ordinateur.'" 4 vols. (Ph.D. diss., Université de Paris, 1994). Jean-Pierre Deregnaucourt has focused on wills in a series of studies culminating in his recent doctoral thesis: "Autour de la mort à Douai: Attitudes, pratiques et croyances, 1250–1500" (Ph.D. diss., Université Catholique de Lille, 1993). Catherine Dhérent has completed two theses using, principally, marriage contracts: "Histoire sociale de la bourgeoisie de Douai de 1280 à 1350" (Ph.D. diss., Ecole des Chartes, 1981) and "Abondance et crises: Douai, ville frontière 1250–1375," 3 vols. (Ph.D. diss., Université de Paris, 1993).

9. In particular, Robert Jacob, *Les époux, le seigneur et la cité: Coutume et pratiques matrimoniales des bourgeois et paysans de France du Nord au Moyen Age* (Brussels: Publications des Facultés Universitaires Saint-Louis, 1990).

family finances. All of these, we shall also see, were as central in the Douaisien drama of marriage and property as were the marriage agreements themselves.

The technical question underlying the *Le Libert v. Rohard* case involved the relation between written documents such as the marriage contracts and wills issued by the Le Libert family and the customary law of inheritance and succession, the unwritten law of Douai. According to Douaisien customary law, marriage created a unitary conjugal fund that was, in its commitment to the marital pair, radical. It gave the head of the conjugal household absolute ownership and managerial rights over all property in the fund. During his life, the husband held these rights alone, but if the marriage had been fertile, the widow assumed these powers, as heir of her husband. She could manage, alienate, and even destroy all conjugal property as she saw fit, just as the husband could have done during his life. According to this custom, all children of either surviving spouse, no matter of what marriage they had been born, were the equal heirs if the parent died intestate (without a will), but the children had no control over either spouse's disposition or use of the property while he or she lived and no automatic right to interfere in any testamentary bequests the parent made before death.[10] If a property owner died without living heirs—either a spouse or children (or their spouses)—the assets reverted first to the ascendant kin (the parents) and only thereafter to siblings.

These were in many ways extraordinary provisions, and we will return to their history and their complexities in the chapters to follow, especially in chapter 1, which focuses on the legal reformation itself. For all its idiosyncrasies, however, this custom was loyally upheld in Douai, by échevin and ordinary citizen alike, until the very end of the Middle Ages, and it was to these norms that Franchoise Rohard made her successful appeal against her three stepchildren. Under custom, Wattelet's property had ascended to his father, since Wattelet had died without having married or having produced legitimate offspring. Jehan Le Libert's property, in turn, had passed to Rohard when he died, for as his widow she was treated as his customary heir. By the custom of Douai alone, then, Rohard was perfectly within her rights to claim the property, and the échevins were perfectly correct to grant her the property.

But custom did not rule alone in this case, for in the years preceding

---

10. If a marriage had not been fertile (if no live birth had occurred), the surviving spouse was heir to only half the estate, and the other half passed to the natal family of the deceased spouse.

the suit the Le Libert family had issued many written documents explicitly intended to overrule custom. Jehan Le Libert's 1402 gift of the houses and cash, which had been recorded in the same month as the marriage contract he made with Rohard, seems to have been written precisely to assure that the property would pass to the children at his death, that it would be excluded from the conjugal fund being established by his new marriage.[11] The marriage contract between Rohard and Le Libert had implicitly endorsed the transfer of the goods out of the new conjugal fund, for it had not mentioned the properties, either as part of the goods Le Libert would contribute to the marriage or as a reserved portion of the estate. The 1416 marriage contract of Marie Le Libert, Jehan Le Libert's daughter from his first marriage, had also implicitly acknowledged her ownership of these properties, by recognizing her rights to trade her share in them for a marriage portion.[12]

To judge from these documents alone, all of the parties to this case thought that Le Libert had intended the children of his first marriage to have these properties, and none of them disputed the justice of this gift. Even in the court case of 1434–35, Rohard did not claim otherwise. Her assertion was simply that the properties had reverted to Le Libert after his son's death and then to her. In her interpretation, Le Libert's intentions had been fulfilled when Wattelet was given his share of the property; what happened to the assets after Wattelet's death was a matter for custom, not a matter for the document, since it had said nothing about the properties' disposition at Wattelet's death.

Although we, along with Douai's échevins, might concede that Rohard had the law on her side in claiming that Wattelet's estate had rightfully passed to Le Libert, we might pause longer before granting Rohard's claim that she was, as custom decreed, Le Libert's heir. She had, after all, written a marriage contract when she wed Le Libert, and that document granted her no such status. It provided her only return of the property she had

---

11. The document has not survived. The date of the transfer—during the same month as the marriage of Le Libert and Rohard (presumably *before* the May 29 date of the marriage contract)—seems to support the children's interpretation. The children also argued that Jehan Le Libert did not have the right to the share he had given Wattelet, for the father should have had only lifetime use, not ownership, of his deceased son's property, and the property of Wattelet should have come to them when Jehan Le Libert died: "Et non est le dit Jehan Le Libert que viagier seulement Et a cest cause et par ce quil avoit joy desdis heritage sen vie durant il estoit tenu de paier et rendu retournes viagerment les dis maison en fin de son vie": AMD, FF 289, fol. 134v.

12. AMD, FF 606/1628 (20 January 1416).

brought to the marriage, along with an increase on it, in this case another 200 francs.

Yet Rohard seems to have been right on this point as well. It had long been and would long remain the practice in Douai that widows married under contract were not obligated to accept as their widow's portion the distributions promised in their marriage contracts. Instead, they could elect to "stay" ("demeurer" or "rester" in the French texts) in their husbands' estates. Just what it meant to "stay" was, however, never made clear in the records Douaisiens have left. In some cases the term appears to have implied only use (usufruct) of the property, not ownership of it. In other cases, however, it was interpreted to mean ownership, exactly the rights custom allowed widows. This was Rohard's claim—that in choosing to stay in the estate, she had the same rights as a woman married under custom, that she was her husband's heir.[13] The échevins upheld her.

We do not know exactly what Rohard did with the property she inherited. We do know, however, that soon after the settlement, she made a generous marriage gift to Marguerite, a daughter of her marriage to Jehan Le Libert, and we might assume that Marguerite was thus, indirectly, the deceased Wattelet's beneficiary.[14] We might also suppose that some of it also went to a son, Alixandre, who married just three years later and went on to found a prosperous dynasty of artisan-entrepreneurs and to serve the city as échevin.[15] We might, of course, speculate that had Jehan Le Libert lived to see his estate used in this way, he would not have objected. Both Marguerite and Alixandre were his children, after all, and he may have thought them worthier than the four children of his first marriage who had already received their original shares. But the three children who sued to reclaim their brother's property would certainly not have agreed. The property had explicitly been given to them, clear evidence, they charged, that Rohard and her children had no rights to their brother's money. Unsaid, but surely understood by everyone in the case, was a fur-

---

13. Thus, to judge from the outcome of *Le Libert v. Rohard*, widows married under contract in Douai had the best of both worlds. They could choose to exit the estate, taking their own property plus the contracted increase—before any creditors claimed their shares—if that option was preferable. Or they could renounce their claims to the payments and stay in their husbands' estates, with full obligations for the debts of the estate. For a discussion of the implications of this choice, see Jacob, *Les époux*, 165–66 and 181–89, chapter 1 below, and Appendix A.

14. AMD, FF 613/2059 (22 September 1435).

15. AMD, FF 614/2159 (10 November 1438).

ther argument. The property Le Libert had left for the children of his first marriage could be considered the portion of the conjugal fund attributable to Le Libert's deceased wife, roughly her "share" in their conjugal goods. By sequestering the houses and cash as he had and marking it for his first wife's children, Le Libert had, in effect, recognized that their mother had rights in the fund and that her children inherited her rights. By claiming those properties as her own, Rohard was thus trespassing on the rights of Le Libert's first wife.

The case of *Le Libert v. Rohard* is an illuminating episode in Douai's transition from one form of marital property law to another, from what legal historians have characterized as an aggressively "conjugal" system to one more "lineal," even "patrilineal," in emphasis. When the reformation had been more fully accomplished, at least a century after *Le Libert v. Rohard*, Douaisiens had in effect abandoned the old notions that allowed Franchoise Rohard the privileges she won in court. Under the law Douaisiens eventually fashioned, the property originally left to Wattelet would have been divided among the surviving children when Wattelet died, thus not even ascending to his father and certainly never passing to Rohard, the woman he married after Wattelet's mother had died. Thus, under the law Douaisiens would adopt, the conjugal pair would be displaced, and lineal kin, represented by children and parents, would take firmer control of marital property. Simultaneously, widows would lose full authority over their husband's estate, for it would come to pass that widows who chose to "stay" in their husbands' estates would do so not as their full heirs but only as dowagers (i.e., as holders of rights to the income from the property rather than the property itself; at the dowager's death, the property passed to predetermined heirs). Women would not be the only losers, however. Husbands would give up some of the autonomy they had enjoyed as heads of household, for they would not be allowed to do as they wished with the property their wives had brought to the marriage; they would be obligated to hold it or its equivalent aside, along with the promised increase on it, for the widow's portion.

The legal transition was not an easy one. The reform took about three hundred years, beginning some time during the thirteenth century and not ending until late in the sixteenth, even into the seventeenth, century. The reform was not the work of higher courts, learned lawyers, or superior political authorities. It was accomplished by Douaisiens themselves over long years of experimentation, by means of documents precisely like those that make up *Le Libert v. Rohard,* and the history progressed unevenly and by unexpected routes. The peculiarities of this legal history are necessarily part of the story I will tell in the chapters to follow, but my interest is in the social and gender history the legal history can reveal, not in law itself. Thus, while beginning with the technicalities of law in Douai, this book concentrates on the world in which Douai's custom and the legal norms that eventually replaced it both acquired and gave meaning, the world in which people combined assets at marriage, shared them during wedlock, parceled them out at birth and death, and then recombined them into new households.

Methodologies

This book is an effort to tease social and gender meaning out of the legal sources left in the wake of this reformation: to reveal what it meant in Douaisien social life and to the relations among Douaisien men and women that people once married and passed property according to a conjugally inflected marital property regime and then later followed a more separatist regime. As historians very well know, however, it is no easy task to derive social meaning from law. By their nature, legal sources are formulaic, normative, sometimes very distant from the social world they purport to regulate, and always hostile to inquiries about social meaning. They are often imported from other cultures and are little understood (or little observed) in their new homes. Even when homegrown, as I will argue the Douaisien laws were, they reveal almost nothing directly about intentionality, interest, or effect, almost nothing, that is, about the very issues on which statements about social meaning turn. They tell us, for example, that inheriting widows such as Franchoise Rohard could exist in Douai, but they leave us utterly ignorant about how the figure of the inheriting widow bespoke a certain conception of gender, about how this inheritance system sustained or disrupted a particular social order, or about how it benefitted particular individuals.

Despite these difficulties, some legal historians have nonetheless argued as though the property relations inscribed in marital property law mirrored social and gender relations. In such an interpretation, the custom with which Douaisiens began the late Middle Ages was "egalitarian" because it made widows the equal of widowers and made daughters and sons equal heirs in intestate successions. By extension, women were more "equal" in such a society than in one where they did not inherit or succeed as men did. In contrast, more "lineal" regimes were "hierarchical" because they gave men—especially men in the father's line—more property rights.[16] The chapters that follow implicitly pursue this issue, and in chapter 8, where I place the Douaisien regimes in a larger historical context, I explicitly return to this argument. Here let me simply point out that "egalitarian" does not correctly characterize the radical equivalence between husband and wife imposed by Douaisien custom or the relative position of children in inheritance; nor is the term "hierarchical" sufficiently precise to describe the particular kind of inequalities structured by the new legal regime propertied Douaisiens adopted in these centuries.

Legal historians are not alone, however, in venturing to link law with social structure. Social historians of the family have also frequently posited connections between the two, although they tend to describe different kinds of connections and to make their arguments more implicitly than explicitly. In these kinds of arguments, marital property relations are treated as one of the many components that make up family "structure," and "structure," in turn, is bound up with the quality of personal relations among family members. In general, historians working in this way begin by pointing out that structural shifts of momentous importance occurred in the late medieval and early modern centuries, for this was the age that gave birth to what has come to be called the "European nuclear family." Usually, this family unit is defined demographically, as a family composed of a conjugal pair who lived with their minor children and, at most, a

16. Legal historians regularly characterize community property regimes, for example, as "egalitarian." See, for example, Paul Ourliac and Jehan de Malafosse, *Le droit familial*, vol. 3 of *Histoire du droit privé* (Paris: Presses universitaires de France, 1968–1971), and Philippe Godding, *Le droit privé dans les Pays-Bas meridionaux du 12e au 18e siècle*, in *Mémoires de la Classe des Lettres, Collection in 4°*, 2d ser., pt. 1 (Brussels: Académie royale de Belgique, 1987), especially pt. 3, chap. 3. Also see Jean Gilissen, "Le statut de la femme dans l'ancien droit belge," in *La Femme, Recueils de la Société de Jean Bodin pour l'histoire comparative des institutions*, vol. 12 (Brussels: Editions de la librarie encyclopédique, 1962). As several scholars have pointed out, however, such terms have meaning only from the fixed perspectives of certain categories of individuals and thus do not accurately describe the tendencies of any system with respect to *all* actors—sons, daughters, husbands and wives, widows and widowers. See, for example, David Sabean's warning in "Aspects of Kinship Behavior and Property in Rural Western European before 1800," in *Family and Inheritance: Rural Society in Western Europe, 1200–1800*, ed. Jack Goody, Joan Thirsk, and E. P. Thompson (Cambridge: Cambridge University Press, 1976), 96–112. In his "Family Structure and Inheritance Customs in Sixteenth Century France," in *Family and Inheritance*, to mention one example that illustrates the imprecision of any such terms, Emmanuel Le Roy Ladurie, following Jean Yver, labels the Norman customs "egalitarian" *and* "lineal"—"egalitarian" in that all *sons* inherit equally and "lineal" in that the *male* lineage is preferred over the father himself and over the mother's lineage.

dependent relative or two, along with servants.[17] But the term is generally understood in an economic and legal sense as well—nuclear families are not just self-contained residential units but are, in addition, independent property-holding units headed by the conjugal pair, which founds and governs the nuclear household. It is no accident, these scholars have gone on to argue, that the epoch in which this family structure took shape was also the age that gave birth to the "companionate" or "affectionate" marriage that so typifies the West, the marriage based on mutual consent, on partnership, even on love.[18] The two developments are, moreover, often thought to be related: household "nuclearity," in most narratives, is closely associated with conjugal "affection."[19]

The Douaisien evidence, however, makes explicit a problem that is often obscured in this discussion: nuclearity in the demographic sense does not presuppose a specific legal or economic nuclearity, and it has even less direct implications for the emotional content of married life. All the Douaisiens households we will encounter in this book, whether rich or not-so-rich, were nuclear in demographic structure in its most literal sense, in that they were headed by a single conjugal pair and contained only the couple, their offspring, and servants. But Douaisien families became less, not more, nuclear in both the legal and the economic sense as the fourteenth century slid into the fifteenth and then the sixteenth. The legal reformation that occurred in these centuries separated property be-

17. This system was first identified by J. Hajnal in "European Marriage Patterns in Perspective," in *Population in History: Essays in Historical Demography,* ed. D. V. Glass and D. E. C. Eversley (London: E. Arnold, 1965), and has been most thoroughly investigated by the so-called Cambridge school of social historians. See, in particular, Peter Laslett and Richard Wall, eds., *Household and Family in Past Time: Comparative Studies in the Size and Structure of the Domestic Group over the Last Three Centuries in England, France, Serbia, Japan and Colonial North America, with Further Materials from Western Europe* (Cambridge: Cambridge University Press, 1972).

18. The notion of "affective individualism" was introduced by Lawrence Stone, *The Family, Sex, and Marriage 1500–1800* (abridged ed., Harmondsworth, England: Penguin Books, 1985).

19. The argument has been most forcefully made for late medieval and early modern England. See, in particular, Alan MacFarlane, *Marriage and Love in England: Modes of Reproduction, 1380–1840* (Oxford: Blackwell, 1986). Also see Barbara Hanawalt, *The Ties That Bound: Peasant Families in Medieval England* (Oxford: Oxford University Press, 1986), and Richard Houlbrooke, *The English Family 1450–1700* (London: Longman, 1984); for additional references, see note 21, below. For a contrasting view, one that emphasizes the tensions that developed in marriage in late medieval urban cultures of Flanders, see Myriam Greilsammer, *L'envers du tableau: Mariage et maternité en Flandre médiévale* (Paris: Armand Colin, 1990). For a critique of the notion of "nuclearity" itself and the idea that an ostensibly "nuclear" domestic structure is associated with affectionate conjugal relations, see Miranda Chaytor, "Household and Kinship: Ryton in the Late Sixteenth and Seventeenth Centuries," *History Workshop* 10 (1980): 25–60.

tween husband and wife, tended to exclude women from certain manage-rial tasks they had once shared with men, and gave men greater responsi-bilities for the financial well-being of children.[20] Yet, only the legal records produced by the new marital property law provide any evidence that Dou-aisiens considered conjugal bonds "companionate" or "affectionate." To judge from this evidence alone, then, we would have to argue that demo-graphic nuclearity in itself has no particular implications for personal rela-tions of the affectionate kind and that it is only in situations where marital property arrangements are *less* nuclear that we encounter a rhetoric about marital love.[21]

20. However perplexing it may be to find Douaisiens shifting from a more conjugally inflected, a more "nuclear," form of marital property law to one less so just when the nuclear family is thought to have taken firm demographic shape in Europe, they were not the only people to undertake such an odyssey in this period. As part of a social process that some historians have called "lineal regrouping," many Europeans of the day made similar changes in the way property was managed in marriage and passed at death.

For this argument, see Henri Bresc, "Europe: Town and Country (Thirteenth–Fifteenth Cen-tury)," in *A History of the Family*, vol. 1, 430–66 (Cambridge: Polity and Blackwell, 1996), p. 432:

Students of the later medieval centuries long ago gave the lie to the general impression that the family progressed steadily from the extended model of the early Middle Ages to the nuclear family of modern Europe. On the contrary, family relationships were consolidated among the lower orders of society, as legal texts show; historians call the process 'linear regrouping' and connect it with the demographic crisis in particular the void following on the Black Death and the recurrences of plague in both town and country. We are thus faced with two competing explanations: a gradual juristic liberation of the individual as he became progressively more aware of his rights and master of his fate; or a malleable set of relationships manipulated by an extended family which used them to occupy new territory, gather capital and useful connec-tions, and build up a power base.

Also see, for a close study of this process in practice, Anthony Molho, *Marriage Alliance in Late Medieval Florence* (Cambridge: Harvard University Press, 1994).

21. Stone's own argument is consistent here. He argued that marriages of an "affectionate" kind developed in the late seventeenth and eighteenth centuries and that the nuclear household of earlier decades was sternly "patriarchal," both in structure and emotional content. In this view, it was not until the father's domestic authority had been eroded as the state assumed many of the functions once performed by the household, as the market became more clearly differentiated from the household, and as a more sentimental notion of marriage took hold, that marriages of the kind historians have labeled affectionate or companionate were common. Such marriages did not originate, however, in the nuclear households of ordinary people—people like the Le Libert family—but first took root among Europe's gentry and *haute bourgeoisie,* only later becoming the norm for Europeans of lower social rank.

While acknowledging the patriarchal character of the late medieval and early modern family, both elite and ordinary, some scholars have also thought these families not incompatible with "affectionate" interpersonal relations. See, for example, Steven Ozment, *When Fathers Ruled: Fam-ily Life in Reformation Europe* (Cambridge: Harvard University Press, 1983), and idem, *Magdalena and Balthasar: An Intimate Portrait of Life in 16th Century Europe* (New York: Simon and Schuster, 1986). Also see Michael Mitterauer and Reinhard Sieder, *The European Family: Patriarchy to Partnership from the Middle Ages to the Present,* trans. Karla Oosterveen and Manfred Horzinger

In this study I have not presumed a direct relationship between marital property or inheritance rules and social or gender meaning. Rather, I have sought to uncover such meanings, treating the legal sources from Douai as records of a struggle both to capture a vision of social and gender order and to impose it, rather than as direct representations of social experience. To do so, I have taken several routes. Let me briefly review the various ways I have approached these sources and the principal methodological issues my inquiry raises.

I began as historians usually begin, asking questions about the genesis of the legal norm and the fit between the legal norm and social practice, questions that essentially concern enforcement, intentionality, interest, and benefit. In doing so, I assumed that legal norms to some extent reflect the interests and the intentions of those who write the law. I also assumed that the effects of law must be measured partly in terms of enforcement. We must know who wrote the law, how it was written, and why they wrote it. We must know whether legal norms were generally followed, by whom, and when.

To ask questions in this way, however, is risky. The approach too easily leads us to assume that interest, benefit, and intention can be collapsed— that those who write law do so in their own interests (directly or indirectly) and that the actual beneficiaries of a particular legal norm are the intended beneficiaries of it. In fact, most historians readily acknowledge, this is rarely if ever so. As we shall see, there is little evidence from Douai that a single set of "interests" was at stake in this city's marital regime or in its transformation. No single social group "authored" the legal norms and it is not clear that the reform "benefitted" or advantaged a single group of people. There is no evidence, for example, that custom's "intention" was to benefit widows such as Franchoise Rohard. There is ample evidence, however, that many widows in Rohard's position did *not* in truth benefit from the rule that made them heirs of their husbands' estates, for with

---

(Chicago: University of Chicago Press, 1983); David Herlihy, *Medieval Households* (Cambridge: Harvard University Press, 1985); idem, "Family," *American Historical Review* 96, no. 1 (1991), 1–16; Barbara B. Diefendorf, "Give Us Back Our Children: Patriarchal Authority and Parental Consent to Religious Vocation in Early Counter-Reformation France," *The Journal of Modern History* 68, no. 2 (June 1996): 265–308; and Jean Delumeau and Daniel Roche, eds., *Histoires des pères et de la paternité* (Paris: Larousse, 1990).

Jeffrey R. Watt, *The Making of Modern Marriage: Matrimonial Control and the Rise of Sentiment in Neuchâtel, 1550–1800* (Ithaca, N.Y.: Cornell University Press, 1992) summarizes the debate about the emotional content of family life in the early modern period. For additional references, see chapters 6, 8, and the conclusion of this book.

the assets came liabilities. Many widows in Rohard's position found themselves with businesses they could not manage, shops they could not operate, debts they could not pay, and children they could not support. Widows so burdened, it is fair to say, would have been delighted to have escaped the privileges for which Franchoise Rohard fought.

This approach suffers from another, related weakness as well. It assumes that questions about social meaning can be answered from the top down—that law is the inscription of the powerful, that deviation from the legislated norm is "resistance" to the powerful, that adherence to the law is "compliance," that is, an effect of enforcement. Such an approach can thus obscure the complex relations between legal norms and culture and can reduce law to coercion and its legislators to forces outside the culture.

There is still another related reason, one more specific to this time and place, for caution in reading Douai's legal history as a story of interests being imposed. Law in this culture, family law above all, was not yet institutionalized as it would gradually be from about 1500 on. As a result, it was extraordinarily malleable, not just in Douai but throughout Europe. As a result we cannot usefully pose questions of authorship in this time and place as we might in another. This does not mean, however, that we must thereby abandon quests for historical significance. In fact, I would argue that thanks to the malleability of law in this age, a malleability that derived from law's susceptibility to social pressures, the records of family law we have from this era acquire a historical importance that such texts could not have had in many others. Because the "logic" of marital property law was in this age more social than juridical, more time-bound and concrete than atemporal and abstract, the legal texts that survive register social and cultural struggles with a directness they could elsewhere seldom have had. The late medieval period itself thus emerges less as the transitional moment in the history of marital property law it is often imagined to be, a confusing time when incoherent practice was gradually codified into learned principle, and more as an epoch with special importance in the social history of law.

Hence, while I have not jettisoned the usual tools of the historian in this inquiry, I have not treated Douai's marital property law simply as a set of rules handed down from on high. I have also thought about the legal records as a kind of social discourse. I have attempted to read the rules about marriage, property, and inheritance operative in Douai as expressions of cultural norms themselves, thus often leaving aside questions of origin, agency, and power and focusing instead on culture itself, culture as a system of social practices that produce meanings. Here my emphasis was not on who did what and why, but on how the system "worked."

This approach reveals the old Douaisien custom to have been an expression of a social logic based on a nuclear household that organized economic, social, and biological reproduction. The widow's right in Douaisien custom, which treated women as the equivalents of men (at least at the moment of succession), thus functioned to serve the larger needs of the social whole.[22] Conversely, the new marital property regime that eliminated this widow's right imagined a slightly different kind of household, with a different role in creating social order. Its treatment of widows reflected this new logic; in this social imaginary, widows had different needs than widowers and were thus granted distinctive kinds of support.

This approach has several advantages. It makes it possible to appreciate why the course of legal reform in Douai was so long and tortured, and even more usefully, it exposes issues of social and gender order that are fundamentally at stake in marital property law but are invisible if one looks only for authors, interests, beneficiaries, and intentions. The approach also has risks of its own, however, for it is inherently both functionalist and circular. In searching for the logic of a marital property system, we are assuming that a coherent society with unitary needs inscribes itself in its rules about marriage and, at the same time, that the rules themselves give coherence to the society, in fact that they constitute it as a society.[23]

One effect of this approach is to obscure the contradictions and inconsistencies that inhere in legal codes and the potentially multiple, always incommensurate, social imaginaries they seek to inscribe. Let us look, by way of example, at the widow's rights that Franchoise Rohard claimed. Reading this provision for its logic, we might say—as I will in fact say— that the provision assured the continuation of the household enterprise

---

22. For the anthropological reasoning that informs my own here, see the seminal text by Claude Lévi-Strauss, *The Elementary Structures of Kinship*, trans. J. H. Bell and J. R. von Sturmer and ed. R. Needham (Boston: Beacon Press, 1969). Also see Jack Goody, *Production and Reproduction: A Comparative Study of the Domestic Domain* (Cambridge: Cambridge University Press, 1976).

23. In practice, let me immediately acknowledge, anthropologists, to whom we owe this notion of law as social logic, have been considerably more sophisticated. They have frequently exposed the ways that societies contain competing, sometimes totally contradictory "logics," that the rules that are inscribed are in some sense impositions—either of dominant classes or, even, of the anthropologists themselves. Still, the basic insight prevails: normative "rules," say, about marriage payments, encode an operative social logic. See John Comaroff, introduction to *The Meaning of Marriage Payments* (London: Academic Press, 1980).

beyond the life of the husband. Correct as this reading may be, it ignores the fact that "inheriting" widows were empowered to sell, give away, or otherwise disassemble the workshop, that they might be incompetent to manage it even if they chose to do so, and that they might remarry and merge the property into other men's households. Any reading of marital property and inheritance law that assumes that the law expresses a coherent and widely shared social logic thus masks both the tensions that law itself seeks to suppress and those to which it inadvertently gives life.

Such an approach also threatens to reduce gender to a set of roles, as though Douaisien women (or men) were able simply to enact any roles assigned by the logic of the system, without regard to the way a particular role assumed a specific gender identity. In such a logic, women—to pursue the Rohard example—are either inheriting or non-inheriting widows, depending on whether the imagined social system was centered on a particular kind of nuclear household economy or not. That an "inheriting" widow does not occupy the same gender position as a "non-inheriting" widow— that the former is powerful, charged with responsibilities, encumbered, as the latter is powerless, denied responsibilities, unencumbered—does not emerge from this kind of analysis.

In short, such an approach ignores the fact that social logics create social actors. To be sure, these actors do not have the full agency imagined when historians think of "authors" and their "intentions," but they nevertheless have the capacity to enact, to enrich, and even to disrupt the system as they perform their assigned roles in it. Social logics are in practice therefore inevitably rife with tension.[24] To get at these tensions, I have thus subjected these legal documents to yet a third kind of study. I have read them, not just as inscriptions of roles, but as vehicles for establishing gender norms that, paradoxically, both constituted identity and failed to contain it. The texts in which Douaisiens recorded their legal principles, I hope to show, also scripted gender codes that sought to reduce gender to the roles assigned. Necessarily, the effort failed. Gender is not solely the product of a particular legal discourse but of multiple and competing discourses, and it thus cannot be reduced to the personal attributes necessary to a single role defined by law. Thus, we shall see, the people actually assigned these roles in late medieval Douai did not fully inhabit the gender

24. For a useful analysis of the process I have in mind, see the introduction to Nicholas B. Dirks, Geoff Eley, and Sherry B. Ortner, eds., *Culture/Power/History* (Princeton: Princeton University Press, 1993), and the essay by Sherry Ortner in the same volume.

identities scripted for them. Still worse, the law empowered these badly cast characters to perform roles other than those assigned. Thus, rather than representing or producing gender order, these legal documents captured—and intensified—the tensions attending to gender in a society that so closely linked gender meanings to property and to marriage.[25]

We see this dynamic at work when we observe, for example, how Franchoise Rohard used the authority granted by law not just to step into her husband's shoes, to use his authority to fulfill his responsibilities and address his interests, to act as "deputy husband," to use Laural Ulrich's term.[26] Women such as Rohard also performed other roles as well; Rohard was, we shall see, not just Le Libert's widow, not just the "deputy" that the *ravestissement* (the legal conditions under which property rights in the conjugal fund were transferred to the surviving spouse) seemed to assume. She was also a mother, businesswoman, stepmother, and citizen, and in each of these roles she necessarily pursued ends often quite different from those of her late husband. Yet she did so with the benefit of the powers ascribed to her as deputy husband, thus potentially threatening the very gender system that could position her as her husband's deputy. Her case illustrates as well another way that the law subverted the gender order, for it exposes the inadequacy of the gender identities created by law. No woman—not even one more eager to perform as the perfect deputy husband than Rohard might have been—could have possessed the combination of personal characteristics required of the oxymoronic "deputy husband." It is, after all, hard to imagine a woman who could totally submerge her interests in her late husband's and, simultaneously, exercise sufficient judgment and skill to manage his financial and business affairs. Inevitably, therefore, any woman in Rohard's position was inadequate—if not as deputy husband, then as woman.

Social Logics/Social Processes

This book thus moves rather eclectically from one mode of analysis to another in search of understanding about what was at stake in marital

25. On the difficult relationship between cultural texts (including legal texts) and social experience and for a balanced summary of historians' efforts in this arena, see Sarah Maza, "Stories in History: Cultural Narratives in Recent Works in European History," *American Historical Review* 101, no. 5 (December 1996) 1493–1515.

26. See Laural Thatcher Ulrich, *Goodwives: Image and Reality in the Lives of Women in Northern New England, 1650–1750* (New York: Oxford University Press, 1982).

property law in Douai in this age and, by extension, elsewhere in late medieval cities. Although borrowing from other disciplines, it is essentially a social history, a study of the social and gender order inscribed by marital property law in a time of profound change both in law and in society. It thus focuses on two questions: first, what were the social and gender implications of the various marital property regimes in Douai and, second, what motivated Douaisiens to change the law as they did.

To address the first question, I have distilled what seem to me the basic assumptions about property, social place, and gender that informed both the old and the new marital property regimes in Douai. Although I will argue that these assumptions were distinct in each regime, neither of these social imaginaries, or social logics as I have called them (discussed in chapters 4–6), is meant to represent Douaisiens' own descriptions of their actions. They serve simply as heuristic devices in my study, tools for analyzing what was at stake in each marital property regime. In fact, it is obvious that Douaisiens did not see these as two distinct logics, for they made no clear choice between them for long centuries. Rather, they combined and recombined elements of each, fashioning ad hoc, necessarily contradictory, and sometimes absurdly baroque mixtures of the two. As we shall also see, the logics of these systems were flawed; not only was each always infected by the norms and practices of the other regime, each was always internally inconsistent and always unable to reduce social complexity to legal simplicity.

In the end, however, propertied Douaisiens did move more decisively from one regime to the other, finally all but jettisoning custom and accepting a new marital property regime, albeit one that was little more consistent than the old. The second question on which this book focuses is why they did so. This inquiry, the specific focus of chapters 2, 3, and 7, turns on how the conditions of daily life in the late medieval urban North made one version of marital property law preferable to another. Cities in this age of European history were, after all, extraordinary places, and there is every reason to believe, as many observers have suggested, that marital property law in cities reflected the peculiarities of the urban condition in this age.

To begin with perhaps the most striking of these peculiarities, cities were unhealthy places, especially so in the post-1300 period, for they were fecund breeding grounds for the Plague and other diseases that then ravaged Europe. People in the cities thus died as adults, but before old age, at rates considerably above "normal," even by preindustrial standards.

Most of these adults were heads of active households—mothers and fathers of young children, artisans with busy shops, merchants with stacks of inventories and unfulfilled contracts. When they died, their most intimate survivors did not look back. Those left behind, in Douai at least, remarried quickly, they set up new households on the ruins of the former, and they brought new children into the world.

Jehan Le Libert's family is typical. He himself married twice; to judge from surviving marriage contracts alone, so did his brother's widow, two of his four known daughters, and two of his three known sons. Some of these people probably married even more often, but like many Douaisiens they may have done so without a contract, so that we have no record of the event; or they may have written a contract that has been lost. We can, therefore, be sure that what we know about the Le Libert marriages is only part of the story, that in all likelihood there were more deaths and remarriages, more children and stepchildren, more combinations and recombinations of households, property, and persons than we can know. There is no doubt at all that the average Douaisien who married was reasonably likely to begin a family with one spouse but combine it into another household five, ten, or fifteen years later, and to add another set of offspring along the way. It was almost as likely that the second spouse would survive the second marriage and then take all the children into yet a third household.[27]

It was not demography alone, and certainly not principally demography, however, that made life—and marriage—in cities different. It was, above all, commerce. A society built on trade, on the constant circulation of goods, put unusual pressure on marital property relations because commercial property's location, form, and value changed so rapidly. Men and women who married could not count on ending marriage with the assets they had had when they began; they could not even count on being able to give their children marriage gifts like those they had been given. The Le Libert family is a case in point—albeit a case that better reveals the possibilities of the system than its dangers. Jehan Le Libert was a butcher, a member of a well-established trade whose members were among the city's most prosperous citizens. Le Libert himself did not begin married

27. Some historians have argued that this demographic crisis was responsible for the shift toward more lineal marital property relations: see Bresc, "Town and Country." Also see, however, chapter 3, below, for evidence that the Douaisien shift did not tidily accord with specific demographic upheavals.

life, however, as an especially prosperous man. When he first married Ellisent Broussart in 1389, Le Libert had just a group of "biens" and "meubles" worth only 80 livres parisis, enough to buy a very small house, plus forty "biestes a laine" (sheep in fleece) to contribute to the marriage. His bride had little more: only some cloth, clothing, and some "biens" all valued at 160 livres, the price of a dwelling only a bit grander than that her husband's cash contribution to the marriage could have bought.[28]

In 1402, Le Libert remarried. His contribution to this marriage is not listed in the surviving marriage contract, but we know that at this time he had at least two houses and 100 francs (165 livres) to give to the five children Broussart had borne him, and we know that his second wife, Franchoise Rohard, was considerably better endowed at her marriage than Broussart had been at hers. Rohard brought 200 francs royaulx (330 livres) in coin, furnishings, cloth, and jewels, plus 5 rasières of land to her marriage—the francs alone were worth twice Broussart's entire contribution to her marriage. Rohard was also much better provided for in her widowhood, another measure of her relatively higher economic status: the value of the property promised her as widow, should she survive Le Libert, was about 650 livres, almost triple the 240 livres that Broussart would have received as Le Libert's widow.[29]

The marriage contracts of Le Libert's children from his first marriage confirm that the Le Libert star rose steadily for years. His daughter Marie, who married in 1416, took 70 couronnes d'or (about 140 livres) as her marriage gift instead of the one-fifth share in the two houses and the cash that would come to her when her father died.[30] The settlement, delivered in coin but claimed in terms of real estate and moneys of account to be left by her father, implies that the properties Jehan Le Libert had bequeathed his children in 1402 were worth about 700 livres, much more than the 240 livres Le Libert had been able to promise their mother for her widowhood just thirteen years earlier.

In the same year as the suit was settled (1435), another son, Nicaise Le Libert, married, both he and his bride for the second time (we do not have records of either previous marriage).[31] The contract for this marriage

---

28. AMD, FF 594/780 (11 October 1389). According to the document, the marriage had actually occurred during the previous August.

29. AMD, FF 600/1258 (29 May 1402).

30. AMD, FF 606/1628 (20 January 1416).

31. AMD, FF 613/2058 (15 September 1435).

does not list the assets Nicaise would bring to the marriage but it does list his bride's: 70 couronnes d'or (130 livres), a house, a stable, and extensive household goods. This was clearly a good marriage for Nicaise, and by the time he wrote his will eight years later, in 1443, things looked better still.[32] Nicaise was still the butcher he had said he was in his marriage contract—or at least he provided that a butcher accompany his bier at his funeral—but he was considerably richer not only than his father had been, but richer than most butchers. He left his widow the property he had promised to her in the marriage contract written in 1435, eight years previously, and he stipulated that his *héritages* (the immovable assets of his family) be divided between his two children (apparently of his first marriage) but went on to make elaborate individual bequests to the church, to his eldest son (who was, it seems, his business partner), and to various kin and friends. In addition, selected members of his parish received 57 sous; candles, votives, and lamps went to his church; 4 sous were offered for each of an unlimited number of masses; 12 rasières of grain were set aside for bread for the poor on each day his "obseques" (funeral services) were said; money was designated for the poor who attended his funeral; and 48 sous were left for the members of his craft who accompanied his bier. Hanotin, the son, also received two new houses plus his father's chief residence, another building lot in Douai, a half interest in another house, 30 sous due on an outstanding bill; numerous rents in kind and money owed Nicaise Le Libert and Hanotin jointly; several small land holdings; some luxury cloaks and outerwear; household furnishings; arms; and jewelry. A few others got special legacies as well: his wife was given all her "habis, cousus, tailles, and joiaulx" (clothing and jewels), plus a lifetime income of 12 livres parisis so long as she did not remarry; a brother received some fine clothing; his half-sister Marguerite (Rohard's daughter) was forgiven an outstanding debt.

The Le Libert story of social mobility is a happy one, surely happier than many others that occurred in fifteenth-century Douai. There is, however, something typical about their tale. The Le Libert family, like all propertied Douaisiens of the day, were traders: they exchanged houses for cash, cash for clothing, clothing for arms, arms for land. And they did so regularly. The marriage contracts and wills that we have to trace these exchanges tell only a small part of the story, but they are eloquent wit-

32. AMD, FF 875 (28 April 1443).

nesses to the ease with which property and people changed place in Douai. Le Libert himself rose several notches in economic status during his life, and his son Nicaise died a truly rich man. Jehan Le Libert's daughters were as aggressive in transforming the assets they had been given. One daughter, Marie, converted into coin the share in the houses that her father had pledged to her; another daughter, Pierronne, turned her share into a promise to pay, negotiable as nuptial vows were being exchanged but payable at an uncertain date in the future.[33] Le Libert's widow indirectly converted the share she took from Wattelet's inheritance into the gifts of "a well furnished bedstead and many other goods, movables, decorations, and furnishings for the bed chamber, along with draperies, clothing, jewels, and adornments for her body," which she gave to her daughter Marguerite at her marriage in 1435.[34] How Le Libert's son Nicaise had parlayed his part in his father's gift into the fortune he bequeathed in his will of 1443 we do not know. We do know, however, that at some point in the course of assembling these lands, rents, houses, arms, clothing, jewels, furnishings, and coin, he had traded away his share in the two houses and 100 francs that had been disputed less than a decade earlier. For their part, the sheep with which his father and mother had begun married life just fifty-three years earlier were long gone. And probably even longer forgotten.

Socioeconomic conditions particular to the fourteenth and fifteenth centuries added to the pressures inherent in economic structure. Like all the great cloth towns of the Low Countries, Douai endured a particular version of the so-called late medieval depression, for its "grande draperie," the very life blood of the city, was decimated in these years, as raw materials became harder to obtain and more dear, as demand patterns shifted, as transportation costs rose, and as new competitors emerged. Douai slipped from first, to second, still later to third rank among northern cities. Its merchant elite lost relative position to capitalists in other, more prosperous and larger cities; its artisans lost renown as makers of luxury cloths. The Douaisien social order was thus sorely tested, as social place became more difficult to obtain and still more difficult to preserve.

Douaisien customary law obviously intensified the mobility bred by demography, by commerce itself, and by the economic difficulties of the age. By making the survivor of marriage the absolute owner of marital

33. AMD, FF 607/1689 (17 December 1417).
34. AMD, FF 613/2059 (22 September 1435).

property, custom allowed the survivor to take all conjugal property when remarrying, thus moving property from household to household, from one set of natal kin (what French historians call *lignage* [lineage]) to another, along with the children of that lineage, just as Jehan Le Libert had done. The assets of one marriage, the property one man or one woman had contributed to a marriage, would thus travel with the survivor of the marriage into another household, possibly into the hands of another surviving spouse—someone like Franchoise Rohard—and then, even, into the hands of children born of the final marriage—someone like Marguerite Rohard. Most northern European laws of marital property relations and inheritance of the age permitted certain asset transfers of this kind, but none more so than the Douaisien. Douaisiens' energetic, almost nervous, attention to matters of marital property relations and inheritance, was to some extent, surely, a response to the uncertainties created by this custom and intensified by economic conditions of the age.

Still, the history of marital property law in Douai cannot be told as a simple story of cause and effect, of how social crises forced alteration of a legal regime that no longer worked. It did not happen that way. Douaisiens did not change law in response to a single economic, social, or political upset or even to a catalogue of such events; rather, they changed their law only in the most indirect, the slowest, way possible. They took so long, I will argue, precisely because they were for centuries by and large content with custom, precisely because they were reluctant to abandon a system that accorded so well with many notions of how property ought to be managed and social relations maintained and precisely because the law that replaced custom could not construct the tension-free social order they presumably desired.

Similarly, I will not claim that gender tensions alone drove the Douaisien legal reform, that Douaisiens rewrote their marital property law because, for example, custom gave widows too much authority. To be sure, custom did grant widows extraordinary powers and, as we shall explore at many points in this book, was replete with contradictions about gender relations. The *Le Libert v. Rohard* case, once again, exemplifies some of these tensions. As Le Libert's heir, Franchoise Rohard was permitted to overturn the principles of inheritance that Le Libert had himself decreed. In effect, she was able to break the bonds of kinship—to disinherit Le Libert's own children, to put hers before them, and thus to deny her step-children the social place Le Libert apparently had sought to guarantee them. Rohard did more, however, than weaken bonds of kinship. As Le

Libert's heir, she also assumed his role as manager of the patrimony. It was now she, not Le Libert or his direct descendants, who chose how money was spent, to whom it was given, when it was invested. Rohard herself seems to have had a real taste for this power. In the contract she issued for her daughter's marriage right after she had won the suit brought by her stepchildren, she promised to her daughter gifts of beds, linens, cloths, clothing, and jewelry but "of such a kind and of such a value as pleased her, not pricing them or giving an estimate of their value."[35] Even filtered through the obfuscating formulas of legal texts, Rohard's voice can be clearly heard: she will not be bound by the usual rules of marriage negotiations that allowed in-laws to judge the worth of proffered marriage gifts and to declare themselves, if satisfied, "pleased" ("contents," as the French texts usually expressed it). She will give what and how much she will; her prospective in-laws can take it or leave it.

Nevertheless, I will not argue that Douaisiens changed custom in order to rid themselves of too powerful widows or "wicked" stepmothers, for it is not at all clear that Douaisiens automatically understood gender in this way. Franchoise Rohard can perhaps make the case for me. She had, let us remember, been married to Jehan Le Libert for as many as thirty-two years before he died; she had reared his children; she had born him at least two more; she had linked his trade with those of her father and brothers. If anyone had rights to Le Libert's estate, we might argue, she did. The Le Libert children themselves might even have agreed, for to judge from the records we have, the suit brought by Rohard's stepchildren did not inaugurate a bitter family feud. We know from Nicaise Le Libert's will that he had loaned money to his half sister, the very same Marguerite whose marriage portion had earlier been enriched by the money Wattelet had left; we also know that Nicaise felt generous enough toward her to forgive the debt when he wrote his will eight years after her marriage. Nicaise also, it seems, quickly restored good relations with his stepmother, for in 1436, about two years after the suit had begun, the two appeared together as joint plaintiffs in a civil suit against another Douaisien.[36] Rather than the cruel stepmother, the usurper and interloper, the *marâtre* of the French fairy tale, Franchoise Rohard might better be thought of— and have been thought of by her contemporaries—as *belle-mère*, the term

35. AMD, FF 613/2059 (22 September 1435).
36. AMD, FF 291, fols. 77, 119, 122v, 123v, 126v, 130, and 130v (1436).

they normally used in referring to women who, like her, had assumed the duties of biological parenthood and were honored for their labors.

Thus, I will insist that Douaisiens were not fashioning new marital property law because the old was inherently unsuitable, because it suddenly seemed so in moments of economic crisis, because it threatened to destabilize the gender order, or because it could not be adapted to meet individual needs. Instead, I will argue that Douaisiens reformulated their law as they developed, in a complex socioeconomic matrix that made change both possible and desirable, a matrix of different social practices that subtly changed the meanings of property, social place, and gender and changed the links among them as well. Their legal reformation is, thus, the record of their efforts to recast these links, not a direct response to inadequacies in the custom they had been bequeathed.

Although closely focused on Douaisiens and their history, this book is also an attempt to place the Douaisien story in a larger history of late medieval marital property law and its relation to social and gender relations in this age. I will argue that although Douai's custom and the process of its revision were unusual and although elements of the city's economic and sociopolitical history were unique, the social and gender history retrievable from this legal archive was not unique to Douai. Throughout western Europe, certainly in the French- and Flemish-speaking part on which this study concentrates, the same issues were at stake—the nature of property, the definition of social place and the mechanisms for securing it, the terms of gender hierarchy. In many places, as we will see in chapter 8, similar choices were made. What is unique about Douai is that peculiarities of its legal history allow us to examine these stakes more closely, more carefully, than we have been able to do elsewhere. This is not to argue that Douai can stand for any other city of the day, not even a city in the southern Low Countries. But it is to insist that what we learn from the history of marital property law in this city can help us understand not just the law, but marriage, gender, and social order themselves, far beyond the walls of late medieval Douai.

ONE

From Custom to Contract

In late medieval Douai, as throughout much of northern Europe in this age, "family law," as it has often come to be called, was regulated by custom. Hence norms were usually unwritten and, for the most part, are known to us only through the descriptions in court cases in which the tenets of custom were disputed or in other, occasional texts of this kind, not by means of written summaries.[1] Principally because it was unwritten, customary law was unstable, constantly subject to emendation as people used it in daily practice, constantly subject to reinterpretation as judges considered it in court, and constantly subject to transformation as it was carried from one place to another.

Douaisien custom surely had this malleable quality as well, but by the fourteenth century when this study begins, custom in Douai—at least the customary rules regarding marital property relations and inheritance—had become rather more fixed than we might expect. This stability had been achieved largely through adjudication as hundreds, even thousands, of cases regarding marital property relations and inheritance had come before Douai's court of échevins and been decided according to increasingly well articulated and fixed principles. So fixed had these tenets become, in fact, that Douaisien sources of the day regularly used the oxymoronic "le loi et coutume de Douai" to refer to custom.

By the late Middle Ages, then, "custom" in Douai had lost much of the flexibility we normally associate with the term. This did not mean, however, that Douaisiens were obliged to adhere to rigid rules about how

---

1. Of course, a great many custumals were written in this age, but they were seldom definitive descriptions of any particular set of practices. See chapter 8 for a fuller discussion of the history of customary law in this region.

property was shared in marriage and passed at death. On the contrary. By this period, Douaisiens had learned to use individual legal instruments such as contracts and wills to intervene in custom, to supersede custom's rules in the particular case covered by the legal document. In effect, we might say, they were restoring to custom the flexibility that had been lost, but they were doing so by extracustomary means. In principle, custom easily accommodated such interventions, but in practice, as we shall see, it is far from easy for us to reconstruct Douai's legal history through the records left in the course of these confrontations between unwritten custom and written legal instruments.

For the historian, the situation is made even more difficult because the individual legal instruments Douaisiens issued were themselves complex constructions, replete with obsolete terminology and apparently contradictory clauses. Because the meaning of any of these documents is comprehensible only in terms of the custom against which they were issued and because custom was originally unwritten (and in Douai, first fully described only in the mid–sixteenth century, when it was no longer exactly what it had been in the fourteenth), the difficulties of the task are compounded. Moreover, we can seldom know the status of an individual document—whether a marriage contract stood alone as a modifier of custom, for example, or whether, as in the *Le Libert v. Rohard* case, other legal instruments controlled some of the property at issue.

Legal historians have for years struggled with these records and their histories, trying to locate Douai's apparently strange custom among others in late medieval Europe and to grasp the relationship between contracts and wills on the one hand and custom on the other. It is only in the last few years, however, that certain puzzles have been solved, only recently that we have been able to be reasonably certain about custom's rules regulating marital property relations and inheritance and about the ways they changed between 1300 and 1550.

The latest, and most thorough, study of Douai's customary marital property system is Robert Jacob's *Les époux, le seigneur et la cité*, published in 1990.[2] In it, Jacob traces the long and complex history of the marriage

---

2. Robert Jacob, *Les époux, le seigneur et la cité: Coutume et pratiques matrimoniales des bourgeois et paysans de France du Nord au Moyen Age* (Brussels: Publications des Facultés Universitaires Saint-Louis, 1990). Also see Jean Yver, *Egalité entre héritiers et exclusion des enfants dotés: Essai de géographie coutumière* (Paris: Editions Sirey, 1966); idem, "Les deux groupes de coutumes," *Revue du Nord* 35 (1953): 197–220; idem, "Les deux groupes de coutumes," *Revue du Nord* 36 (1954): 5–36; and Philippe Godding, *Le droit privé dans les Pays-Bas meridinionaux du 12e au*

contract in Douai, which was, in his view, the primary means for intervention in customary rules of marital property relations and succession in Douai during the Middle Ages. Jacob shows how the contract evolved during the thirteenth and fourteenth centuries, how it came to be widely used at the end of this period, how it emerged as the preferred regulator of property relations in families—at least in those with any significant property holdings—and how its principles came eventually to replace custom. All the technicalities of the legal history he recounts need not concern us here, but there are several elements of his analysis that we must consider in order to understand the social and gender history that marital property law helped construct.

Douai and the Picard-Walloon Custom

Let us begin by locating Douai's custom in relation to others of the day. Douai's traditional custom belonged to what legal historians have labeled the "Picard-Walloon" system, a region that now includes part of the Nord of France, the Pas-de-Calais, and the Somme, along with a section of southwestern Belgium that was then part of the greater Low Countries. Everywhere in this region, customs were marked by the preference they showed the conjugal unit over both the lineage of either spouse or the larger family.[3]

The central feature of this law, as we have seen in the *Le Libert v. Rohard* case, was its grant of absolute property rights to the survivor of a marriage. In the eastern part of the region (roughly, Wallonia), marriage alone conferred these succession rights. In the Picard region, which included Douai, a *ravestissement* was needed—either a *ravestissement par sang*, created by the live birth of a child, or a *ravestissement par lettre*, a

---

18e siècle, in *Mémoires de la Classe des Lettres, Collection in 4°*, 2d ser., pt. 1 (Brussels: Académie royale de Belgique, 1987).

3. Although scholars are agreed that customs in this area were united in their tendency to privilege husband and wife over co-lateral kin, and even over the children born of their marriage, all have nonetheless emphasized the variability of law in this region. See in particular Yver, "Les deux groupes de coutumes"(1953), and ibid. (1954); also, idem, *Egalité entre héritiers*. Emmanuel Le Roy Ladurie summarizes Yver's description of the Picard-Walloon custom in "Family Structure and Inheritance Customs in Sixteenth Century France," in *Family and Inheritance: Rural Society in Western Europe 1200–1800*, ed. Jack Goody, Joan Thirsk, and E. P. Thompson (Cambridge: Cambridge University Press, 1976). For more recent analyses and guides to the literature, also see Godding, *Le droit privé*, and Jacob, *Les époux*.

written document. If no ravestissement—either par sang or par lettre—existed, the conjugal fund was divided equally between the surviving spouse and the kin of the deceased. The ravestissement par lettre was issued by couples who sought to assure the survivor of their union the property rights due the survivor of a fertile marriage; thus, even if their marriage turned out not to provide a live birth, couples in Douai could assure that the entire conjugal fund would be reserved for the widow or widower.

The ravestissement par lettre was thus a written statement of "customary" ideas about marital property, an explicit articulation of what was normally unwritten. The typical ravestissement par lettre followed a simple and rigorously standard form:

> Let it be known to all that Jacquemart De Lommel, who resides in Douai, has made and makes a ravestissement to Jehanne De Sanchy, his wife and spouse of all he has, will have, and might acquire, whether or not there is an heir, according to the law and custom of Douai. And likewise, the said Jeanne De Sanchi makes and has made a ravestissement to Jacquemart, her husband, of all she has and will have or might acquire, whether or not there is an heir [of the marriage], according to the law and custom of the city of Douai.[4]

The Douaisien ravestissement par lettre thus expressed an extraordinarily powerful conception of conjugal property rights. Both spouses, as survivors of the marriage, were to have precisely the same rights. Further, all property of any kind, no matter when or how acquired, was to be included in this conjugal fund.

The Douaisien custom was certainly not the only one in the late medieval North to recognize a conjugal fund that was the absolute property of the married couple and its survivor, but there were few other customs in the North, as we shall see, that were so generous to the conjugal pair. It is, however, when compared with the "dotal" systems that Douai's preference for the conjugal pair seems perhaps most striking. In strictly dotal regimes, like those described in many custumals of the South or preferred by much of Europe's aristocracy in this age, no "conjugal" rights as such were recognized; the property of the bride and groom was kept separate throughout the marriage and, unless there were children born of it, thereafter. The property given a bride by her parents (the dot) was contributed

4. AMD, FF 616/2374 (27 December 1442).

to the marriage only temporarily and, at least during the later Middle Ages, she customarily reclaimed it at widowhood.[5] If the wife predeceased the husband, her properties usually passed to their children or were returned to her natal family, although the widower was often provided usufruct on her dot. In effect, dotal systems made a clear division between the property of each spouse, a division maintained throughout the marriage until the properties passed to the couple's offspring; they were, as legal historians have characterized them, "separatist."

In form and spirit very different from the dotal regimes of the South, Douai's custom, like those of its neighbors in Picardy-Wallonia, was much closer to those used elsewhere in the North. Still, even in the North, there were stunning differences between the Picard-Walloon custom and others. For example, in Flemish-speaking Flanders and much of the rest of the Low Countries—Picardy-Wallonia's closest neighbor—children were *guaranteed* an equal share in their parents' estates, which they received in Douai only if the parents left no will or other legal instrument distributing the property differently. In addition, immovable goods were not usually considered part of the "community of goods" in most of Flanders, but reverted to the natal kin of the deceased; even conjugal property was normally split between the surviving spouse and lineal heirs of the deceased, whether or not there were children born of the marriage.[6]

---

5. In addition, widows in this period often received an increase on their dot or a life income for use during widowhood. The increase on the dot awarded in most southern customary regimes could vary enormously but seems to have ranged between 30 and 50 percent. For a general overview of these systems, see Paul Ourliac and Jehan de Malafosse, *Le droit familial*, vol. 3 of *Histoire du droit privé* (Paris: Presses universitaires de France, 1968–71). Jacob, *Les époux*, briefly reviews the literature on the French medieval "dotal" systems of the South and compares them with the Douaisien system of the contract (which replaced the ravestissement): see pp. 207–15.

Marital property regimes that were formally "dotal" could be much less so in practice. On dotal systems as actually practiced in the late medieval South of Europe, see in particular Jean Hilaire, *Le régime des biens entre époux dans la région de Montpellier du début du XIIIe siècle à la fin du XVIe siècle: Contribution aux études d'histoire du droit écrit* (Montpellier: Causse, Graille and Castelnau, 1957); Jacques Lafon, *Les époux bordelais 1450–1550: Régimes matrimoniaux et mutations sociales* (Paris: S.E.V.P.E.N., 1972); Dominique Favarger, *Le régime matrimonial dans le comté de Neuchâtel du XVe au XIXe siècle* (Neuchâtel: Editions Ides et Calendes, 1970); and J. F. Poudret, "La situation du conjoint survivant en pays de Vaud XIIIe–XVIe siècle," in *Mémoires de la Société pour l'histoire du droit des institutions des anciens pays bourguignons, comtois et romands*, vol. 27 (Dijon: Faculté de droit des sciences économiques de Dijon, 1966).

6. E. M. Meijers, "Le droit ligurien de succession," *Tijdschrift voor Rechtsgeschiedenis* 5 (1924): 16–32, the first important study of this system, traced the affinities between the Flemish custom and those of the Basque, certain Swiss cantons, and other areas, and he grouped them together as prehistoric survivals of both Germanic and Roman influences. See his *Le droit ligurien de succession*, 4 vols. (Haarlem: H. D. Tjeenk Willink & Zoon, 1928–36). His historical narrative has

In their definition of the conjugal fund and their privileging of the survivor of the marriage, the Picard-Walloon customs were, then, distinctive. Not everyone in the region followed these customs, however. Most significantly, the nobility preferred rules that gave considerably less weight to conjugal interests and much more protection to lineal claims.[7] Even among commoners in Picardy-Wallonia, there was no uniformity. In Artois, Liège, and part of southern Flanders, for example, at least in the later Middle Ages, the ravestissement applied only to the movables in the estate, and the surviving spouse held the immovables only in usufruct. In the region of Cambrai (the *Cambrésis*), to mention another variation, the surviving spouse of a fertile marriage had only usufruct on half of the property the deceased spouse had brought to the marriage.

Douai's custom thus stands out, even in Picardy-Wallonia, for its radical attachment to conjugality; it was in Douai almost alone that the ravestissement applied to all property—all, as the ravestissement par lettre typically put it, that the husband or wife "has, will have, or might acquire"— and one of the very few that granted full ownership rights, not simply usufruct, to heads of the conjugal fund. In addition—and this may have been the most radical feature of Douaisien marital property law—the Douaisien custom refused what the French call *dévolution*, the right of children to claim their parents' chief properties. Indeed, as Douai's first printed custom of 1627 so decisively put it:

> When two spouses have made a ravestissement or a ravestissement par lettre, to the survivor of the two belongs each and every good, movable, chattel, and heritage that belonged to them and each to which the deceased spouse was heir at the date of his or her death; the survivor has the right to enjoy, use, and possess as heritable property, as his or her own [all these properties], and the children of the marriage or, in their absence, the kin of the deceased will have no rights whatever in these properties.

been discarded, but his categories and his scholarship on the customs themselves remain generally intact. Yver's "Les deux groupes de coutumes" (1953); ibid. (1954); and idem, *Egalité entre héritiers*, supersede Meijers, but also see Godding, *Le droit privé*. For a close look at how marital property and inheritance law functioned in one city of late medieval Flanders, see Marianne Danneel's study of Ghent: *Weduwen en wezen in het laat-middeleeuwse Gent* (Leuven and Apeldoorn: Garant, 1995).

7. For their part, ordinary people were generally as immune to the customs of the nobility as the nobility seems to have been to their customs. It was only in the early modern period that the norms established by the nobility had any appreciable effects on the customs of their social inferiors: see Jacob, *Les époux*, 13–21, and idem, "Les structures patrimoniales de la conjugalité au moyen-âge dans la France du Nord: Essai d'histoire comparée des époux nobles et routiers dans les pays du groupe de coutumes 'picard-wallon' " (Ph.D. diss., Université de Paris 2, 1984).

By making the surviving spouse the full and absolute heir of all property in the estate, Douaisien custom allowed marital property to move in potentially unsettling ways. It permitted Franchoise Rohard, as we have seen, to take property that her deceased husband had inherited from his child and use it as she saw best, even over the objections of her remaining stepchildren to whom it had been pledged and to whom it would have belonged in most other legal systems of the day. The Douaisien archive abounds with documents that similarly gave absolute property rights to the head of household or its survivor. For example, among the testators whose wills survive in Douai's municipal archive, we find many men like Phelippes Les Lices, who wrote a will that denied his widow the customary ravestissement. Instead, he left her only the linens, clothes, and household furnishings, and he divided their house between her and the children (and reduced her rights in her part of the real estate to usufruct—which she would lose if she remarried).[8] In the same archive we find Marie Le Grand, a woman who had survived three husbands and probably one son and who left all the property she had accumulated in three marriages to twenty different legatees, none of them clearly related to any of her three deceased spouses.[9]

More surprising still, custom permitted men, as heads of household, to take a stepchild's property as his own, even when the child's mother still lived. In a case that recalls the *Le Libert v. Rohard* dispute, for example, Gallois De Noesmielle, the third husband of Jehenne Hordain (twice a widow) was sued by the trustees of the estate that Hordain's second husband had left to be divided between his two children. One of the children had died, but since the man's will had not specifically made the surviving child heir of the deceased, De Noesmielle had claimed the property as his own, as husband and thus "maitre" of the child's mother (who was the property's true heir). Invoking custom's rules of succession and confirming the absolute supremacy of the male head of household, the échevins granted De Noesmielle his claim.[10]

---

8. AMD, FF 861 (August 1307).

9. AMD, FF 869 (13 April 1402).

10. As the échevins put it in their ruling: "If a deceased child owns any money that is being held for him or her by the Ministry of Orphans or elsewhere, when that child (or children) dies, the money passes to the father or mother of the child (or children)" ("se aucuns enfffans meurdans ont aucun some de deniers mise aleur proffit a loffice des orphenes ou ailleurs Et [item] enffans ou enffant vont de vie a trespas eulx pere ou mere de telz enffans ou enffant remporte et apporte telle some de deniers"), AMD, FF 293, fol. 194v (November 1442).

Douaisiens were surely not ignorant of how these customary rules of succession could disrupt certain social relations, but they nonetheless preserved this law from at least 1200, approximately when our records begin, until well after 1500. As we have seen, however, Douaisiens simultaneously took full advantage of custom's logic, which permitted heads of household to manage property as they saw fit. In practice, therefore, Douaisiens regularly issued documents that modified custom's rules. Sometimes they did so in order to intensify custom's inclinations, as when they issued ravestissements par lettre. More often, however—especially in the late fourteenth, fifteenth, and sixteenth centuries—they did so in order to reverse custom's tendencies, to restrict property's movement as custom would not have. Thus, just as Jehan Le Libert had intended to do with his prenuptial gift to the children of his first marriage, Douaisiens removed houses, building lots, gardens, land rents, annuities, and cash from the conjugal fund, protecting them from the radical dispersals to which they would have been subject under custom alone.

The Douaisien Marriage Contract

The most important of these documents, at least as they affected the norms of marital property law itself, was the marriage contract. Although in use as early as the thirteenth century, it was not until late in the fourteenth century that the document was regularly employed in Douai and not until about 1430 or 1440 that the text acquired a stable form. By then it had become the principal mechanism for intervention in custom, even the principal regulator of marital property relations among propertied Douaisiens. In each of the years between 1435 and 1460 (a period when the archival record appears especially complete), about thirty-five to forty marriage contracts in *chirographe* (a parchment recording individual acts) have survived, treating probably about 20 to 30 percent of the marriages that took place in the city and as many as 40 to 60 percent of the marriages among propertied Douaisiens.[11] Although we shall see that the marriage contract did not reign alone in Douai as a means of intervening in customary marital property law, it is this document on which legal historians

11. These statistics do not reflect a probably substantial number of lost contracts or the relatively small number of contracts that were entered in folio volumes (Actes et Contrats, FF 393–413, for the medieval period) rather than written as chirographes.

have concentrated because it was here that Douaisiens worked out the new principles of marital property relations that would later become hegemonic.

The earliest of these contracts, however, bore few of the features that would come to characterize the later marriage contract. Indeed, many appear to be only modified ravestissements par lettre, rather like that written by Jehans Davennes, "tisserand de draps" (drapery weaver), and Maroie Loberielle in 1356. This document began exactly as most ravestissements began, by announcing "that Jehans Davennes . . . has made and makes a ravestissement to Maroie Loberielle his wife of all he has, will have, or might acquire, whether or not there is an heir."[12] Only in a later passage did the text deviate from customary norms, by adding a provision that if Jehans were to die before Maroie, with or without heirs, Maroie would take 50 florins d'or, along with their best bed ("leur milleur lit estofee") in addition to all her linens, draperies, and jewelry, which she could "give and distribute" as she wished. In this section, the document thus explicitly separated marital goods into "theirs" and "hers," as the marriage contract would later do (although, by the technical terms of custom, Maroie Loberielle needed none of the permissions it granted, for the document's opening clause had already granted her these rights).[13]

Even those documents from this period that more closely resembled what would become the marriage contract proper also preserved many traces of custom. The *couvenenche de mariage* (as these early contracts were often called) written between Maroie Le Mounarde and Jehan Hamelle, a boatman, in 1374, for example, listed the property each would bring to the marriage (he brought his boat and two houses; she, cash and personal property) and the goods she would take as widow (her personal property or 80 francs), in the usual form of the marriage contract. The text went on, however, to lay out terms of the estate division that exactly repeated the rules of old custom: if the marriage was fertile, each was the full heir of the other; if not, each split the estate with the "closest relatives by blood and lineage" of the deceased.[14]

---

12. AMD, FF 585/148 (28 April 1356).

13. The intent of the document is not entirely clear. It may have been written to assure the widow testamentary rights that customary heirs might have, in practice, challenged (although according to a strict interpretation of custom—the interpretation Douai's échevins seem always to have upheld—Loberielle needed no such guarantees).

14. AMD, FF 585/194 (28 July 1374). Presumably, the widow could choose between the 80 francs and the share of the estate.

Odd in form and confused by formulas borrowed from custom, the earliest contracts were strange in other ways as well. Most were structured as agreements between the groom and the *avoués* of the bride, men appointed by the bride's father, to whom the groom pledged special properties that would secure the bride's widowhood, rather than as agreements between the bride (or her father) and the groom (or his father).[15] This was a cumbersome system, for it required that property be frozen in place, and it necessitated baroque mechanisms for assuring that the property was recovered when the husband died. Hence, Douaisiens later changed tactics, moving toward what would become the typical form of agreement. This contract was made between the groom and the bride, or, more precisely, between the groom and the bride's legal agent (usually her father or, in his absence, uncles, brothers, and grandfathers, along with her mother). Typically, it did not pledge special properties as guarantees for the bride, but pledged all the groom's property in a general hypothecation.[16] Avoués were thus not eliminated from these documents, but they played much reduced roles, now serving simply as overseers of the financial affairs of the bride, not as parties to the contract.

15. The contract for the marriage of Watier Boiseau and Marie De Marellon, written in 1258, is typical. It obligated Boiseau to assign 120 livres parisis to Jakemon De Lens, Pieron De Hasnon, and Jehan De Mareloon, avoués of De Marellon. Of that amount, 24 livres would be delivered in the form of a one-third interest in a house, the rest within three years in the form of héritages, all to the satisfaction of the avoués. Should Boiseau default, the avoués had the right to seize any of his property. If Boiseau and De Marellon died without heirs, the property would pass to the avoués and then to the next heirs. If De Marellon died first, without heirs, the debt would lapse: AMD, FF 659/5731, in Jacob, *Les époux,* Appendix 2.3.

16. The contract written in 1441 for the marriage of Gille Muret L'Aisne and Ghille De Le Rue was typical: AMD, FF 616/2329 (21 May 1441).

> All their conveyances and each and every one of the things described above the said Gile Muret has promised, and [he has], by his faith and oath, openly and completely held, provided, and fulfilled in each and every respect [these terms] before Andrieu Terlin, Jehan De Servins Dit Loucepoix, and Gile De Le Motte, *avouez* of the said Ghille De Le Rue. . . . And all his goods with the goods of his heirs, movables, chattels, and heritages, present or future, everywhere they are or might be found in country or city, to be executed before [any and] all lords and all jurisdictions at the request of the said Ghille De Le Rue and the said *avouez* or the bearer of these letters, until the intent of this instrument has been fully accomplished.

Once virtually obligatory in the contract—according to Jacob, 90 percent of contracts written in the first quarter of the fifteenth century included avoués—these men appear less frequently thereafter and had all but disappeared by about 1470. By then, the general hypothecation described—"tous ses biens avoeuc les biens de ses hors, meubles, cauteulx et heritages"—either to the bride and/or to the "porteur(s) de ces lettres" sufficed to guarantee the widow the properties due her.

Widows, Children, and Kin

By about 1430 or 1440, contracts had achieved stable form and clear function. In effect, this "mature" marriage contract pursued three objectives:
to secure the widowhoods of women, to assure children an inheritance,
and to protect the marital estate from erratic dispersal away from lineal
kin should the spouses die without living offspring.

The centerpiece of the new marriage contract and the principal mechanism for achieving these goals was the *portement,* the term Douaisiens
used for the properties each spouse brought to the marriage. All but a
few marriage contracts specifically acknowledged the bride's portement,
and most contracts also listed its contents, at least in a summary fashion.
Typically, the contract distinguished personal property in the portement
from cash and from household goods, and it listed immovables and rents
individually. Jehanne Caterent, who married Lyon Regnart, a cloth finisher, in 1441, for example, brought "in goods, movables, and tools . . .
the sum and value of 150 livres parisis monnaie de flandre" along with
"approximately 3 rasières and 1 couppre of tillable land."[17] Catherine Lap-
pense brought 28 livres parisis in cash, her "clothing, jewels, and adornments for her person," and "a house and holding in the city of Douai."[18]
Jehenne Herbert, who married Collard Le Grant, a "laboreur" (worker),
in 1441, had considerably fewer worldly goods, but she nonetheless specified a portement consisting of "many goods and movables such as clothing, jewels, and adornments."[19]

Richer women also grouped their assets according to kind, and sometimes according to origin as well. The portement of Ghille De La Rue
included, as a gift from her granduncle and uncle and from the inheritance
of her maternal grandparents' estate, a one-third share in 4 mencaudées of
land, held in pieces that were scattered throughout the region (excluding 5
rasières of land that her brother William held in fief); 8 rasières of wheat
in a heritable rent; a heritable rent of three capons annually.[20] The bride
also contributed her portion of some property she held with others—two

17. AMD, FF 616/2326 (15 May 1441).
18. AMD, FF 616/2327 (17 May 1441).
19. AMD, FF 616/2324 (11 May 1441).
20. All these properties were currently held by her mother and would pass to the bride and
her siblings only at the mother's death.

houses, one in the Rue du Rivage and another in the Rue de Barlet, which she owned with her brothers; and her share of three houses she held jointly with all her mother's offspring and her stepfather. In addition, she brought one *pre* (a field) consisting of 10 couppres of land; 2 mins of tillable land; 120 to 140 livres parisis monnaie de flandre (m.d.f.), at present invested in the city's trust for orphans; and she contributed 40 gold crowns (valued at 100 livres parisis). At her mother's death, she would also have an equal share in 55 rasières of land. Finally, along with her siblings, she would inherit all the houses and heritages owned by her mother that lay just outside of the Porte Aucherf.[21]

Some brides, like most grooms, did not specify the contents of their portements, although the groom usually acknowledged the portement's existence by pronouncing himself "content" with it, just as a bride normally declared herself "contente" with the portement her groom promised but did not list.[22] Most contracts did, however, list the contents of the bride's portement, and it became increasingly rare to omit these details from the contract, either for brides or grooms, as the fifteenth century gave way to the sixteenth. Until about 1500, between 50 and 75 percent of brides listed their portements while only 10 to 20 percent of grooms did so. The percentages rose dramatically in the first half of the sixteenth century, to 83 percent for brides and 48 percent for grooms, and had risen once again by midcentury, to 85 percent and 51 percent, respectively.

The principal reason for listing the bride's portement was to guarantee her rights as widow, for the portement was the basis of the *reprise,* the property a woman took back from the estate when widowed. Often, the reprise was expressed simply as return of the portement, as in the marriage contract written in 1441 for Jehanne Henemere, whose 110 livres parisis would be returned to her at her husband's death "freely and entirely, without difficulty and without liabilities," whether or not children had been born of the marriage.[23] In other cases, the reprise was expressed in somewhat different goods: Jehenne Dymont's portement consisted of two (attached) houses in Douai plus one garden lot and "many shares in goods, movables and in jewels, clothing, and adornments, and a furnished bed set."[24] If her husband died first, she was to take, as her reprise, "all the

21. AMD, FF 616/2329 (21 May 1441).

22. Or the bride and her father (or other representative of her family) together declared themselves "contents."

23. AMD, FF 616/2331 (9 June 1441).

24. AMD, FF 616/2347 (25 November 1441).

héritages that she had brought to the marriage" plus 3 francs of *rent viagère* (life rent), along with her "furnished bed set, all her clothing, jewels, and adornments that she might have on that day, no matter their value."

In addition to their reprise (or return of their portement), women were almost always granted an "increase," called in Douai the *douaire* or, more often and more precisely, the *douaire, assene, et amendement*. Most douaires were expressed in cash, although some included real estate, sometimes real estate that could be held only in usufruct, making this property claim more like the dower (also—and more correctly—called *douaire coutumier*) traditional in other marital property systems than the simple increase typical of the Douaisien.

There appears to have been no fixed ratio between the douaire and the portement in Douaisien marriage contracts. Jacke De Bimy, who married a carpenter in 1362, was promised a douaire exactly equal to her portement of 40 florins d'or.[25] Marie D'Estree, a widow with two daughters, who married a "goudalier" (a kind of brewer) in the same year, would, however, receive only 30 florins d'or as her douaire, although her portement was 120 florins d'or plus seven houses in Douai.[26] Marguerite Joie, also a widow, married just a few years later with an enormous portement of rents, houses, land, cash, silver, along with personal property that was alone worth 180 florins d'or, but she, like D'Estree, received a relatively small douaire—two houses in usufruct and 300 florins d'or in cash.[27] Jehanne Maubuee, a widow who married in 1375, appears to have negotiated a much better deal. She got 30 florins d'or, usufruct on a house, and her "best cloth" [i.e., bolt of drapery] as douaire, while her portement had been only a house and 20 florins d'or.[28]

As late as the 1520s, no clearer standards had emerged. Jehenne De Denaing brought 120 livres, along with personal property, to her marriage and was promised a total reprise and douaire consisting of her personal effects plus 150 livres.[29] Colle Brouche Dit Caillet brought personal property along with 690 livres parisis and would receive, as combined reprise and douarie, 900 livres parisis.[30] Anthoine Du Four, a widow with one child, brought 300 livres parisis, the tools for making light woolen cloths

25. AMD, FF 585/153 (25 July 1362).
26. AMD, FF 585/154 (12 August 1362).
27. AMD, FF 585/157 (10 February 1367).
28. AMD, FF 585/159 (25 October 1375).
29. AMD, FF 649/5126 (5 April 1521).
30. AMD, FF 649/5127 (12 April 1521).

called sayes (which had belonged to her late husband; her new husband was also a saye maker), personal property, 5 couppres of land, and 50 livres that she held for her son; as douaire she was promised 450 livres.[31] Mariette De Villers brought 117 livres, along with one-quarter of a house in the Rue de Foullons, and she was promised in return a reprise of those properties plus her personal effects and all héritages she might inherit from her *lez et coste* ("side," i.e., natal kin) during the marriage plus a douaire of 60 livres.[32] Katherine De Vermeilles brought 1,400 livres parisis, personal effects, two houses, and a life rent of 26 livres parisis; her douaire was 700 livres parisis.[33]

Despite all the care they lavished on defining the reprise and douaire, marriage contracts also assumed that a widow had an alternative to the reprise and douaire: she could refuse these payments and "stay" in the estate. It is not entirely clear, however, just what it meant for women who chose to stay. Franchoise Rohard, as we have seen, claimed the customary rights of ravestissement when she stayed, although her contract had said nothing about such rights, and the court upheld her claim. Contracts written later than Rohard's usually specifically granted the right to stay, as Rohard's did not, but they too were silent about just what the right implied. The contract for Colle Brouche Dit Caillet, written in 1521, for example, provided that she could take 900 livres parisis out of the marriage as her reprise and douaire, assene, et amendement, plus her clothing, her "chambre," and her jewels. Alternatively, she could "hold to the goods and liabilities that the said Jacques [her husband] had left."[34]

Beginning around 1500, Douaisiens introduced the term *douaire coutumier* to refer to widow's right to stay in the estate. The contract written for Marguerite De Farbus in 1548, for example, provided that, as widow, De Farbus could take "all her clothing, knitwear, and all jewels and adornments for her body and person, her furnished bed set . . . all the héritages and goods left for her at the death of her father" (plus those that she might inherit during the marriage), along with 900 florins carolus as douaire, assene, et amendement. Or she could choose the douaire coutumier: "Or she can hold to her right to the douaire coutumier, of which she has the choice and option."[35] Still relatively rare at the end of the fifteenth

31. AMD, FF 649/5130 (6 May 1521).
32. AMD, FF 649/5132 (4 June 1521).
33. AMD, FF 649/5134 (10 August 1521).
34. AMD, FF 649/5127 (12 April 1521).
35. AMD, FF 654/5541 (5 July 1548).

century—only one contract in four mentioned the douaire coutumier—
the clause regularly appeared in contracts written fifty years later; 80 percent of the contracts in one sample from the 1550s included the clause.[36]
Although it is not certain just when the right to stay in an estate was first
interpreted to mean only usufruct on the estate, it seems likely that the
term *douaire coutumier* always had this meaning in Douai, just as it did
in the Parisian region and everywhere else in France that the phrase was
used. In fact, the clause was probably adopted precisely to clarify the confusion caused by the ambiguous terminology of the past, the confusion
that had produced the case against Franchoise Rohard with which this
book opened.

As it evolved, the marriage contract thus served both to protect widows
and to limit their property rights. By guaranteeing widows return of their
portement (or its rough equivalent) and an increase, it shielded them from
the risks of losses their husbands may have incurred during the marriage
and from debts he might have left when he died. Simultaneously, however,
particularly by the time the right to stay in the estate had been clearly
defined as usufruct alone, it eliminated widows' claims to succession rights.
No longer could they share in the gains of the marriage; no longer could
they assume full managerial control over the conjugal fund when their
husband died, for the property was now explicitly marked for heirs and
thus unavailable for sale or mortgage without the approval of those heirs.

In addition to protecting widows (and simultaneously limiting their
rights), the contract also served as an explicit guarantor of children's inheritance rights. Contracts written by widows or widowers with children
commonly included clauses setting aside monies from the new conjugal
fund for these children when they reached majority or married, or they
simply labeled certain immovables as the children's after the death of their
natural parent. Thus, when Anthoine Du Four, widow of Henry Simon,
remarried in 1521, she specified that she and her new husband were obligated to "govern and feed and to teach a trade to" her son Silvans until
he had reached an "estate honnorable," when he would be given 50 livres.[37]
When Jehan Carlier, a fuller and a widower with children, remarried in

36. For the figure of one in four, see Jacob, *Les époux*, 187–88; the figure of 80 percent is
based on contracts sampled in AMD, FF 914 (*contrats en papier*); fifteen of nineteen contracts
contained a clause explicitly granting the douaire coutumier. See Appendix A for a fuller discussion
of the property rights of widows who refused their reprise and douaire.

37. AMD, FF 649/5130 (6 May 1521).

the same year, he brought one-half a house and tenement as his portement and passed the other half to the children of his first marriage, apparently as the contract of the previous marriage had required.[38] Marie Hanouse reserved 12 livres parisis from the estate she would leave her new husband, stipulating that the money go, at her death, to the son of her first marriage.[39] Thus, the marriage contract came to put children of prior marriages before spouses of the present marriage.

More common still in the mature marriage contract were clauses protecting the inheritance rights of children to be born of the present marriage. Gillette Cardron's marriage contract of 1549, for example, provided that the house, garden, and tenement with 12 couppres of land she would bring to the marriage, as well as an orchard of 3 couppres 4 quarraux, would go to her husband at her death (as custom would have dictated), but only for his life (a limitation foreign to custom); thereafter it would pass to their children, or to her "nearest kin."[40] Other clauses required that widows pass both their own assets and their late husbands' properties on to their children.[41] Still others distinguished among children from different marriages in dividing the conjugal estate, as custom did not. Noel Martin guaranteed support to the four children of his bride's first marriage and promised them as well some land the woman had brought to the marriage along with 100 livres parisis each at maturity; in addition, if there were no children of the new marriage, the children "of the first bed," as Douaisiens usually put it, were promised all the héritages that the woman owned.[42]

If a specific clause of douaire coutumier had not been included in the contract, other clauses were sometimes inserted to similarly limit the widow's control over the estate. In 1553, Jehan Henne, a maker of sayes, stipulated that his share in his father's estate would pass to the

---

38. AMD, FF 649/5136 (25 November 1521), records his remarriage; there is no surviving record for his first marriage.

39. AMD, FF 639/4323 (1496).

40. AMD, FF 654/5542 (2 May 1549).

41. See, for example, AMD, FF 655/5556 (30 January 1555), which required Franchoise Gaudin, bride of Robert Le Roy, to pass all her heritages on to her children and, in their absence, to her plus prochains and specifically made any children born of the marriage the direct heirs of movables that had been left to the bride by her mother. Another stipulated that a specified sum in the woman's estate go to plus prochains and that, if widowed, she was obligated to pass the surplus of her husband's estate on to the husband's children: AMD, FF 655/5562 (17 November 1556).

42. AMD, FF 655/5549 (16 December 1553).

children of his marriage, not to his widow.[43] In 1558, Jehan Vallin L'Aisne wrote a modified ravestissement par lettre that granted his estate to his widow, Marie De Paradis, but only in usufruct, stipulating that the properties would then be split between their "nearest kin."[44] Many contracts were like the Vallin–De Paradis document in that they did not specifically label property for children but seemed to regard children as the "nearest kin" for whom the property was nominally reserved. For example, Jehenne Bauduin's marriage to Vaast Hennicque in 1559 carved 50 livres parisis out of the estate her widower would inherit and labeled this money directly for her *plus prochains* (closest kin), never specifically mentioning any children, but surely including them by implication.[45] Franchoise Fourbert's marriage contract granted her a reprise and douaire of 450 carolus d'or and her personal goods but established that if she died first, 150 carolus d'or would go to her plus prochains and that all property she inherited from her lez et coste during the marriage would go to them as well.[46]

It was typically widows, not widowers, however, who were specifically obligated in such contracts to provide for children; the documents rarely charged fathers with the task of holding property for their offspring, apparently assuming that the men, unlike the women, would do so automatically. The contract between Jehenne Bauduin and Vaast Hennicque, a draper and "parmentier" (maker of specialty trimmings), for example, provided that he would inherit all his wife's estate, less a small cash payment to plus prochains (in this case, obviously not the children, for they would not have been limited to a token payment of this kind).[47] Clearly, the children would become his responsibility, but—like the father of custom—he was not bound by any rules about what property should be held for them. Unlike his wife, he was treated as capable of making that decision by himself.

Although the security of wives and widows and the protection of children, whether of this or a previous marriage, were important concerns of the marriage contract, the claims of lineage itself loomed behind both. Almost invariably, clauses that passed a wife's heritages on to her widower in usufruct and then reserved them for their children went on to provide

43. AMD, FF 655/5544 (17 January 1553).
44. AMD, FF 655/5564 (8 November 1558).
45. AMD, FF 655/5570 (10 June 1559).
46. AMD, FF 655/5577 (23 May 1562).
47. AMD, FF 655/5570 (10 June 1559).

that in the absence of children, the closest of her kin should take them (her plus prochains or her lez et coste). Similarly, contracts that gave widows usufruct on their husbands' properties also reserved the assets for the man's plus prochains at the woman's death. Pollet Du Pentich's contract of 1555, for example, provided that if there were no children born of the marriage, all his immovables would be held by his wife for life and would then pass to his plus prochains; the movables, in contrast, would be entirely hers. If there were children, the entire estate of Du Pentich's own father (whose heir Du Pentich was) would pass directly to the children born of his marriage.[48] The douaire coutumier automatically accomplished this task of preventing widows from transferring their husbands' property outside his "line," for the clause assured that once the woman had died, property would pass first to children or, in their absence, to the husband's kin.

The marriage contract thus imposed a marital property regime quite different from old custom's. Under it, husband and wife were not treated as common owners of all conjugal property and the equal survivors of one another, as they had been under custom. Now, widows had ownership only of specified assets—those they had brought to the marriage (or their equivalent) and those pledged as an increase. Alternatively, they could claim life use, but not ownership, of all marital property. Under this new regime, men did not suffer so costly a decrease in their survivors' rights as did women, but as husband, a man was constrained by special clauses that labeled specific items as the property of his bride, forbade their sale without her consent or that of her avoués, and required their return to her lez et coste at her death. In effect, the new marital property regime in Douai was "separatist" in spirit, rather more like those of the South of Europe, which the Douaisien had once so little resembled.[49]

Children were net winners under the new regime. Those born of previous marriages as well as those not yet born won secure claims to their mother's heritages (should she predecease her husband) and, indirectly, also obtained rights to their father's property as well (should he die first), usually by means of the douaire coutumier. In combination, these clauses added up to a set of powerful protections for the lineage. Brides and grooms were now tied to their natal kin during their lives—and beyond. The children they bore were similarly bound to them, and the conjugal

48. AMD, FF 655/5557 (7 March 1555).
49. Jacob develops this comparison more systematically in *Les époux*, 207–15.

unit, with its small household, was made directly responsible to a larger community of ascendant, co-lateral, and descendant kin.

Writing Custom/Rewriting Marital Property Law

By the mid–sixteenth century, marriages among propertied Douaisiens were more often made by contract than by old custom; so common had it, in fact, become to replace custom with written contracts that when Douaisiens first wrote their custom down around 1550, they included the rules associated with the marriage contract alongside those of custom. Hence, the first written form of custom provides us the first clear evidence that custom no longer ruled alone. By then, this document shows, the marital property regime inscribed in contract was not only serving as an alternative to unwritten custom, as it long had, but was beginning to re-place custom.

The written custom of the mid–sixteenth century did not, however, do much more than begin the process of replacement. The text opened with a recitation of the old rules, and not until much later in the document, in Section V, did the new conceptions of marital property relations make an appearance. Even then, they were expressed so clumsily, so vaguely, that historians have only recently deciphered the meaning of the clause at issue. The first known printed custumal, which followed in 1627, was somewhat clearer in this regard, but it too published both the old rules alongside some of the new, making no obvious distinction between them. Although historians seem agreed that by this time it was extremely rare for propertied Douaisiens to marry without a contract and thus under the old legal regime, it is nonetheless clear that even at this late date, old custom survived, if only as the norm preserved by those with little property to call their own.[50]

Thus, Douaisiens made their way from old custom to the new laws of marital property relations and succession slowly, hesitantly, haltingly. The journey's languid and uneven pace appears to have been deliberate. It is certain in any case that the reformation's pace was not the result of Douai-siens' ineptitude with law, their inability to devise sophisticated legal in-struments. Douaisiens seem to have been willing and canny manipulators

---

50. For a fuller discussion of these editions, see Appendix B.

of their law; they were authors of more wills, marriage agreements, and business contracts than survive from any other comparable city of the late medieval North. It is hard to believe that they could not have devised clear formulas for overturning old custom on their own, but even if they had needed help in constructing tidy legal agreements, they had models ready at hand—from Paris, for example; or, should they still have been without solutions to the technical problems of rewriting law, they could have sought legal counsel or gone to higher courts for advice. They took none of these routes. Instead, they simply fiddled with old custom, trying various forms of marriage contracts, and only very late in the Middle Ages settled on formulas that produced a marital property law that was "separatist" as custom was not. It was still much later that they allowed these notions of marital property law to be generalized as "custom," in effect as an alternative to and then replacement of the old, once unwritten custom.

Still, if the tortured path of legal reform in late medieval Douai cannot be told as a story of confusion about law, there is no doubt that this is a confused story. It is, in fact, only with the help of legal historians and the benefit of hindsight that the long and labored legal process can be rendered as a purposeful narrative, a story of how Douaisiens moved from archaic custom toward a more lineal regime. Hence, while we must surely acknowledge that law changed as legal scholars have described it as changing, we might be pardoned for wondering whether fourteenth- and fifteenth-century Douaisiens knew they were embarking on anything so radical as overturning custom when they began to modify their ravestissements. We might even be permitted to doubt that they ever fully intended what they wrought. Rather than setting out to replace old custom, we might suspect Douaisiens simply gradually found themselves preferring their emendations to it. Over time, as one generation gave way to the next and as the fifteenth century slid into the sixteenth, Douaisiens came to consider the new rules of marital property relations they had devised more natural, more logical, and more fitting than the old.

The Social Context of Custom

The social history of Douaisiens' move from old custom to new marital property law is fully as complex as the legal history. It is even less easily told as a purposeful narrative, for, as we shall see, the empirical record that Douaisiens left yields little evidence that a single set of social actors or a single socioeconomic event caused Douaisiens to move away from old custom. Rather, propertied Douaisiens of all ranks not only long tolerated but actively sought to combine old norms with new, never clearly preferring one system over another until well into the sixteenth century. Even the most energetic modifiers of custom seldom fully abandoned it. A merchant, for example, may have married once under custom, another time under contract; an artisan may have married under custom but later written a will that modified the succession rules implied by custom; an échevin may have married by contract but afterward written one of the strange, hybrid documents that were devised in the course of this transitional period to preserve some of the old ways of doing things. A woman may have been married by custom but later, as widow, written a will that subverted custom.

If Douaisiens were not engaged in an effort—albeit a clumsy one— to rid themselves of custom, what then were they doing? The simplest answer is that they were making use of the legal resources available them—old custom, of course, but new legal instruments as well, along with various principles of marital property law drawn from other regimes—to fashion ad hoc arrangements that seemed to fit the particular circumstances of their lives. To understand this legal reform as social history, we must, then, look more closely at what these circumstances were. We must examine the social world in which the documents were written—the world where men and women married, produced, and reproduced; the world where property was acquired, used, shared, and exchanged. This world, we shall see, was a profoundly commercialized one, and it was this quality, above all, that established the conditions in which Douaisiens acquired and managed wealth.

The View from Outside: Cloth and Trade, Boom and Bust

At the center of Douai's economy stood the drapery. Medieval Douai was one of the great cloth towns of the original county of Flanders, a manufacturer of northern Europe's most luxurious woolens and the home of some of the region's best known merchants of wool and cloth. Located on the Scarpe River, which flows from Artois into southern Flanders before joining the Scheldt just south of Tournai, Douai was linked by water both to the great grain-producing region of Artois and Picardy and to the mercantile centers of Ghent, Bruges, and Antwerp, which lay to the north and east.

The area of the Low Countries in which Douai was located was the earliest to develop economically, the most densely populated, and the best served by ecclesiastical and political institutions. Hence, although Douai was not the largest of the Low Countries' cities—at some 15,000–20,000 residents, the city was only about one-third the size of Ghent and half the size of Bruges—it was one of the wealthiest cloth towns, and it had a cultural and political importance that its size alone did not portend.

Douai has been well known to historians at least since the early part of this century, when Georges Espinas published his authoritative studies of the medieval city.[1] Espinas concentrated on the period from about 1150 to 1300, when the city had emerged as a leading industrial center and, along with neighbors such as Arras, St. Omer, Ypres, Bruges, and Ghent, dominated the European market for luxury woolens known as drapery. The best of these textiles were made exclusively of fine shorthair English wool, which was imported directly by Flemish merchants who traveled to England to buy it from monasteries and other large producers. These

---

1. Georges Espinas, *La vie urbaine de Douai au moyen-âge,* 4 vols. (Paris: A. Picard et fils, 1913). Also see idem, *Les finances de la commune de Douai des origines au Xve siècle,* 2 vols. (Paris: A. Picard et fils, 1902), and *Les origines du capitalisme,* 4 vols. (Lille: E. Raoust, 1933–49).

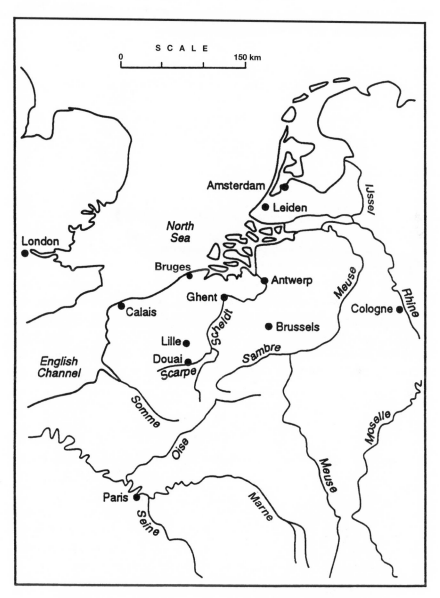

Map of late medieval Low Countries. Drawn by Brian Hollen.

merchants then arranged for the manufacture of the cloths and, finally, sold them, principally through the Champagne fairs.[2]

Douai was especially well known for its "scarlets," the finest and most precious of all luxury woolens in the period.[3] The cheapest such scarlet contained in a shipment to the English royal wardrobe in 1438–39 cost more than fourteen pounds sterling—the equivalent of two years nine months wages of a master mason; the most expensive was about double that.[4] Lesser broadcloths, even those called "luxury," sold at much lower prices, usually at about half that of a scarlet. Even in this exalted company, Douai's drapery stood out. At Provins (in Champagne), for example, one el (about 0.7 meters) of Douaisien dyed "drap" sold in 1294 at between 9 sous 9 deniers tournois and 13 sous 3 deniers tournois, while cloths from Ypres, Châlons, Lilles, Orchie, Paris, Ghent, Poperinghe, and Arras were priced as low as 2 sous 9 deniers tournois and no higher than 10 sous tournois per el.[5] Twenty-four yards of Douaisien drapery sold in Spain in 1394–1410, on average, at more than 6 English pounds, a price matched by few and exceeded only by some Italian cloths.[6]

2. This history has been well studied. See, in particular, Georges Espinas, *La draperie dans la Flandre française au moyen-âge*, 2 vols. (Paris: A. Picard et fils, 1923); G. de Poerck, *La draperie médiévale en Flandre et en Artois*, 3 vols., nos. 110–12 of *Werken uitgegeven door de faculteit van de wijsbegeerte en letteren, Rijksuniversiteit te Gent* (Bruges: De Tempel, 1951); Georges Espinas and Henri Pirenne, eds., *Recueil de documents relatifs à l'histoire de l'industrie drapière en Flandre des origines à l'époque Bourguignonne*, 4 vols. (Brussels: P. Imbreghts, 1906); H. E. de Sagher, ed., *Recueil de documents relatifs à l'histoire de l'industrie drapière en Flandre: Deuxième partie, le sud-ouest de la Flandre depuis l'époque Bourguignonne*, 2 vols. (Brussels: Kiessling, P. Imbreghts, 1951–56). For more recent commentaries, see John Munro, "Medieval Woollens: Textiles, Textile Technology, and Industrial Organization, c. 800–1500," and "Medieval Woollens: The West European Woollen Industries and Their Struggles for International Markets, c. 1000–1500," both in *The Cambridge History of Western Textiles* (Cambridge University Press, in press); Patrick Chorley, "The Cloth Exports of Flanders and Northern France during the Thirteenth Century: A Luxury Trade?" *Economic History Review* 40 (1987): 347–79; Marc Boone and Walter Prevenier, eds., *La draperie ancienne des Pays-Bas: Débouchés et stratégies de survie (14e–16e siècle)* (Leuven and Apeldoorn: Garant, 1993); and Negley Harte, ed., *The New Draperies* (Oxford: Oxford University Press, 1997).

3. For a description of this process and the term *scarlet* as used in contemporary sources, see John Munro, "The Medieval Scarlet and the Economics of Sartorial Splendor," in *Cloth and Clothing in Medieval Europe: Essays in Memory of Professor E. M. Carus-Wilson*, ed. N. B. Harte and K. G. Ponting, no. 2 of Passold Studies in Textile History (London: Heinemann Education Books, 1983), 13–70.

4. Munro, "Medieval Scarlet," 66–67.

5. Chorley, "Cloth Exports of Flanders," 355.

6. John Munro, "Industrial Protectionism in Medieval Flanders: Urban or National?" in *The Medieval City*, ed. H. A. Miskimin, D. Herlihy, and A. L. Udovitch (New Haven: Yale University Press, 1977), 143.

As Espinas told the story of Douai during these glory years, the luxury drapery totally dominated the city's economy, and the drapery itself was totally dominated by rich merchants who brought wool to the city and then exported the cloths made from it. They controlled production as well, for it was they who hired weavers, fullers, and dyers, sometimes even they who directly arranged for the spinning, sorting, and carding of the wool. In Espinas's interpretation, these men were northern Europe's first true capitalists, for by combining trade and production, they concentrated capital in their own hands, utterly monopolizing the entrepreneurial role.[7] While Espinas emphasized that this story of protoproletarianization and early capitalism was repeated throughout the textile towns of Europe, it was, in his opinion, nowhere more perfectly enacted than in Douai. From this city, almost alone in the medieval Low Countries, we have very little evidence of worker resistance: few records of serious uprisings and only scattered indications that artisans tried to form guilds or other corporate bodies to protect their social and economic interests. As Espinas pointed out, the few documents of this nature that we have are pathetic in their timidity, their hesitancy, their scarcity.

There are, to be sure, a few isolated records of artisanal resistance dating from the late thirteenth century, a time when similar revolts were breaking out elsewhere in the urbanized Low Countries.[8] In Douai, however, the revolt seems to have had only limited success, and by the early fourteenth century, Douai's artisans had been firmly put back in place.[9] The only recorded popular uprising of importance during the rest of the Middle

---

7. See his *Les origines* and idem, "Jehan Boine Broke: Bourgeois et drapier Douaisien," *Viertel-jahrschrift für Sozial- und Wirtschaftsgeschichte* 2 (1904): 382–412.

8. The earliest well-documented moment of artisan resistance in Douai came in 1275, a few months after new drapery ordinances were issued, the first since the middle of the century. By 1280, the situation had apparently further deteriorated, for a document of that year records the condemnation of twenty-three artisans, five of them identified as weavers, the rest unnamed by trade, who had organized a work stoppage. Two of the weavers were permanently banished from Douai, on threat of death if they returned, along with eighteen others; the remaining three weavers were decapitated: For Espinas's arguments, see Espinas, *La vie urbaine*, 2:1109 ff. Also see Espinas and Pirenne, *Recueil des documents*, doc. 289, 2:141–43. For a discussion of this evidence, see Martha Howell, "Achieving the Guild Effect Without Guilds: Crafts and Craftsmen in Late Medieval Douai," in *Les métiers au moyen âge: Aspects économiques et sociaux*, ed. J.-P. Sosson (Louvain-la-Neuve: Publications de l'Institute d'Etudes Médiévales, 1994): 109–28.

9. Monique Mestayer, "La ville, entre le roi at le comte," in *Histoire de Douai*, ed. M. Rouche and Pierre Demolon, vol. 9 of *Collection histoire des villes du Nord/Pas-de-Calais*, ed. Y. M. Hilaire (Dunkirk: Westhoek-Editions, 1985), 48, 53–55; Franz Funck-Bretano, ed., *Annales Gandenses* (Paris: A. Picard, 1896), 37.

Ages occurred in a different context, when, in 1322, eighteen individuals (sixteen men and two women) were charged with inciting a riot against rich grain merchants. All were banished, some with the threat of death should they return; in addition, the women's tongues were cut off (their crime had been incendiary speech), and they were threatened with live burial should they return.[10]

The men who governed Douai so despotically formed, before 1300, what historians have traditionally called a "patriciate," a term coined to describe urban elites who ruled by right of birth. Douai's patriciate was, like the governing bodies in other northern cities of the days, almost entirely in the hands of a few rich families, almost all merchants or "rentiers," the latter of whom had left trade and put their money in real estate or finance. They monopolized power as families: sons often followed their fathers on the bench; nephews ruled concomitantly with uncles; young men were selected as sons-in-law precisely because they were from échevinal families and would later join their in-laws in rule.[11]

This was the world in which the Douaisien custom first took root. The society was rigidly stratified and dominated by a single industry, but it was, nonetheless, a world of easy and rapid social mobility within social rank. Work was easy to get, workers always needed; the precious English wool was plentiful, its monopoly securely in the hands of Flemish merchants; the demand for luxury woolens was strong; and distribution was conveniently arranged through the booming Champagne fairs. After 1300, as we shall later see, much would change. Douai would be taken by the French for a good part of the fourteenth century and even after the city was restored to the Low Countries' sovereigns in 1369, Douai would never again enjoy the autonomy it had once had. Its economy would also suffer in these years, as the so-called depression of the late Middle Ages took its toll in Douai and as dramatic shifts in the luxury cloth industry forced a reorganization of Douai's system of production. The difficulties in these years would obviously alter the context in which Douaisiens made decisions about marriage, remarriage, and inheritance.

---

10. Espinas, *La vie urbaine*, 2:633–34: doc. 1006.

11. On the late medieval patriciate, see in particular Max Weber, *The City*, trans. and ed. Don Martinale and Gertrud Neuwirth (New York: Free Press, 1958); also see Hellmuth Rössler, ed., *Deutsches Patriziät 1430–1740: Schriften zur Problematik der deutschen Führungsschichten in der Neuzeit*, vol. 3 (Limburg/Lahn: C. A. Starke, 1968), and for the fullest study of an urban patriciate in Flanders, see Fr. Blockmans, *Het Gentsche Stadspatricaat tot omstreeks 1302* (Antwerp: de Sikkel, 1938).

Yet, these rude changes would not come so suddenly—or be received by a populace so certain about their implications for social order—that they would elicit an immediate or a single response. In fact, they would have their effects in quite subtle and multiple ways. For long, very long years, Douaisiens would go on as they had—marrying, setting up households, running businesses, endowing their children—in the ways they had learned when the city was flourishing, when elites seemed secure, when artisanal labor was easily sold and profitably bought. More fundamental things remained the same as well, for Douai never lost its identity as an industrial and commercial center. Whatever changes the last centuries of the Middle Ages brought to Douai, they did not alter its citizens' corporate investment in production and trade. These activities remained the basis of their social existence and their political identity. To understand why Douaisiens arranged marital property relations and inheritance as they did, we must thus understand the nature of this economy and the sociopolitical order built on it; we must understand something of what it meant to live in a commercial society such as Douai's.

The View from Inside: Circulating Goods

Douaisiens' commitment to trade meant not only that the city's economy was built on commerce itself and trade of the products made in Douai and not just that the city's social and political elite was dominated by merchants and financiers or that its ordinary citizenry was made up of artisans and shopkeepers. It also meant that Douaisien society was fundamentally different from the social world that surrounded it and from the worlds that had come before.

Unlike most of their contemporaries and all but a few of their predecessors in medieval Europe, Douaisiens were producers for the market, not for subsistence. They did not grow grain or raise many animals for food. They bought grain that had been distributed to retailers through the city's staple, and they usually purchased meat from the city's butchers. They built houses made of brick constructed by local artisans, and when they replaced their straw roofs with tiles, as they did during the last centuries of the Middle Ages, they hired tilers to do the work. Most Douaisiens probably made their own clothing, and some probably spun the wool and wove the fabrics they needed to make clothing, but many other Douaisiens

bought even their simplest fabrics from local artisans, and the richest Douaisiens hired dressmakers and tailors to fashion clothes, slipcovers, draperies, and bedlinens for them. Douaisiens purchased—they did not make—
the buckets, shovels, knives, and other implements for their shops and
kitchens; they commissioned their shoes, saddles, harnesses, purses, and
belts.

Although it is the general standard today—and was commonplace even
by the seventeenth and eighteenth centuries in northern Europe—Douaisiens' commercialized way of life was not a commonplace in medieval
Europe, not even as late as the fourteenth and fifteenth centuries. Douaisiens' dependence on commercial exchange, whether of goods purchased
for trade or of goods produced for trade, made Douai—and all similar
cities—different from the world that surrounded it, different from much
of the past. For centuries, all Europeans had imagined that wealth derived
from rights to use the land and from control over the labor necessary to
work it, not from trade. Even in the last centuries of the Middle Ages,
when cities such as Douai had emerged to challenge traditional practices,
all but a few Europeans still worked to feed, clothe, and house themselves,
not to trade. And all still equated political power with land rights, social
status with control of agricultural labor, wealth with leisure.[12]

Of course, by the late Middle Ages, the rural economy was no longer
entirely a subsistence economy. Both peasants and their lords sold surplus
produce, especially in the Low Countries, where urban demand for these
commodities was consistently high. By then there were even some fully
commercialized agricultural exploitations in the region. Industry was itself
also widely dispersed through the countryside; as early as the fourteenth
century, for example, urban merchants and drapers in the Low Countries
employed peasants to help make cloth for export. Nevertheless, the vast
majority of rural residents, even in the Low Countries, did not produce

---

12. The "commercialization of Europe" is, of course, one of the central themes of late
medieval–early modern historiography. Harry Miskimin's *The Economy of Early Renaissance Europe, 1300–1460* (Cambridge: Cambridge University Press, 1975) and *The Economy of Later Renaissance Europe, 1460–1600* (Cambridge: Cambridge University Press, 1977) provide overviews;
the introductory chapters of Lester Little's *Religious Poverty and the Profit Economy in Medieval
Europe* (Ithaca, N.Y.: Cornell University Press, 1978) efficiently summarize the story; R. H. Britnell's *The Commercialization of English Society, 1000–1500* (Cambridge: Cambridge University
Press, 1993) offers a schematic analysis of the process in England and a reliable guide to the
literature. Also see Richard A. Goldthwaite, *Wealth and the Demand for Art in Italy, 1300–1600*
(Baltimore: Johns Hopkins University Press, 1993).

chiefly for the market.[13] As peasants or sharecroppers, they grew food mostly for subsistence, whether their own or their lords'; as landlords they may well have sold much of the produce they received as rents or they may have taken their rents in cash (realized by their peasants' sales of surplus production), but they did not directly organize production for trade. Even those rural people who did piece work in textiles lived principally from their holdings; work for the market was marginal to their material existence, not the core of it.

The relative underdevelopment of commerce in the countryside is not, however, the principal distinction of importance here. The crucial divide between country and city in this age turned on the nature of their respective productive assets and on the way the character of productive capital in each economy shaped social relations. In the countryside, the asset that mattered was land. No matter how land was used—whether to grow crops for the market or for consumption; to graze sheep and cattle; or to exploit for game, wood, peat, or other raw materials—land had permanence and substance, extension in space and time, which urban capital did not. Land might be bought and sold, it might be divided and redivided, it might be put to multiple and various uses, even misused; it might be mortgaged, and the rents from it might be bought and sold like the herrings, wool, cloth, and spices that urban people traded. It would certainly pass from hand to hand, but it did not disappear. It as always there, to be viewed, worked, walked upon. If sold, perhaps eventually repossessed. While its products might circulate and disappear, while its earnings might be traded away like herrings, land itself remained in place.

Urban assets were very different. A huge portion of urban wealth was invested in tools, equipment, jewels, furnishings, clothing, and cash, which Douaisiens usually described simply as *biens*. The rest—all but a small portion—was made up of a category of goods neither quite biens (although Douaisiens often called them such) nor quite héritages (although Douaisiens called them that too): urban dwellings such as houses, warehouses, and sheds. Whatever their precise physical or legal character, however, these goods were in economic fact "movable," some more than others, but all more than land. Tools, materials, and inventories did not have permanent values; they were not fixed but working capital, and they

---

13. See Adriaan Verhulst, *Histoire du paysage rural en Flandre* (Brussels: La Renaissance du livre, 1966). Also see Alain Derville, "Le grenier des Pays-Bas médiévaux," *Revue du Nord* 69, no. 273 (1987): 267–80.

had to be in some sense consumed—used up—in order to realize value. Warehouses, shops, even residences (which were the usual sites of production and trade) did not of course turn over in the same way as did these goods, but they also depreciated as land did not, and in the mind of contemporaries they were more closely allied with the market and the marketable goods they housed than they were with land, which was in this age still thought of by most people as being outside the market. Thus, a warehouse full of cloth or wool; a shop bursting with spices, pots, clothing, and fabrics; a workshop equipped with looms, stretching frames, and rare dyes; or a residence filled with beds, chests, linens, plate, clothing, and jewelry—all had measurable and realizable worth principally in terms of what they could produce for exchange or could themselves be exchanged for. Douaisiens were fully conscious of their wealth's movability, and they worked assiduously to keep their goods circulating—or at least able to be circulated.

Because it had to circulate to acquire value, and had to be imagined to circulate to be imagined valuable, such property was infinitely fungible. Potentially, it was one day a warehouse full of inventories; another day a chest of precious coins; a third day a dress, a silver goblet, a house, or a bushel of grain; and a sixth a portfolio of rents payable in perhaps a dozen different currencies. Unlike land, which was itself a lasting source of subsistence—a fixed and unchanging asset extensive in space and time—the movable wealth at the heart of the urban economy had no immutable form, no secure location, and no permanent existence.

As fungible property, movable goods were inescapably ephemeral. Something could be sold for too little, bought at too high a price, entrusted to someone who did not know its value, lost. The inefficiency of markets in late medieval Europe heightened the insecurities inherent in such an economic system. One day, food might cost a day's wage, another day two days' wages. Douaisien grain prices, for example, rose by more than 500 percent in the fifteenth century, a record no worse than any other city's and probably better than most.[14] A Douaisien scarlet—the cloth that had made the city's reputation as a premier manufacturer of luxury woolens—was in one century the cloth of kings and in the next only the

---

14. See Monique Mestayer, "Le prix du blé et de l'avoine de 1329 à 1793," *Revue du Nord* 45 (1963): 157–76, and Martha Howell and Marc Boone, "Becoming Early Modern in the Late Medieval Low Countries: Ghent, Douai, and the Late Medieval Crisis," *Urban History* 23, pt. 3 (December 1996): 300–24, for a discussion of grain prices in this age and relevant bibliography.

poor cousin to Lucca's silks. Douaisiens who lived through parts of the late medieval centuries could see the worth of their gold plate change so much that what once bought a house later bought only a few years' rents on it, for gold prices, as expressed in the Douaisien money of account, rose almost steadily—in total, by 500 percent—in the century and a half between 1317 and 1477. The gold-silver ratio rose 100 percent between about 1320 and 1350.[15]

Because urban assets were movable, fungible, and ephemeral, as land never was, the social order built on this asset base was fundamentally different from the social order built on land rights. It was, necessarily, more mobile, for in cities such as Douai social place could shift as rapidly as assets could change location, form, and value. Douaisiens, like urbanites everywhere in this period, did not of course regard the social mobility that resulted as an unalloyed good. They, like all their neighbors, sought to secure social place in a way that mere money emphatically could not. For example, they restricted the market so that assets changed hands less

---

15. Although these are hypothetical examples, they do not misrepresent probable realities. Wheat prices in Douai, for example, rose from 0.387 livre parisis in 1336 to 1.625 livres in 1343, fell from 1.25 livres in 1409 to 0.9 livres in 1410 and 0.582 livres in 1411, and rose from 0.782 livres in 1436 to 1.90 livres in 1437 and 3.05 livres in 1438, only to fall to 1.44 livres in 1439: Mestayer, "Le prix du blé."

Money and bullion values in Douai were as volatile. The livre parisis, Douai's money of account, was equal to one-twelfth of the livre gros of Flanders throughout this period. The Florentine florin, with an almost constant bullion context (of 3.46 grams in 1317) bought only 13 gros 3 mites in 1317 but 27 gros in 1365 and 40 in 1409. By the 1430s–50s, it was trading in the high 40s to high 50s and reached 60 gros in 1477 (with a still virtually constant bullion content). The gold-silver ratio in the first half of the fourteenth century varied between about 1:9 (around 1350) and about 1:18 (around 1320). In Venice, the rate fluctuated between 1:9.4 and 1:14.2 between 1305 and 1509. For all these monetary conversions, see Peter Spufford, *Handbook of Medieval Exchange* (London: Royal Historical Society, 1986), lxi, lxii, 36, 12, 215, 217.

J. H. Munro has most thoroughly documented the wide variations in the prices and qualities of Flemish woolens during this period: see in particular Munro, "Medieval Scarlet," and idem, "Wool-Price Schedules and the Qualities of English Wools in the Later Middle Ages, c. 1270–1499," *Textile History* 9 (1978): 118–69. Exact comparisons between the market values of Flemish woolens and Italian silk in the fifteenth century are not available, but see idem, "The Flemish 'New Draperies': The Death and Resurrection of an Old Industry, 14th to 17th Centuries," in *The New Draperies*, ed. N. B. Harte (Oxford: Oxford University Press, 1997). Munro's data indicate that the best silks sold for 20 percent more than the best scarlets of cities such as Douai, and at more than ten times the price of the average short, dyed broadcloth. For a general account of luxury demand for silks in the late Middle Ages, see Jane Schneider, "Peacocks and Penguins: The Political Economy of European Cloth and Colors," *American Ethnologist* 5 (1978): 413–48. For illustrative prices, see A. van Nieuwenhuysen, *Les finances du duc de Bourgogne, Philippe Le Hardi (1384–1404): Economie et politique* (Brussels: Editions de l'Université de Bruxelles, 1984), 392–95.

quickly and prices held steadier; they allowed birth, education, residence, and dress to mark and preserve social status; they created craft associations, drinking clubs, and shooting fraternities to nurture and guarantee privilege; they bought noble titles, copied the lifestyles of landed gentry, and arranged aristocratic marriages for their children. And, as we shall see, they adjusted marital property law. Still they did not abandon commerce. Whatever they might have done to lessen the instabilities inherent in commercial society, they did not cease to trade.

Let us look more closely at Douaisien commerce. This city, like most of its contemporaries, has left us few sources that allow a statistical analysis of the economy—none of the tax records, property surveys, toll receipts, or the like with which historians of other times and places have been blessed. For Douai almost alone of late medieval cities, however, we are not entirely bereft. Instead of the fiscal records available from other periods and places, we have from Douai the astonishing collection of private agreements concerning debts and property transfers, the documents generally catalogued in the archive as *contrats divers*. From them, along with the marriage contracts and wills that Douaisiens wrote in such abundance, we can obtain a very good, if general, idea about how Douaisiens handled their property, one much more complete than we can get from most other contemporary cities. These records leave little doubt about the extent of Douaisiens' devotion to commerce.

Douaisiens' commitment to commerce can be most easily examined by looking at their capital, beginning with land, medieval Europe's principal form of capital, which in law and common speech alike was referred to as an "immovable." Douaisiens, even the relatively prosperous Douaisiens who wrote marriage contracts, owned surprisingly little such property outside of Douai. One collection of seventy-five marriage contracts from the mid–fifteenth century, for example, contained only seventeen (23 percent) that mentioned rural properties as part of portements, reprises, or douaires. Among the nine richest people in the sample, people I have labeled "rentier" precisely because they lived from rents and capital, eight owned land or real estate outside Douai—no surprise, since ownership of such properties helps define the category "rentier." But only eight of twenty-three principal actors who were labeled "prosperous" (people who had more than the usual cash, furnishings, and tools that defined the least wealthy category of "propertied" Douaisiens) and only one of forty labeled "householder" owned any rural property.[16]

Even for the wealthiest Douaisiens, properties of this kind made up only a part of portements and douaires. In one of the most splendid matches of the 1440s, for example, Ghille De La Rue brought as her portement a one-third share in 4 mencaudées of land, 8 rasières of wheat in a rental payment, and another rent in kind of three chickens annually; 10 couppres of land; 2 mins of land; and, at her mother's death, an equal share in 55 rasières of land. In addition to these lands and land rents, however, she brought a share in two houses in Douai; a share of another group of houses held with her siblings and stepsiblings, 120 to 140 livres parisis and 40 couronnes d'or. Finally, along with her siblings, she would inherit all the houses and heritages owned by her mother that lay in Douai's immediate suburbs, just outside one of the city's medieval gates.[17] Her husband, Gille Muret, brought cash only, valued at 1200 livres parisis.[18] De La Rue's brother married soon after she did, and his portement was made up of his share in many of the same properties his sister had named: 5 rasières of tillable land held in fief, a third share in 3 muids, 7 rasières of land; a third share in 8 rasières of grain per year; a third of three capons per year; and a manor just outside the city walls. Like his sister, however, he also brought nonlanded wealth, chiefly a collection of rental properties in Douai, and his bride brought no rural holdings at all—just two houses in Douai, 500 livres parisis, and personal properties such as clothing, furnishings, and jewels.[19]

Less wealthy Douaisiens obviously owned smaller amounts of land. Admittedly, a few of them had a surprisingly large portion of their wealth in land holdings. For example, when Peronne D'Aubricourt married Jacquemart De Bourlon, a draper, in 1441, she brought a half share in 19 rasières, 3 couppres of land with a house, a half share in 3 rasières 2 couppres of a field in Auby, along with personal property.[20] Jehanne Caterent Dite Lalloe, who married Lyon Regnart, a "rapeillions de draps" (cloth

16. See chapter 3 for a fuller explanation of these categories and a tabular presentation of the material.

17. AMD, FF 616/2329 (21 May 1441).

18. Ibid.

19. AMD, FF 616/2366 (21 September 1442).

20. AMD, FF 616/2337 (6 September 1441); her husband contributed, however, only two houses in Douai plus "meubles" and his "utensilles d'ostel" (tools of the trade).

finisher), brought 150 livres parisis plus 5 couppres of land in one place and 3¼ rasières in another; her groom brought some land in Flines, which he held of the Duke of Burgundy, plus another holding of 3 couppres elsewhere, along with 20 francs and the equipment for his trade.[21] But such people were not the rule in Douai, certainly not among the artisans and merchants who wrote all but a few of the marriage contracts we have.

Even those for whom such holdings *were* the norm do not seem to have used them as Europe's landed aristocracy used their lands. Rural properties owned by Douaisiens were in this age seldom primary or even secondary residences; land was not a direct source of subsistence; land rights did not imply control of labor. For most of these people, as for most of their fellow bourgeois of this age, land rights were simply investments, property acquired for its economic value. In contrast, then, to medieval Europe's traditional landholding class, urbanites such as Douaisiens regularly bought and sold land and land rights. The collection of contrats divers provides some hint of just how active Douaisiens were in the nascent land markets of the day. From one sample of contrats divers from the mid–fifteenth century, for example, we have a sale of 34 rasières 2 couppres of land, plus 2 rasières of meadow, in exchange for a life rent of 14½ couronnes, payable to a third party, the wife of Jehan De Brebie. The sellers were Jacquemart De La Pappoire and Marye Alandeluyne, who, presumably being obligated to pay the annuity to the woman, chose to raise the money by liquidating some of their land.[22] In a more complicated transaction from the same sample, Eurade Piquette and her husband ceded their half share in a manor to the widow of Piquette's brother, Agnus Artus, now the wife of Hermin De La Pappoire, for the course of her life. Artus had acquired the half share in the manor as her douaire coutumier. As holder of the douaire coutumier, Artus had only life use of the property, but it is clear that her former sister-in-law did not want to share it with her. In exchange for taking the other half share, De La Pappoire agreed to pay Piquette and her husband a rent of 4 livres parisis per year; each of the parties also agreed to pay half the 4 livres parisis of perpetual rents due on the manor, but Artus and De La Pappoire would collect all revenues from the property while they held it. The deal was made, as the document explained, "to assure good relations among the parties and avoid questions" (that is, to disentangle the financial affairs

21. AMD, FF 616/2326 (15 May 1441).
22. AMD, FF 740 (20 April 1441).

of the separate families) and had the ultimate effect of returning the property to the male line, which had acquired it in the previous generation. To achieve these results, however, all parties agreed to treat the property simply as an income-producing asset that could be divided up and rented out at will.[23]

A last example underlines my point. The manor held in fief that Collart, bastard son of D'Antoing of Bonbecht, brought to his marriage with Jacque D'Auby, daughter of Thomas, in 1441 was pledged for return to his father's line when he and his wife died. It would then be exchanged for 400 francs, which would be given to any children born of the marriage. Although this was, surely, hardly a voluntary exchange of land rights for cash (Collart would probably have been delighted to have kept the manor for his descendants rather than return it to his father's legitimate heirs), the agreement illustrates how easily Douaisiens transferred land rights into cash.[24]

Most transfers of real property recorded in Douai's archive were much simpler than these maneuveurs, but all equally reveal Douaisiens' willingness to treat rural properties as mere assets, not as markers of social role or emblems of status. The widow of a "mercier" (grocer), for example, sold a rental payment on a house in Douai, which earned 2 couppres of oats and 6 sols of perpetual rent, for a cash rent of 6 livres parisis, which would be paid to her annually for life.[25] Another widow, Mahieu Launrignart sold 8 rasières of land to a group of buyers.[26] The variations are endless, the theme constant: land in this urban culture bore little of the social meaning it is often thought to have had in traditional Europe.[27] It

23. AMD, FF 740 (21 June 1441).
24. AMD, FF 616/2323 (8 May 1441).
25. AMD, FF 740 (30 December 1441).
26. AMD, FF 740 (19 December 1441).
27. In medieval Europe, land—the rights to hold it, the rights to work it—was the basis of the social order. The nobility held land; peasants worked the land. Land was, thus, not merely an asset, not simply economic capital as we might understand it today, but the principal form of cultural, social, and political capital as well. By the early modern period, to be sure, this was changing. Land was coming to be thought of and managed as an economic asset with marketable value (and people such as the Douaisiens featured in this book were important agents of that transformation). But the transition was very slow in coming. Until at least the French Revolution, historians have long pointed out, land not only retained much of its traditional meaning but acquired new importance as a social and cultural marker of class. To own land was, presumptively, to join the aristocracy—to adopt a particular lifestyle, to abandon certain kinds of productive labor, to take up distinctive leisure activities.

What is interesting about Douai is that its late medieval bourgeois seem to have treated land much as any kind of economic asset, not the vehicle for social mobility it was for so many other

was a store of wealth, a medium of exchange, a standard of value. Like plate, jewels, clothing, and furnishings, which, we shall see, Douaisiens collected with considerably greater energy, land was principally a form of money.[28]

These transactions reveal more, however, than Douaisiens' willingness to buy and sell their immovables: they also suggest that trades were made, in part, to settle inheritance claims. Douaisien customary law, and Douaisien practice as well, made inheritances partible—that is, custom provided that all heirs of the same rank divide property equally; even the wills or other legal instruments written to modify customary inheritance rules did not dispense with them. Thus, like the house and land that came to the Piquettes, inherited assets in Douai had regularly to be divided, and in order to be easily divided, they often had to be turned into divisible properties—into cash or financial instruments that could be expressed in money. Douaisiens' willingness to buy and sell real property was then a product of both their legal and economic institutions: law made it necessary to sell land; the market made it easy to do so.

Land was not the only form of real property in Douai, however. Alongside their rural property holdings, many Douaisiens also owned urban real estate, and some of them had the bulk of their wealth in this form. This

urbanites. This is not to deny that some Douaisiens of the late medieval period used the money won in commerce to buy their way into the regional nobility or that the city's early modern elite did, in fact, acquire land rights as part of an effort to establish aristocratic status. (See chapter 7 for a fuller discussion of this process.) But it is to point out that the Douaisiens who bought and sold land rights in the late medieval centuries more often acted as though land had little of this social or cultural meaning.

The literature on the social meaning of land in medieval Europe is vast. Important general statements include such seminal works as Marc Bloch's *Feudal Society,* trans. L. A. Manyon (Chicago: University of Chicago Press, 1961) and Otto Brunner's *Land and Lordship: Structures of Governance in Medieval Austria,* translated from the 4th rev. ed. by Howard Kaminsky and James van Horn Melton (Philadelphia: University of Pennsylvania Press, 1992). On the transition to early modern society and the meaning of land in the transition, readers might usefully consult Karl Polanyi, *The Great Transformation* (Boston: Beacon Press, 1957) or Perry Anderson, *Lineages of the Absolutist State* (London: Verso, 1979); or for an introduction to the historiographical controversies about the nature of the transition, *The Brenner Debate: Agrarian Class Structure and Economic Development in Pre-industrial Europe,* ed. T. H. Aston and C. H. E. Philpin (Cambridge and New York: Cambridge University Press, 1985). On the distinctive meaning of land in medieval Europe, also see histories of property law such as Sir Frederick Pollock and Frederic William Maitland, *The History of English Law before the Time of Edward I,* 2d ed. (London: Cambridge University Press, 1968).

28. See Hugo Soly, "The 'Betrayal' of the 16th-Century Bourgeoisie: A Myth?" *Acta historiae Neerlandicae* 8 (1979): 262–80.

property was not, however, treated as fixed patrimony. Like land, it could change hands quickly, especially those houses and lots owned by Douai's substantial landlord class. The bride in a marriage contracted in February 1496 for example, brought shares in seven houses as part of her extensive portement, all of them surely let to renters.[29] Caterine Meurisse, who married just a few months later, brought two half shares in rented houses to her marriage.[30] Like the real estate magnates of later centuries, Douaisiens often treated their houses, warehouses, and shops as fungible wealth. There were, of course, plenty of Douaisiens who held on to their city houses and lots throughout their lives and passed them, intact, to the next generation.[31] But they did so, typically, only if the house was their residence and a rather grand one at that. The rest of the houses in Douai changed hands often and easily, and Douaisiens stood ready to let them, sell them, or otherwise exchange them at almost a moment's notice.

Even the Douaisiens who acquired urban real estate for their own use— and a surprisingly high percentage of Douaisiens seem to have owned the houses in which they lived—did not display the attachment to their homes we might expect; they sometimes also bought and sold their domiciles as though they were commercial assets, not homes. Forty-four of the fifty-seven contracts taken in one sample of contrats divers from 1497 to 1498, for example, treated sales or mortgages of houses by ordinary Douaisiens, people who were for the most part not members of a true landlord class.[32] Many of them were like Jehan De Hem Dit Petit, a butcher, who sold a quarter share in a house and adjoining residence, which he had presumably inherited but could not use in this form. Bartien Tanerurer, also a butcher, and his wife were probably also heirs of the quarter share in a house they sold to another butcher, for one-fourth of 84 livres parisis plus unspecified "rentes foncières" (ground rents).

But many of the Douaisiens who appear in these documents were not simply converting their shares of inherited property into cash. Many— like the "tisserand de draps" (drapery weaver) who sold a house for 24 livres plus assumption of life rents of 12 livres parisis per year (its total

29. AMD, FF 639/4312 (February 1496).

30. AMD, FF 639/4298 (2 August 1495).

31. See, for example, Oeude Pieffors, daughter of one of Douai's échevins, whose claim to her parents' home, called the "Vieux Greniers" on the River Scarpe, constituted a principal part of her portement, both in her first marriage, of 1381, and in her second, of 1390. AMD, FF 588/408 (26 August 1381); FF 594/808 (2 September 1390).

32. AMD, FF 796, 26166–234, excluding 26223–32.

present value was thus about 132 livres parisis)—were selling the domicile to buy another in Douai, to move to another city, or to invest in a business.[33] Others seem to have been trading in real estate markets simply to produce cash incomes, with no intention of reinvestment. Jehan Du Gardin, for example, a "tainturier" (dyer), and his wife sold their house and holding for 30 livres in life rents (payable during the lives of their three children) plus the assumption of outstanding perpetual rents (of four capons, 2 deniers douaisiens, 3 sols parisis, and 3 couppres d'avoine per year). The buyer was Collart Le Phillipe, a "fruitier" (fruit retailer), who took possession of the house in exchange.[34] In total, six of the forty-four contracts for house sales in this sample were explicitly written as such annuity agreements, but many others that were more conventionally expressed as sales may also have disguised such mortgage-like deals. Such transactions directly expressed Douaisiens' commitment to commerce, for in these deals, a "house" was perfectly abstracted as a commodity: the physical residence remained in place, whole, but its market value was divided and traded.

The forty-four real estate transactions described in this particular sample of contrats divers included twenty-eight conventional house sales between Douaisiens; another eight were between a Douaisien and a foreigner—someone from Arras, Lille, or Ghent perhaps, or even from a nearby village such as Ostricourt, who was moving to Douai or who was simply buying property for investment.[35] Most of these people were artisans or small merchants, just ordinary citizens like those we have already met in the archive of marriage contracts. In total, 68 percent of the fifty-seven contracts in this sample named an artisan as one of the two principals to the transaction; only four (7 percent) named a member of the elite (fourteen [25 percent] provided no indication of the social position of the principal actor on either side of the transaction, and most of these people must have belonged to the elite).

Although hardly representative of all Douaisiens, the people who appear in these contracts—the artisans who sold houses, the widows of

33. Other house sales in the sample were priced between 24 livres parisis and 750 livres parisis; the average for the year was about 125 livres parisis.

34. AMD, FF 796/26222 (10 January 1498).

35. The rest (eight in number) were either sales and leasebacks or transactions of indeterminate character.

"merciers" (grocers), "marchands" (merchants), and "mannouvriers" (day workers) who bought life rents by selling their homes, the out-of-towners who bought building lots from residents of the city—were not anomalies. Douai's archive has preserved about eighty to one hundred contrats divers for each of the years between about 1350 and 1550 (and beyond), the overwhelming majority of them treating real estate transactions of this kind. A few people appear in the archive more than once in a given year; still more reappear three, four, or even five and six times over a longer period, and these were the true landlords and real estate tycoons of the day. But it is nonetheless safe to assume that most of the people named in these contracts were ordinary citizens. On average, about 150 different Douaisien men were named as principal actors in such contracts each year (assuming at least two men per transaction—one buyer, one seller). In a total population of, let us say, 17,500, this represents almost 3 percent of the adult men, possibly 6 to 10 percent of the male citizenry.[36]

Thus, although a huge proportion of Douaisien wealth was invested in urban real estate, what was technically immovable property, much of this wealth was treated as movable property, at least in an economic sense. In some nearby cities such as Lille, Ghent, or Antwerp, it is worth noting, urban properties of this kind were not even classed as "immovables" in law; instead, houses in the city, in some places along with their lots, were treated as movables. As such, they were subject to different, more liberal rules about how, when, and how often they could be transferred.[37] In Douai, no such legal accommodations had been made—in Douai, houses and urban real estate were always called "heritages" or "immeubles"—but the practice was no different. Douaisiens, like Ghentenars and Antwerpers, were free to buy and sell urban real estate as though these assets were "meubles."

---

36. Only citizens could own real property in Douai, and the male citizenry was always only a portion of the population of male residents.

Assuming that 150 men appeared annually in these records so that over a ten-year period 1,500 separate men would be named in these records, we can reckon that almost a quarter of the adult men who had lived in the city during that decade would have been named in such transactions. This calculation assumes a population of about 17,500 (about 3,500 of them adult men) and that 2,000 new adult male names (200 per year) joined the ranks, either by immigration or by having come of age. (replacing 2,000 who died).

37. See Philippe Godding, *Le droit privé dans les Pays-Bas meridinionaux du 12e au 18e siècle,* in *Mémoires de la Classe des Lettres, Collection in 4°,* 2d ser., pt. 1 (Brussels: Académie royale de Belgique, 1987).

Movables as Wealth

A possibly even larger portion of Douaisien wealth was stored in goods that were truly movable, not just in economic terms, but in physical and legal terms as well. The typical portement in a Douaisien marriage contract was, let us remember, not made up of land, land rents, or even urban real estate. It consisted of movable goods. Sometimes the lists of such goods were long and explicit; Jehenne Noiret, for example, specified that her portement contained "50 livres monnaie de flandre in gold or silver and . . . a bed, two pairs of bedlinens . . . two pillows . . . a screen, a box . . . a slipcover, four cushions, an outer cloak, a dressing gown, a cross, and a fur worthy of [her] social position."[38] About 75 percent of the eighty-five marriage contracts in the collection from which this came, all from the 1440s, read similarly, if more simply: "24 livres monnaie de flandre with her personal furnishings. garments, and tailored clothing"[39]; "the sum of 100 livres parisis monnaie de flandre, composed both of goods, movables, and household furnishings"[40]; "draperies, clothing, decorations, and jewels; a furnished bed set, the best that they have."[41] The better-off among them added a house to the listing, but they too counted movables as principal components of the portement. The widow of a fuller, for example, brought personal property and the tools of her late husband's trade along with "a house and holding used as a fullery" to her marriage with a "manouvrier" (day worker).[42] Others added a rental income, a garden plot, a share in a building lot. Few, very few, however, had much more to offer.

Matters were little different at death. When Marie Le Grand, a member of Douai's substantial "householder" class, wrote her will in 1402,[43] for example, she had just sold a house worth 40 florins d'or, which she had inherited from her last husband. From him, she also had an income of 3 rasières of wheat and the furnishings of his house. In addition, she had all the property she had brought to her last marriage: another house, a life income of 6 rasières of wheat, and all her "draps, cousus, tailliez et

38. AMD, FF 616/2405 (25 January 1444).

39. AMD, FF 616/2386 (11 May 1443).

40. AMD, FF 616/2381 (8 February 1443).

41. AMD, FF 616/2404 (24 January 1444).

42. AMD, FF 616/2359 (26 June 1442).

43. AMD, FF 869 (13 April 1402). In her case the testament was employed to distribute her entire estate.

joyaux." These clothes and jewels added up, however, to a huge portion of her estate. I enumerate below, as Le Grand's will enumerated, the assets in her estate (including the cash realized by sale of her late husband's house). I have assigned approximate market values to each item to help assess the economic importance of the movables she owned.

6 livres parisis in cash	6.0 livres parisis
1 good outer cloak ("houplande")	8.0
1 richly decorated bed ("sen bon lit estofe de 2 paire de linchoelx, 2 oreiliers et le couverture de sarge de 2 estains")	30.0
1 cloak ("cotte hardie")	9.0
1 dressing gown ("cotte a chambre")	6.0
1 rabbit-fur cloak ("plinchon de connins")	5.0
1 slip-cover ("banquier") and 6 cushions, her best	3.0
1 bed	10.0
1 pair of linens ("linceulx") and 1 stitched coverlet ("keutepointe"), her best	12.0
1 flat basin ("plat bachin") and 1 cauldron, her biggest	1.5
1 fur cloak ("cotte hardie fouree"), of average quality ("que on peut dire le moylenne cotte dicelle")	8.0
1 cap	2.0
1 average quality flat basin	0.5
1 ivory pot	1.0
1 pewter pot, her best	1.0
1 copper pot	0.5
1 frying pan ("payelle")	0.2
1 cauldron	1.0
1 pair of linens	2.0
1 white stitched coverlet	5.0
1 pair of linens	2.0
1 frying pan	0.2
1 frying pan, the biggest she owns ("le plus grande de son maisnage")	0.4

1 belt decorated in silver	3.0
1 stitched coverlet	4.0
1 ivory (writing?) table and silver writing instrument ("taule d'ivoire et le graffe dargent a ce servans")	6.0
1 silk purse ("bourse de camecalz")	2.0
1 purse trimmed in silk	1.0
1 coin ("courrone de Roy") worth 40 gros	2.0
1 amber rosary	4.0
1 head scarf ("couvrechief")	0.5
1 (linen?) garment ("quenuse")	1.0
1 cauldron without handles	1.0
1 pair of pillows	0.5
1 head scarf	0.5
1 cap	1.0
1 head scarf, her best	0.5
1 basin	0.5
1 frying pan	0.2
1 coin ("courrone de Roy") worth 40 gros	2.0
1 coin ("courrone de Roy") worth 40 gros	2.0
her house in the Rue des Cappelles ("se maison seans en le rue des cappelles")	80.0
Total	226.0 livres parisis

With an estate valued at more than 200 livres parisis, Le Grand was not a rich woman, but she counted as one of Douai's sturdy householders, and, as this analysis makes clear, she owed her financial standing principally to the movables she owned. Dresses, cups, and coats made up over half of her estate's value; real estate—even generously taking the net value of her house (after discounting any rents due on it) to be 80 livres—counted for surprisingly little. And Le Grand, like most Douaisiens of the day, owned no land, no land rents, and only a small cash hoard. Her estate, like that of most of her contemporary testators, was overwhelmingly in objects.

Even the richest Douaisiens had an extraordinary amount of wealth in objects like Le Grand's. Ysabel Malet, a member of one of Douai's most prominent families, who died a half-century before Le Grand (in 1359), left a huge estate, which had more than 1,300 écus (then worth about 1,300–2,000 livres parisis) in coin, plate, jewels, clothing, linens, and kitchen equipment—an amount equal to between thirteen and twenty years' work by a master mason at 8 sous per day. Just one of the fur cloaks listed in the inventory was worth 6 écus, at a time when a single écu could buy up to four days' work by a highly skilled artisan and sixteen days work by an unskilled laborer. An azure blue cap trimmed in squirrel was priced at 3.5 écus, a coverlet and bolster at 5 écus, a pair of bed linens was valued at 2.75 écus; her largest copper pot was valued at 3.5 écus, a washbasin, pot, and stand, at 2.25 écus.[44]

Douaisiens thus collected movables—tools, furnishings, clothing, jewels, and cash—with at least the energy they devoted to assembling houses and tracts of land. To a certain extent, they were hoarding wealth by storing it in such objects—an argument to which I will return—but they were not necessarily thereby giving up potential liquidity. These assets were more like cash than such luxuries are considered today, principally because there was, in reality, no such thing as "cash"—perfectly liquid fiat money—in this or any other contemporary society. There were only goods. Douaisiens, of course, expressed exchange values in money terms, and they often actually exchanged coin when they traded, but they did not do so quite as we might imagine. Prices in Douai were set in the livre parisis monnaie de flandre (here the livre parisis or simply the livre), the local money of account, or in the franc (equal for most of the period to 33 sous in the livre).[45] Payment of small amounts of livres or francs was normally rendered in "black" money, coins made of copper and other base metals of insecure values that were recognized only locally. Large transactions, particularly between Douaisiens and non-Douaisiens, were settled in gold or silver coins. Prices were also commonly expressed in kind as well—in Douai most often in chickens (*capons*), sometimes in units of wheat or other grain. But Douaisiens did not, of course, actually buy their dresses or wine with chickens. Instead, they paid in coin, and the amount of coin they paid was determined by the conventional exchange rate be-

---

44. Douaisiens were not, of course, unique in this regard. The personal effects of Jan Van Melle, chief tax collector of Ghent, which were sold in 1477, brought 37,033 groten (1,852 livres parisis): see Walter Prevenier and Wim Blockmans, *The Burgundian Netherlands* (Cambridge: Cambridge University Presss, 1986), 177.

45. The livre parisis m.d.f. was made up of 20 sous or 240 deniers. See the "Note on Money, Dates, and Names" for additional information about the Douaisien monetary system.

tween the produce and the money of account; payment was rendered in coins.

The rates at which these coins were exchanged—the prices they fetched—was not fixed, however. They varied as the gold-silver price ratio varied, as the bullion content of coins was altered by issuing authorities, and as the "real" or market value of the commodity, bullion itself, varied. Hence, although coins of the realm were the only legal tender in this age, they were an imperfect money. All of them were one small step removed from goods—bullion, foodstuffs, products made of bullion-like plate and jewelry, and even products such as silks and furs easily exchangeable for bullion, plate, or jewelry.

Money in Douai was, thus, just another movable—it was a good whose value could be expressed only in terms of another good, a good whose economic value was unstable because it was actuated only in exchange— exchange for other goods of equally hypothetical value. In this regard, Douaisien money was not unique, for by definition money's value is its exchange value. But the instability that was the consequence of this market dependence was more pronounced in late medieval Douai than in different times and places because the markets that gave money value were so unstable. Still worse for the security of money prices, trade in Douai was not normally conducted on a cash basis, but on credit. Houses, for example, were not paid for at purchase, but over time, as buyers assumed outstanding "rental" payments and pledged new ones to past owners. Thus, the typical buyer simply consented to take on outstanding "rents" (in effect, outstanding mortgage payments) and, usually, to pay an additional semi-annual rent to the seller, who was, in effect, providing a new purchase-money mortgage.[46] Wool, horses, cloth, dyes, and wine were normally also bought on credit; service people such as carpenters, seamstresses, tailors, masons, and tile-layers were paid on time; wages and salaries were normally paid in arrears. The thousands and thousands of contrats divers that fill Douai's archive are witnesses to these arrangements; most of these documents are, in fact, nothing but records of such credit. Just how these credit instruments would ultimately be honored, whether in gold or silver coin, whether in wheat or chickens, whether even in jewels, wine, or cloth,

---

46. For an explanation of the housing market in Douai, see Martha Howell, "Weathering Crisis, Managing Change: The Emergence of a New Socioeconomic Order in Douai at the End of the Middle Ages," in *La draperie ancienne des Pays-Bas: Débouchés et stratégies de survie (14e– 16e siècles),* ed. Marc Boone and Walter Prevenier (Leuven and Apeldoorn: Garant, 1993).

was never fully predictable. Still less certain was what the gold or silver, wine or cloth, would bring in its next trade.

Douaisiens' commitment to commerce thus produced a heady mixture of possibility and risk. Fortunes could be made, incomes acquired, households and trades established with an ease unusual even for the age. But disaster could strike just as easily. Douaisiens had to worry about more than the wars, pestilence, and famine that justifiably terrified all medieval people. For them, other dangers lurked as well: money values could collapse, trade routes could close, raw material supplies could be cut off, markets could suddenly shift.

Let me not overstate the case. Douaisiens were not alone in their devotion to commerce, their dependence on trade. Nor were they alone in facing risks of market collapse, monetary failure, or industrial demise. Their condition was, surely, typical of urbanites in all commercial centers at that time. My point is simply that people like them were the distinct minority in Europe of the day—that even with the commercialization of agriculture and the spread of cottage industry, the countryside was still fundamentally a subsistence economy in which land was the principal form of capital and that the institutions of trade and finance that would to some extent protect markets in later centuries were, as yet, fragile and small.

What I want to emphasize, then, is not that Douai was unique. Instead I wish to point out that when Douaisiens married, when they gave birth or saw their kin give birth, or when they contemplated death, they had to think more carefully than Europeans had traditionally thought about the ways property would flow as a result of these events. To understand the social meaning of the Douaisien legal reform, we must, therefore, not only understand the legal system in which they operated. We must also understand what property meant in Douai: how wealth was created and managed, how it secured social place, and how its value was protected. We must keep in mind that the wealth on which the Douaisien sociopolitical order was built was movable, fungible, and ephemeral in a way that was new to most other Europeans.

THREE

Legal Reform as Social Engineering

Given the inherent fragility of a social order so tied to commerce, it is no wonder that Douaisiens worked so energetically to manage the property flows that resulted from marriage, birth, and death. And no wonder, we might conclude, that they chose more conservatively during the centuries that closed the Middle Ages. After all, these were hard times in city and countryside alike, times when it might well have seemed prudent to tie property more closely to male lines of descent. In his authoritative legal history of the Douaisien reformation, Robert Jacob has made a suggestion along these lines, although his interpretation also depends upon a complicated sociology and a specific institutional history.[1] In some important ways my own interpretation will parallel his, but the close links he would make between social position and legal preference, between institutional change and legal choice, and between socioeconomic conditions and legal reform do not withstand sustained scrutiny. Nevertheless, his argument merits such scrutiny precisely because the process of investigating his hypothesis leads us to other, even more productive questions.

The Late Medieval Crisis

Let us turn, first, to the chronology of legal change and its relationship to socioeconomic developments in Douai. Douai's medieval history has traditionally been divided into two periods, one of expansion dating from

---

1. Robert Jacob, *Les époux, le seigneur et la cité: Coutume et pratiques matrimoniales des bourgeois et paysans de France du Nord au Moyen Age* (Brussels: Publications des Facultés Universitaires Saint-Louis 1, 1990).

about 1150 to 1300, and another of crisis and contraction, from about 1300 to 1550. In the first, we have seen, Douai emerged as one of the powerful, semiautonomous urban centers of industry and trade in the Low Countries, a source of the region's fame and prosperity—and a principal source of its sovereigns' wealth. During the second, Douai would slip to second rank in the Low Countries, even to third rank on the European scene.

The decline of the luxury drapery was both the most visible and the most devastating aspect of the crisis in Douai. In the words of Georges Espinas, "The drapery [of Douai] lost its distinctive mark as a major producer for export markets [in these years]; it fell to the rank of simple producer for local markets, the same role that most cities had always played, and even then that role gradually diminished in importance."[2] Accompanying these crises in the economic base, as Espinas characterized them, were a series of political upheavals with far-reaching consequences. The late thirteenth-century wars between the Count of Flanders and his titular overlord, the French king, began the troubles. The rich Flemish cities were immediately drawn into the conflicts, for they were prizes and combatants in the battles, and their citizens had direct interests in the conflicts. Urban citizenries were not, however, united in their interests. The urban patriciates generally supported the French king, while lesser men—smaller merchants and artisans—preferred the Flemish count, who promised lower taxes and continued access to the English wool on which the cloth industry depended. The result was a series of revolts within the cities themselves, and almost everywhere the internal uprisings led, as they did in Douai, to a reform of the échevinage. Patricians were banished, their property confiscated, and their offices taken by others.

In some cities of Flanders—most famously, in Ghent—these revolts presaged years of unrest that eventually led to a formal restructuring of

---

2. George Espinas, *La vie urbaine de Douai au moyen-âge*, 4 vols. (Paris: A. Picard et fils, 1913), 2:668. Espinas based his conclusions on extensive studies of Douai's voluminous archive, which, as we shall see, offered strong support to his argument, but his interpretation was influenced just as profoundly by the ideas of Belgium's great historian, Henri Pirenne, with whom Espinas frequently collaborated. According to Pirenne, the crisis in Douai was not unique to this city. During this period, luxury textile production left all the old cloth towns of Flanders, moving to the surrounding countryside, to the North, to England, and to Italy; at the same time, foreigners took over long-distance commerce itself, once the domain of Douai's own elite. For Pirenne's argument, see, in particular, *Histoire de Belgique*, 4 vols. (Brussels: Renaissance du Livre, 1972–75), and "Stages in the Social History of Capitalism," *American Historical Review* 19 (1914): 494–514.

government, to the age of so-called guild rule. In Douai, however, things happened differently, less dramatically and with less revolutionary effects. Soon after settlement of the late thirteenth-century revolts, Douai's échevinage was reopened to the old patrician families who had been exiled, but these men never regained the control they had once enjoyed, and the body never reacquired its character as a closed society. In the usual meaning of the term, it was no longer a patriciate, but became instead an oligopoly of the rich and rising rich, one that functioned as authoritatively as the old but that was more open to "new" men, including artisans, than it had been before 1300 and was thus less caste-like than the old patriciate.

Another, still more significant consequence of the French-Flemish wars was Douai's separation from the county of Flanders. When the wars dragged to an end after the famous battle of Courtrai in 1302, where an army of French knights had met ignoble defeat at the hands of Flemish commoners, Flanders was divided into two parts. The bulk of the old country remained in the hands of the Flemish count, but a portion of the French-speaking area that contained Douai, Orchies, and Lille was in 1305 formally ceded to the French crown. Douai remained a French possession until the marriage of the Valois Duke Philip to Marguerite of Male, daughter of the Flemish count, in 1369. The city and the administrative district into which it, Orchies, and Lille had been formed by the French were part of the marriage settlement, and when Philip assumed his title of Duke of Burgundy in 1384, the district was formally joined to his domain. Douai and its sister cities of Lille and Orchies were held continuously by the Burgundians and then the Hapsburgs until the late seventeenth century, when Louis XIV finally took them. Throughout these long years, however, until the 1667 conquest of Douai (the annexation was in 1668), the district was kept separate and administered as a distinct entity, much as the French had first established it in 1305.

During the "French" period of the fourteenth century, Douai existed in a sort of liminal position, neither French, though French-speaking, nor Flemish, though proudly "flammand" in spirit. Politically separated from all but Lille among the "bonnes villes" of Flanders to which it had originally belonged, Douai was now dependent on and subject to its sovereign in a way it had never been. The city was compelled to pay a huge portion of urban revenues to the crown, first to the French and then, after 1384, to the Burgundians. Its elite increasingly sought royal office or performed functions for the municipality at the behest of the crown, and in foreign affairs, Douai was—prudently—a constant and dutiful supporter of royal interests (no matter who the royalty was at the moment). Although Douai retained much of the prestige bequeathed by its history as one of Flanders' original "bonnes villes," managing even to preserve the right to select its own échevins, make and enforce its own law, and collect its own taxes, it was no longer quite what it had been. Its citizens were probably less prosperous on average and less optimistic about their prospects than they had been, and its elites were less secure in their own power at home and less independent of their sovereigns, whose clients they were inexorably becoming. It is no wonder, then, that the fourteenth and fifteenth centuries have been seen as a long period of economic and political decline in Douai.

Social Class and Legal Preference

Jacob has proposed that this climate of uncertainty propelled the Douaisien reform (although, as we shall see, he also argued that it was only after some unrelated institutional changes that the reform could be realized). His hypothesis has several parts, the first of which depends upon a particular understanding of social stratification in Douai. In Jacob's view, the Douaisien legal reform was led and dominated by the rich, who stood at the very top of the city's social hierarchy, the merchants and financiers who ran Douai after the revolts of the 1290s. In Jacob's words, "It is the established bourgeois, [who] lived from commerce or their rents, whom we find among the very first to use the clause of reprise."[3] Ordinary people of Douai, in contrast, came to the contract much later, and with much less energy, than did their more privileged fellow citizens; they clung instead to the old ways of doing things: "The small craftsmen, workers, finishers, and nailmakers resisted, clinging to the ravestissement."[4] If, as Jacob admitted, artisans, retailers, and workers often "were marrying under entirely classical forms of the conventional regime" (i.e., the marriage contract) by the mid–fifteenth century, it was nonetheless true that "the increase in numbers of clauses of reprise unrolled largely as a conquest of the lower ranks of society by those at the top."[5] Looked at a bit more closely, however, the Douaisien evidence does not fit this pattern as well as it first seems:

3. Jacob, *Les époux*, 205.
4. Ibid.
5. Ibid.

ordinary people did not refuse the contract as the hypothesis requires, and the rich did not "turn their back" on the ravestissement as predicted.[6]

Let us look first at the behavior of ordinary people. Even the earliest contracts were written by weavers and butchers as often as they were by merchants or knights; in fact, ordinary people were emphatically the majority of contract writers, even in the earliest years, when the contract was in embryonic form. Of the thirty-five surviving marriage contracts written between 1351 and 1374, for example, (the earliest significant collection of contracts that exists), only eight were written by families that I have labeled "rentier." The term is somewhat imprecise because it includes people still active in commerce and a few men in the professions, as well as true rentiers, men who lived from passive investments alone. As will become clear, however, Douai's elite was not so distinctly stratified until after 1500, and so for the purposes of distinguishing among Douai's propertied residents, I have thought it reasonable to use the term "rentier" to refer simply to those whose marriages were financed by portements consisting principally of land and rents or of large holdings of cash, urban real estate, inventories, and personal property.[7] Thus, examples of rentiers in Douai include people such as Katherine D'Aubi, who brought 400 francs to her marriage in 1374, and her groom, Jacquement Pourcelet, who contributed the same amount of cash plus five houses in Douai, 6 rasières of land in Bermaincourt, 12 rasières in Wasiers, and an annual rent of 10 livres parisis m.d.f.[8]

Most couples writing contracts were not, however, rentiers. Most were considerably less well off. Sixteen of the couples involved in the thirty-

---

6. The phrase is from Jacob, who remarked that "a desire to preserve their assets in the family by turning their back on the old customary law began first among the ranks of the rich." Jacob, *Les époux*, 204–5.

7. AMD, FF 586 (period ending March 1376). There were a total of seventy marriage agreements in this sample.

As rough measures of socioeconomic standing, I have divided writers of marriage contracts into three categories, "rentiers," "prosperous householders," and "simple householders." "Rentiers" were people with extensive landholdings or urban real property, rents, and large cash portements (roughly, over 200 livres parisis in the fourteenth century, 300 livres parisis in the fifteenth century, and 600 livres parisis in the sixteenth century). "Properous" contract writers owned some real property, sometimes a small portfolio of rents, and extensive collections of personal property valued, along with cash, at about 20 to 200 livres in the fourteenth century, 100 to 600 livres in the sixteenth. "Simple householders" made up the residual category; these were people with personal property and cash valued at less than 20 livres in the fourteenth century and 100 in the sixteenth, along with, perhaps, a small house or a share in a house.

8. AMD, FF 585/189 (11 July 1374).

five marriages in this sample could be counted only "prosperous." Like Robe La Verines, these brides contributed mere modest portements—in her case, a half share in a house in Douai, 7 couppres of land in Quiery, and 80 florins d'or—and they married men who, like La Verines's groom, had only cash, "moebles, fer et hostiaulx de son metier" (movables, iron, and tools of his trade) all worth 80 florins d'or.[9] The remaining nine couples of the thirty-five were more ordinary still. Like Maroie Losote, who brought 8 francs francais d'or in cash and some cattle, they had almost no immovable property and only a modest collection of chattels and movables.[10] In total, as table 1 summarizes, more than 80 percent of the sampled fourteenth-century contract writers (133 contracts) were only "prosperous" or merely "householders." Almost by definition, the men of this group were not professionals, merchants, financiers, nobles, or men of leisure; rather, they were weavers, fullers, finishers, nailmakers, laborers, butchers, shopkeepers, carpenters, and brewers.

Only a few marriage agreements actually tell us the occupations of the men who married or whose daughter they were marrying, however, so we must usually deduce social role simply from economic rank, as I have just done. Those that do provide specific occupational identifications or other indications of social status (in addition to the information about their wealth) confirm what the financial data suggests: it was not the leisured, the professional, or the merchant classes who wrote the majority of the fourteenth-century contracts. In total, seventy of the seventy-nine principal actors actually identified by occupation in the 133 marriage contracts sampled for the entire fourteenth century were artisans or small retailers (table 1).[11]

Thus, however incomplete our information about the occupations of those Douaisiens who chose to marry by contract, it is certain that the

9. AMD, FF 585/162 (16 November 1373).

10. AMD, FF 585/210 (4 January 1375).

11. To be sure, many of those people who were not identified by occupation (a large group of some 187 men), whether writers of contracts or of ravestissements, must have been merchants, professionals, or even men of leisure. In this period, it was still uncommon for men of such status to identify themselves or be identified by occupation or social role; their wealth alone apparently sufficed to place them socially, while more ordinary people needed an occupational label in addition to their name. Among the twenty-two men in the fourteenth-century samples of marriage contracts who were counted as rentiers, only seven were identified by social role (see table 1). Two called themselves artisans—which probably meant that they were merchant-artisans, people who had once produced the goods they sold and now oversaw both production and commerce; the rest were called "marchand," "drapier," or "escuyer."

Table 1

Economic and Occupational/Social Status of Writers of Marriage Documents (Fourteenth-Century Samples)

	Total	Economic Status			
		Status Not Measurable	Rentier	Prosperous	Householder
Total contracts	133	8 (6%)	22 (17%)	59 (44%)	44 (33%)
Contracts indicating occupational/social status of at least one principal actor	64	3 (5%)	6 (9%)	30 (47%)	22 (39%)
Number of principal actors identified by status	79	4 (5%)	7 (9%)	40 (51%)	28 (35%)
artisans and retailers, nontextile	50 (63%)	1 (2%)	2 (4%)	24 (48%)	23 (46%)
artisans and retailers, textile	20 (25%)	3 (15%)	0	12 (60%)	5 (25%)
drapers	1 (1%)	0	1 (100%)	0	0
merchants	2 (3%)	0	1 (50%)	1 (50%)	0
other	6 (8%)	0	3 (50%)	3 (50%)	0
Total ravestissements	80				
Ravestissements indicating occupational/social status of at least one principal actor	32				
Number of principal actors identified by status	34				
artisans and retailers, nontextile	22 (65%)				
artisans and retailers, textile	8 (23%)				
drapers	1 (3%)				
merchants	0				
other	3 (9%)				
Total documents	213				

Note: Occupational status refers to occupational or professional identifications provided in the document itself, usually as part of personal identification (e.g., "Jehan D'Auby, drapier"). It also includes labels of social status, presented in the same form (e.g., "Jehan D'Auby, ecurier," "Jehan D'Auby, maitre," or "Jehan D'Auby, clerc"). A small number of identifications were derived from other information in the document, as, for example, in a marriage contract listing the tools for making sayes as part of a groom's portement. Occasionally, two occupations were given for the same person (e.g., "charpentier et manouvrier"). In these cases, I took the first unless it was less specific than the second (e.g., "clerc et tisserand").

Sampled documents: AMD, FF 585/141–213 (April 1351–April 1375); FF 586/214–305 (May 1375–January 1378); FF 596/888–923; (April 1393–May 1394).

majority of them were ordinary citizens, even in the early days before the contract was commonly used. To insist on the importance of ordinary people's role in changing marital property law is not, however, to deny that Douai's elites wrote marriage contracts *relatively* more frequently than did more ordinary people. In all, 16.5 percent of the 133 contract writers from all fourteenth-century samples could be positively identified as members of the social elite, a percentage much higher than their likely representation in the population at large and probably a bit higher than their representation among Douai's propertied classes.[12] Among the male principal actors in contracts who could not be identified by occupation or social status—more than 180 men—the percentage of elites was surely higher still.

Nonetheless, even if ordinary citizens issued marriage contracts in these years relatively less often than merchants and professionals, the fact that they chose to do so in such substantial numbers signifies their independent interest in changing marital property law. After all, they paid handsomely for the privilege of having a contract drafted and transcribed, almost certain evidence that the contract was valuable to them, that they were not simply imitating their social betters.[13] To be sure, they were not independent authors of their contracts. They learned the techniques of revising custom from others—presumably indirectly from the rich, who seem to have written the very first contracts—but this does not mean they were slavishly copying texts written by others, or that they were coerced into doing so by their political leaders.

In a sense, of course, their documents were not original compositions. Marriage contracts were highly formulaic texts; no one, not even the fantastically wealthy, devised the contract's formulas or gave the document language at will. Writing a marriage contract was in many respects much like filling in the blanks of a standardized form. There was, moreover, only one standard form in Douai at any time; all marriage contracts were written before the same board of échevins and were thus not subject to the variations that historians have sometimes found in areas where such

12. This calculation assumes 266 male principal actors (conventionally, the groom and the father of the bride) in 133 contracts, 79 of whom were positively identified.

13. There is no direct evidence about the cost of registering marriage contracts (and similar documents) in the fourteenth century, but we know that the clerks and the échevins who handled the registration were paid fees for their services. A document from the early sixteenth century suggests that such fees then totaled about 10 percent of the assets covered: AMD, BB 72, fol. 1027r and v.

documents were drafted by several different private notaries. Certainly the form of the marriage contract changed over time, as Douai's échevins and their clerks made adaptations they thought legitimate, but from the point of view of a couple writing a contract, there was very little room for individual variation.

Nonetheless, contracts were not all alike, and those of ordinary people differed from those composed by the rich in ways that reflect their particular situations and their interests. Let us compare, for example, the terms of the contracts written by ordinary people with those drafted by Douai's elite in the collection surviving from 1375 to 1378.[14] There are fifty-nine such documents, twenty-two of them written by people positively identified as members of artisan families, two written by people known to be members of elite families (one "marchand," one "chevalier").[15] All but twelve of the fifty-nine contracts provided the widow her portement (or they contained a separate clause of reprise); all but twelve of these forty-seven granted the widow a douaire in addition to return of the portement or the reprise. Not all the douaires were, however, the standard increase on the portement. In the case of the marriage of a chevalier, for example, the douaire was in the form of usufruct on properties in the husband's estate.[16] In a marriage contract written for a "prosperous" butcher, the douaire was also granted only in usufruct if there were children of the marriage (if not, the widow received her douaire outright).[17] A marriage contract written by a mere "householder" provided that the douaire be split with any children born of the marriage.[18] In total, three of the four rentier contracts among the thirty-five providing both return of the portement and a douaire went on to restrict the douaire in some way, either by granting it in usufruct or by dividing it with others. Among the seventeen contracts of this kind written by "prosperous" Douaisiens, three limited the douaire in this way; two of the fourteen written by "householders" did so.

In one sense, this pattern confirms our expectations. The richest Douaisiens appear to have been the most concerned to hold property in the lineage; they devised the most elaborate clauses (with the various provis-

14. AMD, FF 586 (1375–78).

15. Of these fifty-nine documents, thirty-five provided no occupational status identifications for either principal actor.

16. AMD, FF 586/224 (17 June 1375).

17. AMD, FF 586/236 (9 September 1375).

18. AMD, FF 586/248 (21 January 1376).

ions of usufruct or shared ownership of the douaire), and they added such clauses at a higher rate than did ordinary Douaisiens. Looked at from another point of view, however, these documents reveal a surprising commitment to forms of "patrilineality" on the part of ordinary people. Of course, it is clear that whether "householders" or "prosperous," these people did not so aggressively track property through lines of descent, assiduously labeling it for the lineage, as rentiers frequently tended to do. But it is equally clear that they would have had little reason to write clauses exactly like this. These people had very few immovable assets at all, the very kind of goods that are most easily imagined as belonging to future generations. They owned tools, livestock, furnishings, and clothing instead, and they were thus considerably less likely to look ten, twenty, or thirty years ahead, to label these goods for return to natal kin or to suppose that they would still be intact when the time came for the estate distribution.

If they had no land and grand houses that they could readily track through future generations or back to the ancestors from whom they had come, ordinary people did, however, use the contract to protect "lineal" interests in other ways. Gillotte Descaillon, who married Jehan Aymon in 1375, reserved her small portement of 75 livres parisis, which was made up of cash and movables, and her douaire of 25 livres parisis for her father or, in his absence, her children or next of kin, thus assuring her natal family (rather than her husband's kin) her estate.[19] Agnes Creneche, an apparently childless widow who married a prosperous "peintre" (painter) in the same year, specified that many of the items she brought to the marriage—a bed, a coverlet, some clothing, and other household goods— be given to a niece at her death.[20] The marriage of Jehanne Merlin and Pierot De Berenlin Dit Motin, a "mulquinier" (miller), which took place about the same time, provided that half of the widow's douaire be left for the bride's niece.[21] Jaquemon De Courchielles, daughter of a "manouvrier" (day worker), reserved any heritages she might acquire for her children or, in their absence, the next of kin (the plus prochains).[22]

Among the twelve contracts in this group that provided no douaires and listed no portements, thus clinging very closely to the old notions of

19. AMD, FF 586/214 (1 May 1375).
20. AMD, FF 586/215 (May 1375).
21. AMD, FF 586/218 (12 May 1375).
22. AMD, FF 586/220 (20 May 1375).

marital property relations (these twelve documents were, in fact, little more than modified ravestissements) we also find traces of new ideas about lineality. All the twelve contracts, whether written by people labeled householders (five), prosperous (three), or unidentified (four), moved away from the grant of full property rights provided by old custom; some (six) simply allowed each spouse to write a will for a limited amount of property, but others split the estate with children or other kin, thus much more seriously undermining old notions of spousal succession rights.

Hardly the passive imitators of their social superiors, Douai's artisans and small retailers were thus aggressive rewriters of marital property law, eager pupils of the clerks who must have guided them as they drafted their contracts. These contract writers were not as quick as the very rich to grant property in usufruct or to encumber their gifts with elaborate clauses directing its subsequent disposition. They were, however, every bit as quick to adopt the marriage contract to their own perceived needs. And, like the rich, they defined their needs to be lineal.

If ordinary people confound our expectations by having turned away from custom with an eagerness that approached the elite's, the rich themselves similarly perplex us by having clung to old custom and the ravestissement much longer than we might have anticipated. The échevins themselves chose to marry by custom surprisingly often. Of the twelve échevins who served in 1390–91, for example, most appear to have married by the old rules. Only five left marriage agreements of any kind, and three of them were ravestissements par lettre: Jehan D'Auby, a "tondeur de grans forches" (a shearer of drapery); Jehans Paniers, husband of Reusselle Boinebroque, a member of the family that Espinas made infamous as one of Europe's earlist capitalists; and Alixandre Caron, whose widow would later remarry—and do so very well indeed—with a contract.[23] The archive contains no record of marriages for the remaining seven officials, but some of these men did marry, we know, for we have records of the marriages of their legitimate children, by chance all of them daughters.[24] A few of

---

23. AMD, FF 586/221; 585/172; 592/648; 600/1222. Jehans Gariage and Willaume De Gouy left contracts: AMD, FF 592/647 and FF 599/1165. Of course, they may have issued other legal instruments that weakened the force of the ravestissement par lettre; Jehan D'Auby, for example, wrote a will in 1402 that distributed his goods more widely than the ravestissement provided (AMD, FF 869 [2 May 1402]). He must, however, have had his wife's permission to do so (and she was a major beneficiary of his will) because wills did not not supersede prior marital documents.

24. Bertoul De Sain's (AMD, FF 597/996); Jehan Hongnard's (AMD, FF 585/188); Jaques Pieffort's (AMD, FF 589/503 and 594/808); and Jehans Wallequin's (AMD, FF 590/533).

the seven échevins for whom we have no marriage records may, to be sure, have married by a contract that has been lost, but the odds are better that they either wrote no marriage agreement at all, letting old custom rule their marital property relations, or that they wrote a ravestissement par lettre that has been lost.

The échevins' preferences seem to have been typical of the age. Of the 213 marriage agreements sampled for the fourteenth century, 80 were ravestissements (38 percent), many of them undoubtedly issued by Douai's richest citizens (table 1). The table gives little direct evidence, however, that it was the elite who showed such loyalty to customary notions of conjugality, at least as measured by their use of the ravestissement. Only four of the thirty-four occupational statuses provided in the eighty ravestissements from this period specifically referred to merchants, professionals, or nobles. Still, among the principal actors to the ravestissements who were not named by occupation or social status (about 125 men), there were doubtless a good number of very rich men, for, as we have seen, it was usually men of this status, in contrast to members of the artisanal class, who were not identified by occupational role.

One hundred years later, the situation had significantly changed. In stark contrast to the record of 1391, when few of the échevins appear to have married by contract, ten of the twelve échevins who served in 1497–98 did so. Only two left no contracts, but other sources reveal that both men married and, although we have no sure way of knowing whether custom or written convention governed their marriages, it is reasonable to guess that they did not let custom rule, that they, like their brethren on the bench, wrote marriage contracts or other legal instruments to modify custom. Still, even the fifteenth century did not see the end of the written ravestissement. For the century as a whole, almost 17 percent of the surviving documents in the five series sampled (240 documents) were ravestissements par lettre (table 2). And 40 percent of those whose authors' social status can be identified were written by Douai's elite (eight of twenty). Just as in the fourteenth century, moreover, artisans and small merchants were well represented among those contract writers whose occupations or social status could be identified: almost 80 percent of the 179 named occupations or social positions (close to 50 percent of the principal actors in all sampled contracts).

By the mid–sixteenth century, things had changed once again. About 50 percent of the contract writers identified by occupation or social status in this period were elites, about double the percentage in samples taken

Table 2

Economic and Occupational/Social Status of Writers of Marriage Documents (Fifteenth-Century Samples)

	Total	Economic Status			
		Status Not Measurable	Rentier	Prosperous	Householder
Total contracts	200	28 (14%)	22 (11%)	65 (32%)	85 (43%)
Contracts indicating occupational/ social status of at least one principal actor	129	19 (15%)	13 (10%)	42 (33%)	55 (42%)
Number of principal actors identified by status	179	25 (14%)	20 (11%)	66 (37%)	68 (38%)
artisans and retailers, nontextile	99 (55%)	16 (16%)	4 (4%)	35 (35%)	44 (44%)
artisans and retailers, textile	42 (23%)	4 (10%)	3 (7%)	14 (33%)	21 (50%)
drapers	3 (2%)	0	0	3 (100%)	0
merchants	12 (7%)	3 (25%)	2 (17%)	6 (50%)	1 (8%)
other	23 (13%)	2 (9%)	11 (48%)	8 (35%)	2 (8%)
Total ravestissements	40				
Ravestissements indicating occupational/social status of at least one principal actor	18				
Number of principal actors identified by status	20				
artisans and retailers, nontextile	10 (50%)				
artisans and retailers, textile	2 (10%)				
drapers	1 (5%)				
merchants	3 (15%)				
other	4 (20%)				
Total documents	240				

Note: Occupational status refers to occupational or professional identifications provided in the document itself, usually as part of personal identification (e.g., "Jehan D'Auby, drapier"). It also includes labels of social status, presented in the same form (e.g., "Jehan D'Auby, ecurier," "Jehan D'Auby, maitre," or "Jehan D'Auby, clerc"). A small number of identifications were derived from other information in the document, as, for example, in a marriage contract listing the tools for making sayes as part of a groom's portement. Occasionally, two occupations were given for the same person (e.g., "charpentier et manouvrier"). In these cases, I took the first unless it was less specific than the second (e.g., "clerc et tisserand").

Sampled documents: AMD, FF 609/1770–832 (March 1421–March 1428); FF 616/2320–406 (May 1441–March 1444); FF 632/3705–42; (September 1478–July 1479); FF 639/4284–357 (April 1495–March 1497).

just thirty years earlier (table 3).[25] Whether this change reflects structural shifts in the Douaisien economy—an absolute or relative increase in the number of rich—or simply a fall-off in the number of artisans and retailers who wrote marriage agreements is hard to say with certainty. We can, however, identify two patterns without difficulty. First, many fewer of the Douaisiens who wrote marriage agreements after about 1500 chose the ravestissement par lettre (only 6 of 111 agreements [5 percent], only 2 of them written by elites [none by men calling themselves "marchand"]). Second, artisans and retailers were then rapidly disappearing from the entire archive of marriage documents (only 55 percent of identified occupations in all sixteenth-century samples, and only 45 percent in the samples taken in the 1550s, as compared to 79 percent in the fifteenth-century samples).

Yet, the virtual disappearance of the ravestissement and the decline of ordinary people in the archive of marriage agreements are not necessarily different measures of the same process. The ravestissement par lettre had never, let us recall, been the sole possession of ordinary Douaisiens; it had not even been preferred by those members of the artisanal class who wrote marriage agreements of any kind, and its demise in the sixteenth century thus cannot be attributed to their abandonment of it. Quite the contrary: 8 percent of the artisans and retailers named in the fifteenth-century samples of marriage agreements had chosen to write ravestissements, but 12 percent of those in the sixteenth-century samples did so. In fact, to judge from what are admittedly rather sketchy data, the disappearance of the ravestissement from the Douaisien archive could have been more than accounted for by the elite's (surprisingly tardy) decision to abandon it: 12 percent of the elites identified by occupation or social place in the fifteenth-century samples wrote ravestissements, while less than 4 percent of those in the sixteenth-century samples did so.

The Problem of Turning Points

Jacob's sociological analysis of the legal reform turns out, then, to be misleading, for it does not seem that the move to contract "was led by the rich" and "imposed on ordinary people." Even less satisfying—although

---

25. Taken from AMD, FF 654 (1548–49), 655 (1553–70), and 914 (1557). Of seventy-eight occupational status identifications, twenty-six were merchants and fourteen were "other."

Table 3

Economic and Occupational/Social Status of Writers of Marriage Documents
(Sixteenth-Century Samples)

		Economic Status			
	Total	Status Not Measurable	Rentier	Prosperous	Householder
Total contracts	105	2 (2%)	24 (23%)	42 (40%)	37 (35%)
Contracts indicating occupational/ social status of at least one principal actor	79	1 (1%)	16 (20%)	33 (42%)	29 (37%)
Number of principal actors identified by status	123	1 (1%)	25 (20%)	53 (43%)	44 (36%)
artisans and retailers, nontextile	45 (36%)	1 (2%)	2 (5%)	14 (31%)	28 (62%)
artisans and retailers, textile	23 (19%)	0	0	11 (48%)	12 (52%)
drapers	5 (4%)	0	0	4 (80%)	1 (20%)
merchants	34 (28%)	0	19 (56%)	13 (38%)	2 (6%)
other	16 (13%)	0	4 (25%)	11 (69%)	1 (6%)
Total ravestissements	6				
Ravestissements indicating occupational/social status of at least one principal actor	4				
Number of principal actors identified by status	9				
artisans and retailers, nontextile	3 (33%)				
artisans and retailers, textile	4 (45%)				
drapers	1 (11%)				
merchants	0				
other	1 (11%)				
Total documents	111				

Note: Occupational status refers to occupational or professional identifications provided in the document itself, usually as part of personal identification (e.g., "Jehan D'Auby, drapier"). It also includes labels of social status, presented in the same form (e.g., "Jehan D'Auby, ecurier," "Jehan D'Auby, maitre," or "Jehan D'Auby, clerc"). A small number of identifications were derived from other information in the document, as, for example, in a marriage contract listing the tools for making sayes as part of a groom's portement. Occasionally, two occupations were given for the same person (e.g., "charpentier et manouvrier"). In these cases, I took the first unless it was less specific than the second (e.g., "clerc et tisserand").

Sampled documents: AMD, FF 649/5126–76 (April 1521–April 1523); FF 654/5539–42 (July 1540–May 1549); FF 655/ 5543–86; (November 1551–October 1570); FF 914 [10 docs., unindexed] (March 1521–April 1522); FF 914 [19 docs., unindexed] (April 1557–January 1558).

on the face of it equally commonsensical—is the analogue to Jacob's argument from social structure: his suggestion about why the reform took place when it did. In Jacob's interpretation, the chronology reflected a complex mix of economic and political or institutional factors. Propertied Douaisiens sought to flee custom because these rules threatened their social position in ways that could no longer be tolerated as economic conditions worsened in the fourteenth century. Their flight was less precipitous than it would have been, however, because urban fiscal policy hindered their departure.

Let us look, first, at the surviving marriage agreements themselves, and the precise chronology of change they seem to chart. To all appearances, the archive suggests that Douaisiens abruptly turned away from custom sometime around 1375, just as Jacob observed. Of the 166 marriage agreements dating before 1375, only 24 were contracts (and only 7 of them were written between 1351 and 1373); the rest were ravestissments par lettre.[26] In contrast, 29 of the 54 (54 percent) surviving documents dated October 1373 to January 1375 were contracts; 59 of 91 (65 percent) documents in the collection dated 1375–78 were contracts.[27]

This seems a dramatic shift indeed. The turning point occurred at that moment, Jacob surmised, rather than some seventy-five years earlier when economic and political crises first hit Douai because it was only then that the elite were free to choose a more socially conservative marital property regime. Until then, they could not act upon their preferences because economic conditions were *too* unstable, and under these circumstances Douai's propertied elite did not dare save for the future. In these unsteady times, all that mattered was the present, and so for long years Douai's rich thus had to subordinate one set of interests (in patrilineal inheritance) to another (in the immediate preservation of assets).

For Jacob, it was only around 1380 that the political and fiscal situation had stabilized enough for Douai's elite to opt for lineal inheritance. A key episode in the transformation was the city's definitive abandonment of the *taille*, a form of taxation on households. Douai's échevins had traditionally levied the taille arbitrarily, announcing their imposition of levies without

26. All but eleven of the seventy-five marriage documents in chirographe dating from before 1301 are ravestissements par lettre, texts that *intensified* custom rather than subverted it. Of the sixty-four marriage agreements surviving from 1301 to 1350, only six were marriage contracts proper; the rest were ravestissements of some kind; of the twenty-seven that survive from 1351 to 1373, only seven were contracts.

27. AMD, FF 585 and 586.

warning and setting tax rates at wildly varying levels, depending upon financial needs and political possibilities. So onerous were these burdens, and so unpredictable, Jacob reasoned, that Douai's propertied class had not dared to save capital for future generations because they had not presumed to dream that wealth could survive intact for so long. Only when this taxation method had been discarded, tentatively in the 1320s, definitively in the 1380s, were Douaisiens free to abandon custom and to institute, via their marriage agreements, "the transmission of family values."[28]

Plague and warfare played a role in the choice of marital property regime as well, Jacob proposed, but they worked in the opposite way, because they so put the future in peril that elites were inclined to suppress their longing for patrilineal marital regimes. Again, it was not until the 1380s that their fears had sufficiently subsided. Then, with war at a standstill, plague in hiatus, and fiscal reforms secured, Douaisiens could decisively move toward the dotal-like marital property regime they had longed desired: "Reassured about the safety of their patrimonies, the families of this 'middle' bourgeoisie were able hereafter to dream of a future, a future in which people married younger, and of dotal conventions able to guarantee the transfer of assets among people who shared blood."[29]

Appealing as this reasoning may be, it cannot be supported by the evidence. First, the evidence from the collection of marriage contracts is far too thin. There are only twenty-seven such contracts for the entire generation living before 1373 (just over one per year for twenty-two years), hardly enough to make a claim for sociological significance. Worse, the marriage agreements that have survived in Douai are only a portion—an unknown portion—of those that were actually written, at least to judge from the frequency with which contracts or ravestissements mentioned in other archival records do not appear in the existing collection of chirographes.[30] It is perilous indeed to use records with unmeasureable but certain lacunae of this magnitude for close statistical correlation of the kind Jacob's argument requires.

Second, the marriage contracts that do survive do not unambiguously support Jacob's chronology. The sudden proliferation of contracts that

28. The phrase is from Jacob, *Les époux*, 406.

29. Jacob, *Les époux*, 222.

30. For example, a collection of one hundred contrats divers dated 1391, mentions six marriage contracts, none of which have survived in the archive: AMD, FF 695 (April 1391–September 1391).

he dates from 1380 (coinciding with what he believes was the definitive elimination of the taille) began, in fact, in the early 1370s. While 1380 did see an upsurge in marriage agreements of all kinds, probably reflecting, as Jacob surmised, an increase in the marriage rate in that year, the increase does not necessarily reflect a *new* interest in marriage by contract. As we have seen, 65 percent of the documents surviving from the 1375–78 sample were marriage contracts, 69 percent of those in samples from 1376–77 taken by Jacob. In 1380, in comparison, 73 percent of the surviving documents were contracts. The shift from the ravestissement to the contract continued more or less steadily thereafter: in 1392–93, 79 percent of the surviving agreements were contracts, 77 percent of those from 1408–10, 85 percent of those from 1441–43; and 94 percent of the documents from 1450–51. Seen in this context, the 1380s do not seem a turning point but a moment in a more gradual and more fundamental process of legal reform.

Before the Marriage Contract

Nonetheless, it is almost surely true that fewer Douaisiens wrote marriage contracts before the last third of the fourteenth century than they did thereafter. It is not true, however, that Douaisiens who married before the 1370s were as overwhelmingly committed to original custom's notions of conjugality and succession as the small size of the surviving archive of pre-1375 marriage agreements would suggest. Both the huge archive of contrats divers and the collections of wills from earlier decades in Douai testify that Douaisiens had been aggressively amending customary marital property and inheritance arrangements long before they adopted the marriage contract.

Let us look first at the contrats divers. Of course the main purpose of these miscellaneous contracts, receipts, and records of business deals was not to regulate marital property relations and inheritance; the main purpose was to record a property transfer or the debt attached to such a transfer. Still, some of the contracts reveal that the property transfers were connected with wills or marriage contracts, and they thus indirectly betray the purposes of the property transfers themselves.[31] One such business

---

31. In a sample from the late thirteenth century, for example, house sales were the single most frequently recorded transaction (twenty-six of the seventy-one contracts were of this kind); sales of movable goods or recognitions of debts of an unspecified kind formed a less coherent

contract from the late thirteenth century, for example, acknowledged payment of a promised portement due on a marriage contract (the marriage contract itself has not survived in the archive of chirographes)[32]; another from the same era recorded a second husband's payment of property due his wife from the estate of her first husband (the payment went to his wife's former avoués)[33]; a third was a stepfather's written guarantee of property left by the boy's father.[34]

A later sample of contrats divers, from 1391, contained even clearer evidence that Douaisiens used these contracts to record adjustments of the customary laws of marital property relations and succession.[35] Six of the one hundred contrats sampled in that year specifically recorded payments promised by prior marriage contracts (none of which has survived). For example, Jehan De Flandre, a grain merchant, delivered 100 francs d'or to his daughter, as promised in her marriage contract to Pierot Parsis, a butcher;[36] Jehans Des Mouchieuex, a drapery weaver, acknowledged receipt of 40 livres parisis and 1 gold noble (worth 72 sous parisis) from his wife's mother and brother, from the estate of her father, promised at his marriage.[37] An additional twelve documents in the sample were estate settlements, all of them acknowledging payments promised in wills or marriage contracts that had been written earlier for the express purpose of intervening in customary laws of succession.

Contrats divers surviving from later years contain many fewer references to wills or marriage agreements, presumably because by then the

---

category (thirty-one contracts), but it included many good-sized transactions—108 livres parisis paid for two sacks of wool (AMD, FF 664/6208, [January 1279]); 80 livres parisis for wine (AMD, FF 664/6199 [December 1278]); 30 livres parisis for 5 kierkes of alum ([AMD, FF 664/6179 [July 1278]).

32. AMD, FF 664/6153 (January 1275), reprinted in Espinas and Pirenne, *Recueil de documents relatifs à l'histoire de l'industrie drapière en Flandre des origines à l'époque Bourguignonne*, 4 vols. (Brussels: P. Imbreghts, 1906), vol. 3, doc. 615.

33. AMD, FF 664/6170 (April 1278).

34. AMD, FF 664/6169 (April 1278); in Espinas, *La vie urbaine*, vol. 3, doc. 649.

35. Of course, most of these documents were, like those in the sample from one hundred years earlier, records of market transactions that had no effect on custom's rules about marital property relations or inheritance: of the one hundred contrats divers in this sample, almost half recorded sales of houses or of rents (forty-six), and most of the rest were acknowledgments of debts for sales of movable goods—for example, a debt of 9 francs d'or (worth almost 15 livres parisis) for delivery of cattle (AMD, FF 695/11605 [8 June 1391]); another, 60 francs for sale of a boat (AMD, FF 695/11592 [19 May 1391]); another, 78 francs for a purchase of wood (AMD, FF 695/11604 [8 June 1391]).

36. AMD, FF 695/11629 (15 July 1391).

37. AMD, FF 695/11624 (9 July 1391).

procedures for fulfilling the terms of marriage contracts and wills were so well understood that registering the property transfers required by them seemed superfluous. Of the 109 contrats divers surviving from 1441, for example, there were only 4 that settled marriage contracts or estates, as compared to at least 18 in the sample from 1391; the rest concerned house sales (59), transfers of movable goods, usually business inventories (24), sales of rents (10), or records of unspecified debts (12). A sample from the end of the century contained even fewer documents explicitly altering succession or marital property relations. Of 59 documents, only 1 concerned the settlement of an estate, and none treated marriage contracts; the remainder were house sales (46), sales of rents (7), or debt settlements of one kind or another (5).[38]

As mechanisms for recording property transfers rather than tools for managing marital property relations and inheritance, contrats divers are extremely crude tools for measuring Douaisiens' efforts to change customary rules about marriage and inheritance. The wills that survive from the mid–thirteenth into the early fifteenth centuries are, however, much better indices because they were frequently written specifically for such purposes.[39] Even the earliest wills pursue these goals. All of the nine wills in the city's earliest collection (of pre-1274 wills) that were written by married or widowed men were principally directed at changing custom's most basic rules about succession. Simon Le Cras, for example, left everything to his wife, Marien, as custom would have decreed, but he required that she support their daughter Oede until she came of age and then pay her 13 livres parisis, a restriction custom would not have imposed.[40] Aleaume Le Cambier left his chief residence to his wife Oedain, but only until she remarried; in that event, the house would go to their children.[41] Engherran Brunamont was still more aggressive. He left generous gifts to the church and the poor, and then gave his son Pieron the 500 livres parisis promised at his wedding and a house on the "Grant Markiet"; to the daughter of

---

38. AMD, FF 796.

39. Jacob argues that after about 1370, the will no longer played a significant role in altering customary rules of succession. My evidence suggests otherwise, but it is impossible to know without a much more extensive statistical study just how often Douaisiens used wills to regulate such matters, either before or after the late fourteenth century. In general, I would agree with Jacob that the marriage contract became relatively more important in the fifteenth century and may even have surpassed the testament in this regard.

40. AMD, FF 861 (April 1263), in Monique Mestayer, "Testaments douaisiens antérieurs à 1270," *Nos Patois du Nord* 7 (1962): 73.

41. AMD, FF 861 (April 1248), in Mestayer, "Testaments douaisiens," 64.

his first marriage he left 100 livres parisis; to Oedain, daughter of Bernart Brunamont, he left 40 shillings parisis; to servants and other family members he left additional small gifts; finally, to his grandchildren he made residual gifts of a cash income of 3 marcs per year.[42] Jehans Louskars left his "feme et espousee" his house as long as she remained unmarried in addition to his jewels and his gold plate; to his daughter by Marien Le Fourier he gave 100 sous tournois; and to his son Jakemin, also born of Marien Le Fourier, he gave 20 livres parisis; to a certain Juetain, wife of Jakemon De Soumaing the goldsmith, he left 40 sous parisis and to Jakemon, her son, 40 sous parisis; to his wife and any children they might have he gave all his "moebles" to be divided equally among them.[43]

Nine of the sixteen married or widowed men who wrote wills dated between 1350 and 1367 similarly used the will to rearrange succession. All of the five married men in the group denied their wives some of the property custom would have granted them; all the men who had children made unequal bequests to the children, thus appearing to have overruled custom's preference for equal inheritances.

Of twelve Douaisien men in a sample taken about a half century later, in the very early fifteenth century, all but one used the occasion not just to make gifts to the church but, like their predecessors, also to intervene in customary norms about succession. A few did so, to be sure, only in minor ways. Jehan Hamelle gave everything to his wife except his boat, presumably the chief piece of equipment for his trade, which he left to his son.[44] However slight Hamelle's intervention in custom, he was explicitly overturning not only unwritten custom but the ravestissement he had written in 1374, when he and his wife first married. Then he had agreed that if the marriage were fertile, his wife would be his full heir.[45] His will, in contrast, passed the tools of his trade directly on to their son. But Jacques Ballans, a tanner, a much richer man, wrote a will that more aggressively pursued exactly those lineal interests simultaneously being defined in marriage contracts. He gave huge amounts of property to his children, leaving his present wife only the *sourplus* (residual amount), but he obtained her consent to these gifts and had her agreement recorded in the preamble to the will ("du gre et acord de Jacque Lamant sa femme et espeuse"). To

42. AMD, FF 861 (January 1261), in Mestayer, "Testaments douaisiens," 69–70.
43. AMD, FF 861 (October 1269), in Mestayer, "Testaments douaisiens," 76–77.
44. AMD, FF 869 (13 October 1403).
45. AMD, FF 585/194 (28 July 1374).

the son of this marriage, he left 200 couronnes d'or, several houses, and some furnishings, making the three children born of his first wife the residual heirs of this son, should he die without descendants of his own; to one daughter of his first marriage he left 5 rasières 2 couppres of land and a house; to another, a house; to some grandchildren, 10 couronnes each; to his wife, all his "immeubles" but only for her life, after which they would revert to his children. He also stipulated that none of his children would take the immovables specifically bequeathed to them until their mother's death.[46] Andreieux Piquette, who was apparently unmarried, left a goddaughter a half interest in a house and some equipment and apparel; he left one nephew jewelry and plate; to another man (probably a nephew), some household goods; his maid, one-half of his household linens and a "lit estofee" (fully equipped bed); to his brother-in-law, husband of his sister, he gave a rental income of 30 livres parisis, four houses, another house and garden, and a couppre of meadow land; to his sister herself, he left only three of his best "hanaps" (drinking cups); to a knife-maker, apparently in payment of a debt, he left 50 couronnes, and to the children of a relative, perhaps a brother, he left 10 couppres of land and two small houses with the stipulation that if the children died before marriage or maturity, the property would return to Piquette's own plus prochains.[47]

All these wills were written in chirographe, on individual parchments now stored in the Douaisien archive. In addition to this collection, the archive houses many hundreds of wills in register, volumes dating from 1419 that were kept by the échevins to record testaments taken by priests and clerical notaries. Unlike the wills in chirographe, which were usually written by well propertied citizens, these were typically the testaments of Douai's simpler residents—artisans, retailers, day laborers. Also unlike wills in chirographe, which were usually drafted long before death, these testaments were made by people in a great hurry, for most of them would die within weeks, if not days, of making their statements. These, then, are deathbed testaments.

In form and substance, however, the wills in register are much like the wills in chirographe, although they are considerably less elaborate, reflecting the urgency with which they were made and the modest size of the estates they typically treated. They usually begin with a formula about

46. AMD, FF 869 (19 September 1403).
47. AMD, FF 869 (8 May 1404).

the imminence of death, with token gifts to the parish church and a request for burial. The testators then rush on to express their wishes about the disposition of their remaining estate, and their requests are often very general, for they usually had little to give away and little time to think about it: "my goods should go to my daughter," "all I have will belong to my niece." A few, however, make special bequests or impose restrictions that honor lineal property interests similar to those contained in the wills written in chirographe. For example, Jacquemart Le Libert, probably uncle to the Jehan Le Libert with which this book began, made a testament leaving all his property to his wife on the condition that she not remarry; if she did, she was to pass the children's share of the estate on to them.[48]

Thus, to judge from these records, the shift from what stood as custom had been underway long before the marriage contract had become the principal tool of legal reform, long before we even have reasonably complete collections of marriage contracts. Still, there is no doubt that Douaisiens intervened in custom more often and more aggressively, whether by will, individual property transfer, or marriage agreement, after about 1350 than they had before. For the entire period before 1350, we have only 140 marriage agreements in chirographe (a few others may reside in register in the city's administrative archive) and only about 115 wills, most of them dating from after 1300.[49] The collection of contrats divers is richer for these early years—there are about 1,850 such documents from the period between 1224 and 1350—but in comparison to the next 125 years, when almost 17,000 such documents have survived, this collection too is meager. Although I have argued the shift may to some extent simply reflect the accidents of record survival, so marked an increase could not be entirely the result of losses in the pre-1350 archive. Some combination of circumstances—demographic, institutional, economic, social, or political—produced, we must conclude, so many more wills and contracts after 1350.

---

48. AMD, FF 448, fols. 29v–30 (23 June 1439). She did remarry within a few years. She had her adult children witness the new marriage contract to confirm that she had complied with her first husband's wishes: AMD, FF 617/2410.

49. This count includes only wills in chirographe in the Archives Municipales de Douai. No wills in register, the other important collection of wills in Douai's municipal archive, have survived from this period. There is also a collection of wills (whose size is unknown) in the hospital archives of Douai, which are now closed. Scholars suspect that this is a good-sized collection (previous generations of scholars were granted limited access to these sources), but a great many of the wills in this archive are copies of those held by the city. A small number of wills have also been preserved from the chapter house of St. Amé in Douai: Archives departementales du Nord, St. Amé, Comptes du Domaine.

We can be certain, however, that the increase was not the result of population growth. In fact, most historians have argued that the city's population fell dramatically between about 1330 and 1380 and did not recover until after 1500. Alain Derville has made the most aggressive claim of this kind, contending that the city lost half its residents after the years of Plague, warfare, and economic decline characteristic of the fourteenth century.[50] Most other observers have been more cautious, never putting the medieval population as high as Derville was willing to do—he claimed it reached 30,000—and generally hedging about just how much it declined with the so-called depression of the late Middle Ages.[51] Whatever the precise population figures for either period, however, there is no doubt that Douai's population after 1350 did not, until well after 1500, equal the level reached at the end of the thirteenth.

It is considerably more likely that institutional developments in Douai help account for the burgeoning of the archive in the course of the fourteenth century. Douaisiens generally wrote wills and marriage contracts before other Northerners, in part because the city developed earlier the institutional structure necessary for such record keeping, a development perhaps also indicative of a rising literacy rate. It is also certainly the case that Douai's échevins, perhaps more than échevins in neighboring cities, had good reasons for establishing and maintaining such a system. They personally earned handsome fees for the services they rendered contract and will writers, as did the city itself, and the financial benefits alone go a long way to explaining why the échevins would have been eager to provide this service and why they would have so carefully kept their records up to date. If the échevinage changed in character as it seems to have done after about 1300, if more "new" men and more ordinary artisans joined its ranks, the bench may have become still more assiduous about soliciting this business, for these "newer" men might well have welcomed the extra income as their predecessors did not. In this age, additional reve-

---

50. Alain Derville, "Le nombre d'habitants des villes de l'Artois et de la Flandre Wallonne (1300–1450)," *Revue du Nord* 65, no. 257 (1983): 277–99.

51. I have elsewhere argued that there was less dramatic change between the two periods, taken as wholes; the population of medieval Douai never exceeded 23,000 or 24,000, I have reasoned, and *on average* did not fall below 16,000 or 17,000 in the late fourteenth and fifteenth centuries. See Martha Howell, "Weathering Crisis, Managing Change: The Emergence of a New Socioeconomic Order in Douai at the End of the Middle Ages," in *La draperie ancienne des Pays-Bas: Débouchés et stratégies de survie (14e–16e siècle)*, ed. Marc Boone and Walter Prevenier (Leuven and Apeldoorn: Garant, 1993).

nues for the city's coffers must have also seemed imperative. These were the years, after all, when French and then Burgundian sovereigns skimmed huge amounts off the top of town receipts, when the contributions demanded for support of external wars and diplomacy rose steadily, and when tax revenues from sealing luxury cloths dwindled.

Yet, even if Douai's échevins had both the political authority and the technical infrastructure necessary to produce this astonishing archive, and even if, especially after 1300, they had good financial reasons for doing so, neither kind of institutional reason fully explains why Douaisiens, more than their neighbors, would have taken the opportunity to manage their private financial affairs in this way and why so many more chose to do so in the latter part of the Middle Ages. The conclusion seems inescapable, if tautological: Douaisiens wrote wills and contracts because they had the chance to do so and thought it in their interests. If more did so after about 1300 than before, the increase reflected a generally heightened sense of concern about the issues these documents could address.

If the size of the archive roughly reflects the number of people who sought to employ such instruments of law rather than a demographic revolution or a sudden institutional development of some kind, as I believe it does, we would not, however, expect to find a single turning point away from custom. As we have seen, this is exactly what we find. Instead, we find that from its earliest existence, the archive contained records much like those of later years and that the changes that occurred in the fourteenth century were more in quantity than in kind. We find, in short, that the shift away from custom was a slow process, driven not by a suddenly unfettered desire for a "patrilineal" marital property regime among Douai's rich, but born in gradually altered attitudes about marital property and succession arrangements, attitudes that seem to have been shared by artisan and merchant, worker and man of leisure alike.

FOUR

The Social Logic—
and Illogic—of Custom

The Douaisien legal reform thus did not directly reflect narrowly defined class interests; nor did its chronology tidily accord with abrupt shifts in fiscal policy or sudden socioeconomic crises. Still, Douaisiens' eagerness to write wills and contracts that modified custom was surely produced by their sense that custom did not perfectly meet their needs, and the decision finally to make a new marital property regime hegemonic reflected Douaisiens' sense that the new better accorded with their social values than did the old. This was a subtle process of social accommodation, however, one not easily reduced to simple formulas of economic cause and effect.

To understand it, we need to consider more carefully the social changes that the legal reform both enabled and recorded. Rather than first asking what failures of law Douaisiens were trying to correct or what crises compelled them to change the law, we must step back a bit, asking more fundamental questions: what values, what social good, might Douaisiens have imagined when they married by custom or when they wrote a ravestissement par lettre to extend custom's privileges to an infertile couple? What different values did they ineluctably articulate when they chose to write a contract, when they distinguished the bride's portement from her groom's property, when they reserved marital assets for children or natal kin, or when they deprived husbands of full control over the conjugal fund?

To investigate these issues, we must consider the concrete experiences of Douaisiens who organized their daily lives with the help of these rules. We must look, quite prosaically, at how a household might have functioned under each legal system; at the tasks the married couple, as a unit and as individuals, were expected to perform; and at how subsistence was managed, and how wealth was accumulated, how fortunes were pre-

served. In doing so, we gain new perspective not only on the social significance of the legal reform, but also on the motives of those who chose the
new law.

In doing so, however—in distilling from each of these two legal regimes what I will call their "social logics"—I do not want to suggest that
either the regimes or their logics were as clearly distinguished in practice
as they are in my schematic. Nor do I want to imply that Douaisiens
would have articulated these logics in this way. And I certainly do not want
to suggest that Douaisiens would have seen them as competing logics. In
fact, custom and the marital property regime that replaced it were not
mutually exclusive. They shared many assumptions about social and gender order, especially about the demographic nuclearity of the household,
the strength of the ties between parents and children, the distinction between men and women, and the dominance of men over women. In practice, moreover, Douaisiens arranged their marriages and inheritances in
ways that mixed features of both marital property regimes, and they did
so for many centuries, apparently ignorant of or unconcerned with the
contradictions that resulted. To impose my analytical framework—to describe two different social imaginaries—is, then, to impose logical and
historical order where Douaisiens may have seen little. My justification
for doing so is that it helps us see what Douaisiens may have only dimly
seen—the way law expressed social impulses and came to shape social life.

The Logic of the Household

Let us return to old custom and the social logic it seemed to express. The
chief impulse of custom—the principle that seems to have been at its
heart—was to preserve the household as the unit of production, what I
have elsewhere called a "family production unit."[1] By this term I mean
more than a "family economy." In a family production unit of the kind
that existed in most northern industrial and commercial cities of the late
Middle Ages, men, women, and children did not simply pool earnings
and share consumption goods, as they did in a family economy as it is
usually defined, although they did both. They also shared the same productive assets. In family production units, the household was thought of

---

1. See Martha Howell, *Women, Production, and Patriarchy in Late Medieval Cities* (Chicago:
University of Chicago Press, 1986), 27–30.

not so much as a collection of people as an assemblage of productive properties. In its classic form, this was the "manse" or the land to which the
medieval peasant had use and inheritance rights. In the form the family
production unit took in most urban societies, the properties were the tools,
dwellings, shops, inventories, and even trade rights and business connections that constituted a city dweller's principal assets.

In Douai, as in all cities of the late medieval North, these family production units were organized in demographically nuclear households.
About this fact, there can be no doubt. There is little evidence from Douai
even of "simple" extended households composed of aging parents along
with a younger married couple and their children.[2] Almost invariably,
young people set up new households when they married. If newlyweds
did live with one set of parents, as some few did, they did so only for a
short time, and the privilege was considered so unusual that it was treated
as a marriage gift, a good that had to be counted as part of the portement.
When Richard Des Plasquendare married Marghot Le Hunonne Dite Le
Neuville in 1376, for example, his contract listed his portement as one
year's support plus 7 florins d'or from his mother, along with 7½ couppres
of land in Sin.[3] When Pieronne Le Marchant married in 1443, she was
given 100 florins phillipes d'or, her "habis et chambre," and the promise
that her father would "garder et gouviernier" the couple for three years.[4]
In a lawsuit from the 1430s, we find even clearer indications of how rare
it was for parents to house their married children. In this case, the father
of the bride (she had just died) sued his former son-in-law for the price
of the food and lodging he claimed to have provided the couple during
their short marriage. The son-in-law indignantly protested, claiming that
he and his wife had never lived with her parents ("They had continuously
lived in their own household, providing food, drink, and subsistence from
their own expenses and out of their own household, not at all from the
assets of the plaintiff").[5] Had it been otherwise, had they enjoyed so unusual a privilege, the son-in-law implied, they would have made (and recorded) a special arrangement.

Just as married children lived away from their parents, so did aged

2. On this point, also see Jacob, *Les époux le seigneur et la cité: Coutume et pratiques matrimoniales
des bourgeois et paysans de France du Nord au Moyen Age* (Brussels: Publications des Facultés Universitaires Saint-Louis 1, 1990), 124–27; 326–28; 331–41.

3. AMD, FF 586/261 (25 May 1376).

4. AMD, FF 616/2387 (12 May 1443).

5. AMD, FF 289, fols. 182–83v (29 May 1435).

widows and widowers live apart from their married children. Old people kept their own households as long as they could, even when they were single, or they retired to convents, monasteries, or beguinages.[6] So rare does the practice of boarding parents seem to have been that Douaisiens made any such arrangements formal, just as they made a formal agreement when married children boarded with parents. Amand Deutart, for example, wrote a marriage contract for his daughter in which he gave the couple a gift of animals and household goods in exchange for life support, either from the couple, or from the survivor of their marriage.[7]

If nuclear households like this were the main loci of production in late medieval Douai, the logic of custom's rules about property management and transmission through marriage seems transparent. In such a society, custom's primary concern would not have been individual property rights, not even "family" property rights; the primary concern had to be the rights of the household. Because this household was nuclear, the property rights lodged with the nuclear couple. By making the household the "owner" of property, and the people who belonged to the household only its possessors, custom created social order—or, we might better say, expressed the way this society was ordered.

As Robert Jacob has explained it, a similar logic had informed Douai's custom from its beginnings in the Picard-Walloon countryside.[8] The original custom of the entire region emerged, he has argued, among peasants, and it owed its affection for the conjugal unit to the form manorialism took in this area during the twelfth and thirteenth centuries. In this region of flat, rich agricultural land; powerful lords; and easy communication, peasants endured more seignorial pressure than elsewhere. They were taxed heavily, regularly, and arbitrarily, principally in the form of the *taille* (a property tax on the "manse") and the *relief* (death duties). Never able

6. On Beguines in Douai, see Walter Simons, "Begijnen en begarden in het middeleeuwse Dowaai," *Jaarboek De Franse Nederlanden* 17 (1992): 180–97; and idem, "The Beguine Movement in the Southern Low Countries: A Reassessment," *Bulletin de l'Institut historique belge de Rome* 59 (1989): 63–105.

7. AMD, FF 639/4343 (1496).

8. Jacob, *Les époux.* Also see Robert Fossier, "The Feudal Era (Eleventh–Thirteenth Century)," in *A History of the Family,* ed. André Burguière et al. (Cambridge: Polity and Blackwell, 1996), 1:407–30.

to accumulate enough surplus to imagine a partible inheritance for their offspring, these peasants concentrated on preserving their holding and minimizing taxes. The principle of "death seizes the living" ("le mort saisit le vif") was their solution; accordingly, the marital estate was not divided among the surviving spouse and lineal kin (and charged death duties) when the first spouse died, as it was in most other community property regimes of the day. Instead, the marital estate was held intact until the second spouse—or subsequent spouses—died. Only then was it divided among surviving children. Thus the family holding passed intact from spouse to spouse without division and without death duties.[9]

As wealth increased in the late Middle Ages, Jacob continued, as the manorial system disintegrated, and as peasants became townspeople, however, the social and fiscal logic that gave life to this custom lost its force. Everywhere people began to modify, often to discard, these norms. Most of the changes left no traces; in only a few places are there even isolated markers of the paths taken—a scrap of legislation in one place, a judicial opinion in another, a contract in still another.[10] Alone, they can tell us very little; read together and alongside the much fuller Douaisien record, however, they reveal that everywhere in Picardy-Wallonia, in town and countryside alike, people were adopting the traditions they had inherited to meet the changed circumstances of the day. Of course, circumstances were not the same everywhere: legal mechanisms had developed differently in cities than in the countryside and were not identical even from city to city; local economies had taken diverging routes; social organization was not the same in every city and village; potential political actors—people who could actually change law—were not similarly empowered everywhere. Hence, the disparity of routes followed; hence, the disparity of outcomes.

In Douai, Jacob also argued, change came later than elsewhere principally because for about two centuries the city put the same kind of pressures on the household as rural lords had done. While the evidence does not seem to support Jacob's emphasis on the close link between fiscal change and reform of custom, as we have seen, his general point is correct and important: Douai's original custom imagined the household as a pro-

---

9. This principle was enshrined in Article I of the sixteenth-century Custom of Douai; see Appendix A.

10. In chapter 8, we will return to this process of change and the records it left in the Picard-Walloon area.

ducer of wealth, and it further imagined that the assets of this unit were best protected when held intact by its managers, not when parceled out to or hoarded for residual heirs. Of course, custom and the mores it expressed required that the managers of this household—the conjugal pair—pass this property on to lineal kin when they died. But even those couples who interevened in custom by issuing wills or contracts almost never disinherited children; typically, they merely rearranged the way assets would be divided and the timing of their descent. The point, then, is not that heads of household operating under old custom neglected their lineal descendants, not even their lineal kin. The point is that as long as either spouse lived, he or she had full control over the use and disposition of the property under their care. They could make management decisions, including decisions to sell certain assets, without consulting their children. It was otherwise in areas where custom guaranteed children specific portions of a particular asset pool, where other lineal kin stood in for children who had died, or where the marital property was divided and distributed at the death of the first spouse. Together—and such provisions typically appeared together—all such provisions not only restricted the power of the head of household but they also very much changed the way the conjugal fund was managed during the life of the marriage.

The household imagined by custom was thus independent and radically unitary, formed not by members of extended families, whether lineally or collaterally organized, but by a man and woman who functioned as one. Custom's notions about the household's nature were perfectly expressed in its central text, the ravestissement par lettre. Let us return to the document:

> Let it be known to all that Jacquemart De Lommel, who resides in Douai, has made and makes a ravestissement to Jehanne De Sanchy, his wife and spouse of all he has, will have, and might acquire, whether or not there is an heir, according to the law and custom of Douai. And likewise, the said Jeanne De Sanchi makes and has made a ravestissement to Jacquemart, her husband, of all she has and will have or might acquire, whether or not there is an heir [of the marriage], according to the law and custom of the city of Douai.[11]

11. AMD, FF 616/2374 (27 December 1442).

In this text, the husband and wife are positioned as entirely independent actors, able fully to possess, control, and bequeath wealth, people who could freely choose to make their spouse the exclusive owner of all the assets they held or would acquire. Further, the text treats the husband and wife as one by treating them as exactly identical partners in the marriage. It even uses precisely parallel language to describe their respective donations: "et pareillement laditte Jeanne De Sanchi a ravesti et ravesst ledit Jac-quemart."

Although radical in its insistence on conjugal unity and independence, the image conveyed by the ravestissement was not simply an effect of the text. In seeming replication of the text's verbal message, the rituals of actually making a ravestissement par lettre enacted the themes of conjugal independence, unity, and power. The document was produced by husband and wife alone, who together had it drafted in the presence of two éche-vins. No parents, siblings, or children accompanied the couple to the town hall, where the document was drawn up; no neighbors or friends bore witness. Although a public act in the sense that it required public author-ity, the execution of a ravestissement par lettre was neither a communal ritual nor a familial ceremony. It was a private agreement, made between husband and wife, between the couple and the law, alone.

Material practice seemed also to echo the text. In its assumption that the marital couple was independent of extended family, that marriage cre-ated a distinct economic entity, and that husband and wife were equal contributors to the conjugal fund, the ravestissement par lettre accorded with the social practices of many—even most—Douaisiens. In late medi-eval Douai, as we have seen, marriage was synonymous with household formation (as it was in most northern cities of the period). Brides and grooms, as we have also seen, almost never lived with their parents, and newly married couples ran their own shops and managed their own busi-nesses. Of course, they were initially financed by their parents and often followed the same occupations as their parents, but married sons and daughters were not normally their parents' lodgers, employees, or junior partners.

As the ravestissement par lettre also seems to assume, women were major contributors to the conjugal economy. Wives had chief responsibil-ity for subsistence production in the household, for it was they who orga-nized meals, saw to clothing and bedding: kept house. Not all the work they did was so gender-specific, however, for wives and widows also helped run family businesses and sometimes managed shops on their own.

The extensive regulations issued by Douai's échevins to control production quality were often quite explicit on this point. Some were directed to the wives of craftsmen, as well as to the craftsmen themselves: "And if the wool were not dyed the color the 'drapier' or 'draperiere' had commanded the dyer, his wife or his journeyman . . . ," one ordinance read.[12] Others even implied that women practiced the dyeing trade independently: "no dyer, whether male or female," may work with "alun de glace," intoned a thirteenth-century regulation.[13] Some women even had their own income-producing occupations, usually in those economic sectors typically marked female—making clothes, preparing and selling foodstuffs, spinning wool. A few, however, worked in trades traditionally considered male. Douaisien ordinances are replete with the feminized forms of the words "draper" ("drapière") and "merchant" ("marchande"), the entrepreneurs who organized cloth production or bought and sold both wool and cloth. Less hypothetical references to such businesswomen are equally plentiful. A 1324 list of fees paid by merchants who rented stalls in the Douaisien cloth halls named, for example, sixteen women among the sixty-three lessors; in a list almost its duplicate, thirteen of fifty-two were women.[14] Another document from 1331–32 lists fees due on past sales in the cloth hall and at retail; the hall fees in arrears from 1326 named three women among six delinquents; the retail sales fees from 1327–28 named twelve women among fifty-eight.[15] In this regard, we know, Douaisien women were not exceptional. From other northern cities of the day, we have similar evidence that women even ran workshops where leathergoods were made, that they worked as money lenders and brokers for long-distance traders, and that they made knives, keys, and locks.[16] Seen as a reflection, even an encoding, of these social practices, the ravestissement and the custom

---

12. Espinas and Pirenne, *Recueil des documents relatifs à l'histoire de l'industrie drapière en Flandre des origines à l'époque Bourguignonne,* 4 vols. (Brussels: P. Imbreghts, 1906), doc. 229(32), dated ca. 1250; also see, where a fuller's wife is similarly described as her husband's partner, ibid., doc. 385(11).

13. Espinas and Pirenne, *Recueil des documents,* doc. 229(96, 97), dated ca. 1250.

14. Espinas and Pirenne, *Recueil des documents,* doc. 338, dated ca. 1324. These lists are from the "basse halle," where cloth was sold in small lots; see Espinas, *La vie urbaine,* 2:853–54, for a discussion of this institution.

15. Espinas and Pirenne, *Recueil des documents,* doc. 341, dated ca. 1331–32.

16. Most of this evidence is summarized in Merry Wiesner, *Women and Gender in Early Modern Europe* (Cambridge: Cambridge University Press, 1993); see her bibliographic notes as well. Also see Barbara Hanawalt, *Women and Work in Preindustrial Europe* (Bloomington: Indiana University Press, 1986), for additional empirical data.

it inscribed thus acquire a deeper logic, and the text's positioning of husband and wife as mutually interchangeable partners seems in rough accordance with daily life.

Although the work women did as members of the households they helped run was valuable and valued, their labor status was not, let me hasten to add, the same as men's. A wife's principal job was to manage household subsistence and produce children; the work she did for the market, whether in her husband's trade or in her own, was understood as an extension of her work for the household, not as a separate enterprise to which she had independent rights. As we shall see, the theory did not always match reality, and in many instances theory had to be adjusted to accommodate reality, but in the minds of most Douaisiens, a wife worked under her husband's supervision and by his authority; his widow worked as his agent.

Nor were women imagined as creators of wealth de novo. Like Douaisien grooms, the brides in Douai, whether they married under traditional custom or not, obtained much of their wealth from property given to them by their parents. The distinctive feature of Douai's custom in this regard is not, thus, that women were considered fully independent generators of wealth; the distinctive feature is that women were equated with men in their capacities as providers of wealth. The inheritance customs of Douai provide clear evidence of this conception. Under custom, daughters received an exactly equal portion of the family property in intestate successions. Even when Douaisiens wrote wills, they tended to leave equal amounts to boys and girls, distinguishing between the two, if at all, only in terms of what kind of property was given to each sex, not in terms of its value. Richard Hucquedieu, a tanner, for example, left his son Jehan 200 francs, the same amount he left to his son-in-law, heir of his deceased daughter and father of his only grandchildren, both girls. To each granddaughter, he also left a goblet; to his wife, he left the surplus, providing that if she remarried, she was to give 50 francs each to their son and the same to the heirs of their deceased daughter.[17] Jaque Balloon, another tanner whose will comes from the same period, left his son Thomas a "small house"; to a married daughter he gave a house with 5 rasières 2 couppres of land, and to another married daughter he left a third house.[18]

17. AMD, FF 869 (14 May 1401).
18. AMD, FF 869 (19 September 1403).

Martin Le Tilliers, a draper, left his only child, a daughter, his house and the surplus of his estate.[19]

Wills are, of course, not perfect guides to inheritance practices, for they treat only those properties not under the control of prior instruments (such as marriage contracts) or of custom (in Douai, all property not mentioned in written instruments). Most wills were, thus, only supplementary to, not constitutive of, inheritance, and the will itself was almost never explicit about its relationship to the overall inheritance plan. In some cases, however, it is possible to tell what role the will was intended to play: whether it was intended to supplement custom, to complete an estate distribution begun by gifts *inter vivos*, or completely to substitute for custom. And it is clear that many of the wills written by married men in late medieval Douai played major roles in managing inheritance. When Waltier Piquette wrote his will in January 1402, for example, he used it to give one married daughter 100 francs, an apparent addition to the marriages gifts she had received earlier; to another married daughter he left the same cash gifts plus an income. But he gave substantially more to his son, who had not yet married and had had nothing of his father's estate so far: three houses, 7 rasières of land, and all his rents on Douaisien property. To his wife he left a long list of additional houses, lands, and rents, along with the surplus of his estate.[20]

Like the distributions given them at their parents' deaths, the marriage gifts given daughters were approximately the same as those given sons. This was the norm even in most marriage contracts (we have, of course, no records of the marriage gifts given daughters who married under custom); it was certainly the rule in the earliest marriage contracts, which, as we have seen, were often little more than slightly altered ravestissements par lettre. Among the nine couples whose portements were both listed in a sample of marriage contracts from the 1390s, for example, there were effectively no differences between the portements of females and males. Among the five rentiers in the group, four of the women brought land and land rents as marriage portions, just as did four of the men. Among the four "prosperous" couples, assets were similarly distributed between the genders, in about equal portions: one groom and one bride owned

19. AMD, FF 869 (2 May 1404).
20. AMD, FF 869 (9 January 1402).

land and land rents; two grooms and one bride owned urban real estate; two grooms and four brides had personal property such as furnishings and tools; one groom and one bride had cash alone.[21]

Douaisien wives, whether married to artisans, shopkeepers, or merchants, were thus positioned as adjuncts to their husbands, who cooperated with them in managing and provisioning the household enterprise. Given their roles in household management, it is not surprising to find that women in Douai first married when they were fully adult and that they then married men of almost the same age.[22] This was true even for Douai's most elite families, those from whom the city's échevins usually came. Jehan Caudry, échevin in 1497–98, was married in 1485, and the two sons of that marriage (for whom we have records) first wed in 1510 (25 years later) and 1515 (30 years later).[23] The Du Ponds, another échivinal family, seems also to have married late. Pierre Du Pond, who served with Caudry, married in 1495. One daughter of that union first married in 1513 (18 years later); another in 1525 (30 years later); a son first married in 1520 (25 years later).[24] Amé Pinchon, their colleague, first married in 1456; a son married in 1486 (30 years later).[25] Anthoine Saingler, the fourth member of that year's bench for whom we can retrieve such infor-

---

21. Elsewhere in Europe, brides were frequently very differently endowed at marriage. In Montpellier, for example, brides were rarely given immovable property; instead, they carried cash or household goods, while their grooms brought land, houses, and animals. See Jean Hilaire, *Le régime des biens entre époux dans la région de Montpellier du début du XIIIe siècle à la fin du XVIe siècle: Contribution aux études d'histoire du droit écrit* (Montpellier: Causse, Graille and Castelnau, 1957).

22. The age at first marriage in Douai, at least for women, seems to have been slightly lower than elsewhere in early modern Europe and may have decreased as the fifteenth century waned, although the data we have from Douai are not extensive enough to be certain. For summary information about marriage ages elsewhere in the period, see Richard Houlbrooke, *The English Family 1450–1700* (London: Longman, 1984); Louis Henry, "Schémas de nuptialité: Déséquilibre des sexes et célibat," *Population* 3 (1969): 457–86; idem, "Schémas de nuptialité: Déséquilibre des sexes et age au remariage," *Population* 6 (1969): 1067–122; Peter Laslett and Richard Wall, eds., *Household and Family in Past Time: Comparative Studies in the Size and Structure of the Domestic Group over the Last Three Centuries in England, France, Serbia, Japan and Colonial North America, with Further Materials from Western Europe* (Cambridge: Cambridge University Press, 1972). Also see Joseph Meury and Joël Sorre, *La Fresnais 1525–1802* (Alet, France: Alet Chamber of Commerce, 1985).

23. AMD, FF 635/3966 (28 April 1485); FF 644/4500 (14 April 1510); FF 646/4952 (4 August 1515).

24. AMD, FF 639/4288 (1 May 1495); FF 645/4866; FF 650/5228 (21 September 1525); FF 648/5121 (10 December 1520).

25. AMD, FF 621/2804 (1 April 1456); FF 635/4014 (14 October 1486).

mation, married in 1458; a son of that marriage first married in 1491 (33 years later); another son married in 1497 (39 years later).[26]

The Le Libert family, most of them butchers who occupied a lower social rank than these échivinal families, seem also to have married relatively late in life. Jacquemart Le Libert, Jehan Le Libert's uncle, married Marie Rohard (sister of the Franchoise Rohard with whom this book opened) sometime between 1400 and 1410, when he was well past 30.[27] One of his daughters, Marguerite, first married in 1448 (38 to 48 years after her parents' marriage); in her case, we have confirmation that she was fully adult when she married because we know that she had already reached her conventional majority (probably around age 21) in 1444, when her mother had remarried.[28] Another daughter, Marie, first married in 1440 (30 to 40 years after her parents' marriage); a third daughter, Jehanne, married in 1437 (27 to 37 years later). A son, Franchois, married in 1454, (14 years after his father's death). And since we know that Franchois was still a minor in 1444, but was old enough to attend the signing of the marriage contract when his widowed mother remarried, we can guess that he was in his twenties when he first married.[29] Jehan Le Libert himself first married in 1389. A son, Jacquemart, first married in 1421 (32 years later), and Jacquemart's own daughter first married in 1444 (23 years after her parents' marriage). Pierronne, a daughter of Jehan Le Libert, married in 1417 (28 years after her parents' marriage); another daughter first married in 1416 (27 years after the marriage). Marguerite, Franchoise Rohard's own daughter by Jehan Le Libert, was first married 33 years after her parents' marriage.[30]

---

26. AMD, FF 622/2923 (28 December 1458); FF 637/4154 (28 May 1491); FF 639/4345 (31 August 1497).

27. He had witnessed a property transfer in 1385, when he had to have been at least twenty-one.

28. During the Middle Ages, the legal age of majority was generally taken to be 11 to 14 for girls, 14 to 16 for boys, but in cities of the southern Low Countries, the age of majority was generally considered to be higher, reaching 18, 20, even 25 years. Many of the sixteenth-century custumals of the region formally raised the age to 25 for boys and girls alike. See Philippe Godding, *Le droit privé dans les Pays-Bas meridinionaux du 12e au 18e siècle*, in *Mémoires de la Classe des Lettres, Collection in 4°*, 2d ser., pt. 1 (Brussels: Académie royale de Belgique, 1987), 70–71. Marriage contracts in Douai that leave property to children at marriage or "maturity" regularly take "maturity" to be 18, 20, or 21 years.

29. AMD, FF 615/2307 (20 November 1440); FF 617/2410 (31 May 1444); FF 618/2505 ; FF 614/2138 (8 January 1437); FF 620/2712 (20 October 1454).

30. AMD, FF 609/1783 (2 June 1421); FF 617/2419 (7 October 1444); FF 607/1689 (17 December 1417); FF 606/1628 (20 January 1416); FF 600/1258 (29 May 1402); FF 613/2059 (22 September 1435).

More exact evidence about marriage ages can be derived from the city's *Registre aux bourgeois*, the records of new citizen registrations, which have survived in regular series from 1399 forward. In most years of the fifteenth century, the clerks keeping the registers included the new citizen's occupation, his marital status (all but a few registrants were male), the name of his spouse, and the names and ages of his children. Some of those children grew up to marry in Douai and write a marriage contract, and when they did we can sometimes precisely document their marriage ages. I have made these calculations for three years during the fifteenth century—1438–39, 1451–52, and 1474–75—when 103 men purchased citizenship rights. Sixty-one of the men were married with children, and together they had 123 children. Of these children, 16 left marriage contracts, 8 of them male, 8 female.[31] For the girls, the age at first marriage ranged between 18 and 23; both the median and mode were 21. For the boys, the range was 21 to 37; the median was 27, the mode 25.

Second marriages were, however, a different matter, for older widowers seem frequently to have taken young women as brides, in the pattern depicted in the well-known *Le Menagier de Paris* of the fourteenth century, in which an elderly bridegroom instructs his child bride on household management.[32] Franchoise Rohard, we have seen, was surely a good decade younger than Jehan Le Libert, maybe even a full generation his junior. Anthoine Saingler, échevin in 1497–98, was another "December" groom, his wife another "June" bride. Saingler had first married in 1458; he survived that wife and remarried in 1481. Two years later he remarried again, to a woman who would in turn survive him, living to witness her granddaughter's marriage in 1528. To judge from this evidence, Saingler's widow was probably little more than 20 at her own first marriage, for that would have made her about 65 in 1528; Saingler, himself, we know, was at least 45—and thus a generation his bride's senior—when she married him.[33]

A small number of these second marriages may have reversed the asym-

31. The low number is a striking reminder of the infant and childhood mortality rate in Douai, the social exclusivity of the marriage contract, and the rate of losses in the archive. It also probably measures the rate of geographical mobility in the region, for it is likely that some of these children emigrated from Douai before marrying.

32. Georgine E. Brereton and Janet M. Ferrier, eds., *Le Menagier de Paris* (Oxford: Clarendon Press, 1981).

33. AMD, FF 622/2923 (28 December 1458); FF 634/3868 (10 December 1481); FF 634/3917 (22 October 1483); FF 651/5290 (22 January 1528).

metry, producing "December" brides and "June" grooms. We have, after all, ample anecdotal evidence that women could marry two, three, even four times, and it seems inevitable that some of them would have married younger men. Marie Rohard, the sister of Franchoise Rohard, for example, remarried more than 20 years after her first marriage, when she had to have been more than 40 years old. To judge from a collection of marriage contracts from 1441–43, she was not an exception. These documents named 26 widows, of whom 10 left previous marriage contracts; 5 of them had been first married at least 20 years earlier. Maroye Le Cordewaur Dit Bosset had been married twice before, the second time between 1418 and 1420; even if she was only 20 at her second marriage, in about 1419, she would have been at least 40 at her third.[34] Marguerite De Warlain had previously wed in 1397–98, making her at least 60(!) when she remarried in 1441[35]; Ysabel Leswanier had also been married twice before, once in 1415 and once in 1439, so she was probably in her forties when she made this marriage.[36] Ysabel Selet, who was first married in 1416 (and a second time in 1439), was about the same age as Leswanier, as was Martine Dannphue, another who had first married about 25 years previously.[37]

The Logic of Property

The logic of the household also involved a logic of property, a logic that reflected the nature of Douaisien wealth and the character of the social order built on such wealth. As we have seen, most of the assets in Douaisien households were movables in both a legal and an economic sense— furnishings, jewels, clothing, coin, tools, raw materials, inventories, and the like. Or they were buildings that served to render these movables economically valuable—shops, warehouses, even residences—and so were themselves also movables of a kind. As such, these properties were necessarily fungible, always potentially and often actually exchangeable, one for another. It was this fungibility—with all the risks that accompanied it—that underlay custom's "logic of property." With its insistence that

34. AMD, FF 608/1713 (16 July 1418); FF 616/2378 (19 January 1443).
35. AMD, FF 598/1063 (29 November 1398); FF 616/2399 (3 October 1443).
36. AMD, FF 606/1610 (26 November 1415); FF 615/2269 (20 January 1440); FF 616/2398 (21 September 1443).
37. AMD, FF 607/1666 (ca. 1416); FF 615/298 (ca. 1440); FF 616/2338 (12 September 1441); FF 606/1570 (ca. 1415); FF 616/2381 (8 February 1440).

property could be transferred and transformed as the head of household desired, custom was, in effect, accommodating the mobility essential to commercial wealth, acknowledging the impermanence of Douaisien assets. In some ways this seems a very modern conception of property, for it reflects a notion that property's value inheres in its income-producing capacity, that one "property" is indistinguishable from another except in terms of what it earns. It seems modern in another way as well, for it imagines that the proximate or present owners of a property are its absolute owners, that they alone are responsible for its management, that they owe no accounting, no explanation, to future owners about its present use, that they have every right to use it as they think best.

Although the Douaisiens who appear in the archives of that city were presumably not the only people in late medieval Europe to harbor such notions and probably not the only ones to leave such a clear record of actions that betray these notions, they do not seem typical of premodern people as described by most historians, not even of premodern urbanites. Most Europeans of this day, historians have argued, thought about property in different ways: it was made up of assets with fixed values, values that inhered not only in the assets's economic exchange value or their income-producing capacity but also in the status they bequeathed. Such assets could not be bought and sold like herrings or sacks of wool; they had to be hoarded, held for future generations, labeled as heirlooms, cherished. While they might well produce income and have exchange value—in fact they had social and cultural value precisely because they had such monetary worth—they were managed quite differently than they usually were by the people who populate Douai's late medieval archive of contrats divers, wills, and marriage contracts.

Douai's custom thus seems to reflect practices more modern than premodern. It allowed property to be passed on to spouses, to heirs of any status, even to friends, as the property owner chose. Assets could be transferred whole, intact, if the head or household thought that best, or divided if that manner of succession seemed efficient. In effect, by custom's logic, property could circulate wildly, could go from person to person, from blood line to blood line—all in the interests of keeping it in productive units.

Anachronistic as these notions may seem, they were deeply ingrained, so deeply ingrained that even the early marriage contracts (documents that would eventually undermine custom) reflected these attitudes. The typical portement described in the contracts written before about 1400 betrayed few of the ideas about lineal inheritance, the sacredness of patrimony, or the immutability of "family" wealth that would so mark the marital property regime that would replace custom—and that already so marked the marital property regimes of others in European society. These contracts seldom included, for example, information about the portement's origins or its eventual disposition. Instead, brides simply listed the biens they would contribute to the marriage; it was surely understood that the property had come from the bride's parents, but it was the rare marriage contract that even named the assets' donor. Of the fifty-nine that survive, for example, from 1375–77 only nine named the provence of even a single bien in the portement. Like the contract written for Jehanne Maubuee in 1375, they simply named the goods: "in movables and chattels, the sum and value of 20 florins d'or called francs francois, along with a house and holding."[38] Nor did the contracts specify how the property was to pass beyond the bride. Rather, they usually provided, as Robe La Verines's vaguely did, only that at her widowhood, "the said Robe will have and take, freely and without debt, all the héritages declared above along with the sum of 20 florins d'or frans."[39] As we shall see, these casual practices would be abandoned in the course of the next century, as Douaisiens came to treat marriage goods more as though they belonged to the "line," not to the couple who used them.

Custom had as meaningful implications about the nature of social place, for its willingness to accommodate the mobility and fungibility of commercial property also allowed extraordinary mobility of persons. As we have seen, custom permitted new people into households, as second, third, and fourth spouses, and it delegated to them managerial responsibilities that matched the property rights they thereby gained. By the same logic, it permitted households to be merged into others.

It was as though in accord with this logic that widows and widowers in Douai regularly remarried and they did so promptly, often within months of the death of their deceased spouse, almost always within a few years. From one sample of eighty-three marriage contracts from the early 1440s, for example, we find sixteen widows who seem to have been previously married by custom.[40] By definition, they were entering the new mar-

38. AMD, FF 585/159 (25 October 1375).

39. AMD, FF 585/162 (16 November 1373).

40. AMD, FF 616; Ten of the widows in this entire sample (twenty-six out of eighty-three) had been previously married by contract. Some of the remaining sixteen widows whose previous marriages seem to have been controlled by custom may have been restricted by testaments or

riages with full rights to all the property their deceased husbands had owned and all that had been accumulated in the course of the prior union.[41]

Presumably, men as well as women remarried quickly in Douai, but it is women's remarriage rates that seem most unusual, because there is good evidence that elsewhere in premodern Europe a widow did not easily make a new match, especially if she was burdened with another man's children and if she was beyond her youth.[42] In Douai, however, such women seem to have had no trouble finding new spouses. Eight of the twelve widows who wrote marriage contracts in a sample of forty-one contracts taken

---

other legal instruments (registered transfers of property out of the conjugal estate, for example) that their husbands had written before their deaths, so we cannot be sure that the sixteen widows in this sample actually had unencumbered control over the conjugal estate. All we know is that they did not leave a record of a previous marriage contract.

It is interesting to note that none of the twenty-six widows in this sample, and almost none in several other samples studied, issued ravestissments par lettre—i.e., that virtually all widows married by contract or, if they married by custom, that they did not extend the customary grant of all conjugal property to their new husbands by written ravestissement (thus the new husbands gained full succession rights only if the new marriage was fertile). Evidently, widows had little interest in turning all their assets over to new husbands and were willing to do so only if the new marriage produced offspring.

41. This was a period of extraordinarily high mortality in Douai, and the remarriage rate in these years surely reflects the unusually high number of deaths. Samples from other periods, when the death rate was closer to average, also contain, however, huge numbers of remarriages. In a sample of marriage contracts taken at four intervals (before 1374, 1374–75, 1400, and 1500), for example, Monique Mestayer found that 19 percent (3 percent were in third or fourth marriages) of the brides were widows: see Monique Mestayer, "Les contrats du mariage à Douai du XIIème au XVème siècle, reflets du droit et de la vie d'une société urbaine," *Revue du Nord* 61, no. 241 (1979): 353–79.

42. Most of the evidence we have on remarriage rates comes from the early modern period, rather than from the medieval. See, for example, D. Dalle, "De bevolking van de stad Veurne in de 17e–18e eeuw," *Handelingen van het Genootschap voor Geschiedenis 'Société d' Emulation' te Brugge* 106 (1969): 49–139 (cited in Marianne Danneel, *Weduwen en wezen in het laat-middeleeuwse Gent* [Leuven and Apeldoorn: Garant, 1995], 309); Alain Bideau, "A Demographic and Social Analysis of Widowhood and Remarriage: The Example of the Castellany of Thoissey-en-Dombes, 1670–1840," *Journal of Family History* 5, no. 1 (Spring 1980): 28–43; J. Dupâquier, E. Hélin, P. Laslett, M. Livi-Bacci, and S. Sogner, *Mariage et remariage dans les populations du passé* (Academic Press: London, 1981).

On remarriage rates in late medieval urban cultures, see, in particular, Barbara Hanawalt, "Remarriage as an Option for Urban and Rural Widows in Late Medieval England," in *Wife and Widow: The Experiences of Women in Medieval England*, ed. S. Walker (Ann Arbor: University of Michigan Press, 1993), and the extensive discussion in Danneel, *Weduwen en wezen*, 311–21. Danneel's evidence parallels my findings: citing B. Todd, "The Remarrying Widow: A Stereotype Reconsidered" (in *Women in English Society, 1500–1800*, ed. M. Prior [London: Routledge, 1985]), Danneel points out that remarriage rates for women seem to have declined later in the early modern period: Danneel, *Weduwen en wezen*, 308.

from the early 1420s, for example, had minor children.[43] At least ten of
the twenty-six widows who married in 1441–43 had small children.[44] Anecdotal evidence is as telling. Jehenne Du Mont married for the second
time in 1435, when she already had three small children, and six years
later married for a third time.[45] Jehenne Hordain bore her first husband
four children before he died; she then remarried, in 1436, and bore two
more children; by 1440, she had married a third time.[46] Ghilles Blocquiel,
widow of the échevin Pierre Du Pond, remarried in 1528, when she must
have been in her fifties, thirty-three years after her marriage to Du Pond
To this marriage, she brought a minor son of her first marriage and her
granddaughter, the child of her deceased daughter, whom she was rearing.[47] To judge from this evidence, a woman's property counted for everything, at least in Douai. If she had a shop, a warehouse full of inventories,
a fully equipped household, a house, rents, or land, a woman was marriageable—even a woman with minor children, even a woman in late middle age.

For their part, widows seem to have been as eager to remarry as were
the men who wed them. For them, as for their new husbands, it was
practical matters that weighed heavily in their decision to replace their
deceased spouses. Alone, a widow might not have been able to run the
tannery or handle the looms; alone the shop may have seemed too much.[48]
Even rich women were not free of these constraints, for these were the
days before private lawyers, professional executors, formal partnerships,
corporations, and the like—the institutions of modern economic life that
help separate ownership of an asset from managerial responsibility for it.
In late medieval Douai, a rich woman who had succeeded to a warehouse
full of grain, a stack of contracts for delivery of horses, or a building still
under construction and a work crew waiting for orders thus had just as

---

43. AMD, FF 609.

44. AMD, FF 616.

45. The second marriage is recorded in AMD, FF 613/2072 (18 January 1436); the third in
AMD, FF 616/2347 (26 November 1441).

46. The second marriage is recorded in AMD, FF 613/2069 (ca. 1436); the first and third
are mentioned in AMD, FF 292, fols. 62–64 and 117–18v.

47. AMD, FF 651/5277 (27 August 1528); FF 639/4288 (1 May 1495).

48. We know that some of these widows remarried in the trade of their deceased husbands:
Anthoine Du Four, for example, who married Anthoine Miguot, a saye weaver, in 1521, was the
widow of another saye weaver (AMD, FF 649/5130 [6 May 1521]). Douai's records do not,
however, allow many identifications of this kind, for it is only in the rare instance that the trades
of a woman's several husbands can be traced.

good reasons for finding a new spouse as did her less prosperous neighbors.

A widow who remarried so quickly may have done so with genuine regret for her deceased spouse but she could not have done so entirely unwillingly. For these women, as for the men who sought to wed them, marriage was principally a means of organizing a life, managing a household, and preserving one's status in the community. This did not necessarily mean that they had no concept of conjugal affection or that their affections were so slight that they could be easily transferred from one person to another. But it did mean, at a minimum, that affection was subordinated to practicalities. And it may even have meant that conjugal affection was not then considered an especially important ingredient in the marriage pact.[49]

The Illogic of Custom: Gender and Property

Whatever its social logic or its rough accord with social practices, however, the custom of Douai was laden with contradictions that centered on property, the roles of women, and gender relations themselves. Some of the contradictions were inscribed in the very legal texts written to express custom's notion of conjugality; others emerged in social practice, as Douaisiens went about the business of daily life.

The most fundamental contradiction lay in the notion expressed in the ravestissement that wives could be equated with their husbands. We know, as Douaisiens knew, that women were not the same as men, not in Douai, not anywhere in this or any other period. Women may have contributed significantly to the household economy, both with the property they carried into it and with the work they did, but they did not do so on the same terms as men. In practice, women in Douai had greater responsibility for subsistence production in urban households than men did and relatively less responsibility for market production or for the public roles that

---

49. Just what it meant about the quality of conjugal relations that widows (and widowers) remarried quickly is impossible to say with certainty. Alan MacFarlane has suggested that widows who remarried precipitously must have done so precisely because they sought to recapture the pleasures of their former marriages. My own view is that socioeconomic matters so conditioned the possibilities for remarriage and its desirability that "love" cannot be treated as an independent variable in the equation. See MacFarlane, *Marriage and Love in England: Modes of Reproduction, 1300–1840* (Oxford: Blackwell, 1986).

derived from household status. Moreover, men had privileged access to the skilled trades, men alone had formal political authority, and men were considered the official heads of household.

The contradiction lay not just in the contrast between legal texts and social practice, however, but also within the law itself. While custom defined wives as their husband's partners and widows as their substitutes, it nonetheless gave husbands all authority over conjugal property during their lives, thus effectively denying wives any property rights during marriage. As husbands, men married under custom in Douai could transfer, sell, and even destroy all property in the conjugal fund, including the property their wives had brought to it. Everything a wife earned, every debt she incurred, was the property of her spouse, her "baron," as the sources commonly named him. "Partner" a wife may have been in a limited sense, but "equal" she surely was not.

The conjugal equality portrayed by the ravestissement par lettre, the mutuality on which it appeared to insist, was, thus, only a partial representation. It described a kind of *economic* mutuality, a partnership made up of two members who provided roughly equal economic worth, and whose economic capacities were taken as utterly commensurate. It was decidedly not a representation of partners with identical social or legal capacities. It was, in fact, not a representation of individuals at all—but a representation of the unit husband and wife formed when they headed a household. Custom's logic, therefore, was to represent the singleness of this unit, a unit that could be spoken for only by a single, indivisible person. During his life, this was the husband; after his death, it was his widow.

Paradoxically, the contradictions inherent in this notion of partnership came over time to be expressed by the ravestissement par lettre, the very text that otherwise articulated the notions of conjugal unity and sameness at the heart of custom. As though admitting the absurdity of a law that represented wives as free and equal agents, most of the ravestissements par lettre written after about 1400 added a strange and revealing clause to the standard text:

> Let it be known to all that before the aldermen of the city of Douai have personally come Pierre Hardi and Jacque Huquedieu, his wife and spouse, to whom Pierre has made a ravestissement and by virtue of this document makes a mutual donation to Jacque, his wife, of all he has or will acquire during their marriage whether in goods, movables, chattels, or in heritable immovables, to enjoy after his death by his wife and her representatives. And likewise, this woman, *being sufficiently empowered by Pierre her husband,*

which empowerment she accepts as agreeable, has made and makes a ravestissement to Pierre her husband of all she has or will acquire during their marriage whether in goods, movables, chattels, or immovables for him and
his representatives to enjoy after her death, all according to the custom of
Douai.[50]

Nonsensical on the face of it—why would a woman able to give her
own property away need her husband's permission to do so, especially
if she was giving it to him?—the emphasized clause nicely captures the
contradiction between economic "sameness" and social/legal distinction:
wives were powerful creators and managers of property and, simultaneously, people with no independent claims to wealth.

The key word here is "wives," for it was only as wife that custom denied
a Douaisien woman full property rights. Once widowed, a woman was
fully empowered. She could then act for her husband and for the household estate she now represented. Custom was entirely unambiguous about
this radical transformation; it openly acknowledged women's capacities to
create wealth and to manage property, and it seemed to fully intend that
widows exercise these powers. Still, an insidious inconsistency lurked be-
neath custom's serene exterior. The law granted widows this authority
not as individuals but as representatives of the household, a household
defined as male-headed. Hence, to do her job as custom imagined it,
a widow would have had to act for—to act *as*—her late husband. Of
course, no widow could do so, even if she wanted to. And not all of
them wanted to.

The *Le Libert v. Rohard* case, with which this book opened, is a case
in point. When Rohard took up her role as agent of her husband, manager
of the assets they had shared and guardian of their children, she did so
exactly as custom deemed right. Nonetheless, in assuming her new roles,
she was simultaneously empowered to suppress Le Libert's own voice,
even to deny his children what he had previously given them—hardly
the powers a widow who was acting on her husband's behalf would have
exercised.

Other civil disputes are as revealing. Let us look, for example, at a
suit between two widows, Jehanne Polle and her former daughter-in-law,
Ysabel Cartoy. The suit was initiated in 1434, when Polle, widow of
Thomas Duhamel and mother of the late Bernard Duhamel, was sued by

---

50. AMD, FF 616/2346 (26 November 1441) (emphasis added).

Cartoy and her new husband for a half share in a house. Polle, it seems, had promised the property to Cartoy when Bernard Duhamel (Polle's son and then Cartoy's husband) was on his deathbed. Duhamel was at that time full owner of the house as heir of his father, Thomas Duhamel, and legatee of his father's brother, once joint owners of the house. According to custom, Polle (as surviving parent of Bernard Duhamel) and Cartoy were to have split the house at Bernard Duhamel's death, for the marriage between Duhamel and Cartoy had not been fertile, and they had made no written ravestissement. But witnesses confirmed that Polle had made the promise, as her son had begged, apparently fearing for his young widow's financial security.

He need not have feared. Cartoy remarried immediately after Duhamel's death, and then she and her new husband brought the suit against her former mother-in-law for the remaining half share in the house that her former mother-in-law had not ceded to her. She won. While there can be little doubt that Cartoy was legally entitled to the house (for witnesses verified that Polle had promised it), it is also clear that in taking the house from her deceased husband's estate, into marriage with another man, Cartoy was hardly acting as the loyal widow custom seems to have imagined. Nor was she the vulnerable widow she may have once appeared. Now she was another man's wife, the mistress of another household and thus positioned as predator, not victim.[51]

It is impossible to say what Cartoy felt about the dispute and her role in it. We are perhaps tempted to suspect that Cartoy had never truly been either the pitiful widow her late husband seemed intent on protecting or the righteous trustee of her late husband's property she would have been imagined to be under custom. In remarrying so quickly, thus enabling her new husband to sue her former mother-in-law for property that, by custom, would have been the older woman's, Cartoy seems to have abdicated both roles. We might thus see Cartoy as a tricky operator, a woman who, as wife, pretended vulnerability (perhaps even love and devotion) while her husband lay dying, but then, taking his (and his mother's) house with her, skipped off into another marriage. But we must be cautious. We simply cannot know what motivated Cartoy. Perhaps she simply thought, along with the law, that her role as Duhamel's wife was over and that now she was answerable to another man and another set of interests.

51. AMD, FF 289, fols. 31, 101–103v, 144, 145 (dated 1434–45).

Our confusion about the case arises in part because lawsuits like these were not the product of law's malfunctioning, but of its proper functioning. They were products of a legal regime that tried both to erase women as wives and give them full visibility as widows. In this strange logic, wife and widow were not the mirror opposites they might seem to us; they were both creators of wealth for a household that—in theory—contained them. The problem was that, in practice, women were not contained. Even when they were acting in the interests of the original household, as we might argue Franchoise Rohard had done, they were not exactly the same as the men they replaced. And they were certainly not contained when, like Cartoy, they used their widow's rights to attract a new spouse and to sue their former mothers-in-law.

The contradictions were not confined to the roles women played or did not play; they extended to the definition of femininity and feminine virtue itself. In effect, custom contained two utterly contradictory notions of femininity. On the one hand, it defined a wife as a silent and powerless being, someone unable to take charge even of the property she had brought to the marriage or had earned by her labor. In complete contrast, it implicitly labeled the widow a skilled manager of property, someone able to decide how property was used, how it was to pass to children, and what form it ought to take. The stunning disjunction between these two characterizations—one woman was "dumb" in the literal as well as the figurative sense, the other both speaking and savvy—was, again, not just a textual construction. The contradiction was played out time and time again in daily life.

We see it, for example, in cases where widows were brought to court on charges of owing debts that had come with the estates they inherited. Thus, Sebille Pachelorre, widow of Jehan Du Buisson, a wine merchant, was sued in 1435 for fees due on wine sales made over a sixteen-year period, from 1416 to 1432.[52] Pachelorre protested, and she spent months trying to produce written evidence that the fees had been paid. Unable to locate the documentation, she was charged to pay 4 gros m.d.f. for each of 518 lots sold—a huge sum in fifteenth-century Douai, equal to more than a year's wages for a highly skilled artisan. Whether Du Buisson had, in fact, died without paying these accumulated fees, we will never know. It may well have been that he was derelict, but it is nevertheless suspicious

52. AMD, FF 289, fols. 35v–36, 50v, 51, 158v–159 (ca. 1435).

that the claimants waited until his death to bring suit. And it is significant that the widow did not even know how to put her hands on her husband's papers, or certainly not on any that would have made her case. If, in truth, the fees were due, the suit was "just," but its justice does not justify a system that made women such as Pachelorre responsible for debts about which they had no knowledge, with which they were clearly so unequipped to deal, and over which they had no control.

Some widows were not like Pachelorre, however. There are many cases in the archive that read as though the widow was seeking the position of "dumb" wife in an attempt to avoid debts she knew to be due. Let us look, for example, at a case from the early 1440s, in which Jehanne D'Anzain, widow of Denys Le Thiery, was sued by the holders of a rent due on a house that had come to her with the estate of her deceased husband. She claimed no knowledge of the debt but like Pachelorre could not produce documents showing it had been retired when Le Thiery had bought the house. D'Anzain lost, of course, for—as we have learned from the Pachelorre case—ignorance of her late husband's business dealings (made manifest by her failure to have preserved the written proof, if it had ever existed) was no excuse. It is of course possible that D'Anzain was the innocent she insisted she was—as wife, truly ignorant of her husband's affairs as Pachelorre seems to have been, too unworldly to have known to save the essential document and therefore vulnerable to the dishonest claims of predatory creditors. But it may also be that she had just let the rental payment lapse, hoping that she might be able to claim the role of "dumb" wife in an effort to avoid her obligations.[53]

The contradictions between dumb wife and savvy, speaking widow did more than open the way for predatory creditors and unscrupulous widows. Such contradictions were also at play in the remarriage market, for it was surely the contradiction between the "dumb" wife and the "speaking" widow that made it seem so essential that widows take new husbands. Many widows may have been like Sebille Pachelorre seems to have been: so disempowered by the denial of property rights that their marriage had imposed, they were as widows utterly incapable of managing any property at all—not their own, not their late husband's. In practice, they were the "dumb" wives the law had named them, and as widows, they could not suddenly be transformed into the competent creatures custom imagined.

So they had no choice but to marry. It is thus one of the many ironies of this system that for more than a few women, widowhood was not the long-awaited moment of independence, the time when they, like Franchoise Rohard, could take charge. Instead, widowhood was a precarious interlude in their lives, a terrible moment of vulnerability, a time to be passed through as quickly as possible.[54]

Remarriages in Douai were, then, as much measures of the tensions inherent in custom as they were measures of the opportunities available to women who had property of their own. What is especially interesting about the Douaisien evidence, however, is that these widows rarely, if ever, married as they were so often described as doing in the comic literature of the day. In those texts, women married out of lust for money or sex, and they thus sought either old, rich men or young, virile ones.[55] Although it is extremely difficult to obtain statistically significant measures of Douaisien women's remarriages, the little we can tell from surviving marriage contracts suggests that Douaisien women had different objectives when they entered the remarriage market. Of the seven widows who married by contract in a sample of forty-one documents from the 1390s, for example, at least four married men close to them in age and from similar social backgrounds, and two (about whom we do not have enough information to safely judge) seem also to have done so. Only one man in the group may have married up in the way so gleefully ridiculed in the plays and stories of this time period; his portement consisted of only 10 couppres of land and "tous ses meubles" (all his movables). His bride, the widow of a merchant, brought three houses in Douai, 2 rasières of land in one place, 9 couppres of land held separately, a garden, and 200 florins d'or "en argent, meubles et marchandise."[56] But this marriage was hardly the norm. The norm was set by Maroie Coutel, a widow with three children, who married Gille De Chauny in early 1422.[57] She brought household goods worth 124 couronnes, a house, a garden in Douai, and a half interest

---

54. Danneel, *Weuwen en wezen,* esp. 315–16, emphasizes this ambiguity as well.

55. Chaucer's Wife of Bath is the figure from the period's comic literature surely best known to English readers. She is modeled after "La Vieille" from the *Romance of the Rose* (by Guillaume de Lorris and Jean de Meun). In general, on the theme of gender inversion in the comic and prescriptive literature of the period, see Joy Wiltenburg, *Disorderly Women and Female Power in the Street Literature of Early Modern England and Germany* (Charlottesville: University of Virginia Press, 1992).

56. AMD, FF 596/906 (October 1393).

57. AMD, FF 609/1811 (January 1422).

in a manor, plus 13 rasières of land near Douai. Her groom brought about the same amount: 6 bonniers of land, a house in Auchy, and personal property including grain and animals.[58]

What the Douaisien evidence suggests instead is that the tensions inherent in this city's remarriage practices were not about age and social status per se (although they may have been represented as such), but about property—about the way that custom both empowered the conjugal pair and the household economy that was their responsibility and, simultaneously, threatened the familial order born of conjugality and the gender hierarchy on which the entire system depended. One last story of the civil court records exposes these tensions almost perfectly. The case centers on Jehenne Hordain, a widow who was sued in 1440 by Marie Le Hellin, niece of Hordain's first husband, Nicaise Le Hellin, for an income that Hordain now possessed and was about to carry into a new marriage, her second since Le Hellin's death about five years earlier.[59] The rent had once been Nicaise Le Hellin's mother's, and she had left it to her two sons, Nicaise and Miquel, the latter of whom was the father of the plaintiff. Miquel Le Hellin had left his share to his own son, but the son had died without a wife or legitimate issue. The property then had returned to Miquel; at his death, it had gone to his co-heir, his brother; and at his death to Hordain, as successor to her husband.

There it would stay, for Marie Le Hellin lost her suit. Although she was the daughter of the original owner of the property, she could not sustain the claim of kinship, not even of direct descent, against the force of custom, which made conjugality, even long dead and now very distant conjugality, premier.[60] Jehenne Hordain thus went on to her third marriage, freely taking with her—and sharing with children born of other men—an income that had belonged to Marie Le Hellin's father and that Marie Le Hellin fervently believed should have come to her.

In fiction, there would be many ways to tell this story. Hordain could be positioned as the evil protagonist, as the faithless betrayer of her former husband, as an embezzler of property that belonged to another family and other children, even as a kind of Wife of Bath. The story could also be

---

58. Daneel's evidence, summarized in *Weduwen en wezen*, 319–20, points to the same conclusion.

59. Hordain had married Le Hellin in about 1420. It seems he died in the mid-1430s; she married next in 1436 (AMD, FF 613/2069). The suit was brought when she married yet a third time, in 1440 (AMD, FF 292, fols. 62–64v).

60. AMD, FF 292, fols. 62v–64 (1440).

told entirely differently, however, with Marie Le Hellin as the culprit, a woman greedy for wealth that was patently not hers, wealth that Hordain had honorably earned as wife to Nicaise Le Hellin. How Douaisiens of midcentury would have read the case we cannot say for certain. We know only that the sole "text" Douaisiens produced on the subject—their custom—requires the latter interpretation.

FIVE

An Alternative Logic

In the course of the fourteenth and fifteenth centuries, as Douaisiens is-sued tens of thousands of contrats divers, wills, and marriage agreements, they did more than simply construct a new marital property regime. They institutionalized a new social imaginary. Like the imaginary that informed custom, this one also involved notions about property's meaning and its value, about the household and its economic function, about marriage, and about gender. Although imbedded in complex social practices that combined elements of the old and the new, the main features of this alter-native imaginary are visible in the legal texts Douaisiens left in this period.

Fixing Movables

A redefinition of property and its relationship to social place lay at the heart of the legal reform that expressed this social imaginary. One of its elements is easy to see, for the legal system clearly recorded the change: the new marital property and inheritance system gave relatively greater emphasis to the property rights of kin than to those of the household. The earliest wills from Douai, even those from the thirteenth century, began the process. They tended, as we have seen, to make lineal kin the residual owner of the household production unit instead of the house-hold's survivor. By the mid–fifteenth century, this impulse was fully real-ized in marriage contracts that preserved héritages for lineal kin and some-times earmarked the entire estates for these relatives.

But there were less visible aspects to the reform as well, for the effect of these wills and contracts was not just to privilege kinship over conjugality. To label property for kin was also to make a production choice, a choice to remove production responsibility from the household. In doing so, Douaisiens expressed a new conception of property and of property's role in linking people to one another: they came, in effect, to define their property less as mobile production goods that were to be employed by the residents of the household than as fixed stores of wealth that served to connect people through time. These conceptions were not, of course, explicitly articulated, and they certainly did not appear, fully formed, at a single moment. They emerged slowly, out of practice, as Douaisiens gradually changed the way they acquired and used property.

Let us begin by looking at the most literal aspect of this process—the changes in the kinds of assets Douaisiens held. During the course of the fifteenth and sixteenth centuries, Douaisiens put an increasing proportion of their wealth into land and land rents, assets that were, by their nature, fixed stores of wealth—"immovable," as most Douaisien assets were not. The archive of marriage contracts tracks the change clearly. While less than 20 percent of the contracts sampled from the fifteenth century mentioned land or land rents, just over 50 percent of all portements in contracts surviving from the 1550s were heavily invested in land.[1] To a certain extent, this change reflects the disappearance of artisans and other ordinary folk from the archive of marriage contracts—people who would have held their capital in movables (rather than land)—so we cannot attribute all of this rise to a systemic shift in the nature of Douaisien wealth.[2] Nevertheless, it is certain that a more significant (if not precisely measurable) portion of Douaisien capital was invested in land by the sixteenth century

---

1. Tables 2 and 3 in chapter 3 summarize the information drawn from sampled marriage documents. The figures for landholdings cited here are drawn from that material.

2. The samples from the years from about 1540 to 1560 are smaller than those from earlier decades, a decline that makes comparisons with earlier years difficult, because we do not know how much of the decline occurred across the social spectrum. Some of it, we can be certain, is attributable to an absolute decline in the numbers of artisans in the archive, but it is not clear whether this fall off reflects the disappearance of artisans from Douai or artisans' decision to abandon the marriage contract.

A shift in registration practice also took place in this period, and it may be that many contracts were lost in the process. During this period, Douaisiens were switching from vellum to paper for their chirographes, and the marriage contracts from this period are thus divided between two different collections. In vellum, we have only fifty-eight contracts for the entire period, 1551–1648, and most of them date from the 1550s. There are a few scatterd marriage contracts on paper from the 1550s (AMD, FF 913), but it is not until the very end of that decade that the collection begins to take shape (AMD, FF 914 and, especially, FF 915).

than had been the case in prior centuries. In one sample of seventy-five contracts from the two years between 1441 and 1444, for example, only nine documents listed land and land rents in portements (12 percent); in a comparable sample of forty-three contracts taken from the single year 1522, in contrast, ten (23 percent) owned land. By the 1550s, the percentage of portements including land and land rents had risen even higher, although it is harder to make reliable comparisons between these decades and earlier periods because of differences in the survival rates of contracts and in recording techniques.

The shift to landholding is especially evident among Douai's most elite citizens, its échevins, most of whom belonged to what I have labeled the "rentier" class, people who lived to a large extent from rents on land and urban real estate. Of the eight échevins who served in 1391 for whom we can obtain such information, only five, or 62 percent, held land or land rents. Surely this is a significant number, but it is not as large as we might expect for the sociopolitical elite of a city such as Douai. And it is surely as significant that many of these men—even the richest of them—still had a lot of assets in cash equivalents, urban real estate, and inventories.[3] Let us look, for example, at Willaume De Gouy, who seems to have been one of the richest échevins. Although heavily invested in land and land rents, neither he nor his wife counted as members of a landed aristocracy. They were, instead, investors in assets of many kinds—of which land rights were only one. When they married in 1401, De Gouy's bride brought cash, jewelry, and household goods priced at 1,500 florins d'or, and another cache of 50 francs. In addition, she provided 47 mencaudées of land in St. Aubert, Montrecurst, and Saulzoin; 4 mencaudées in St. Aubert and a rental income of 2 moutons de roi on three houses in St. Aubert; 5 mencaudees in pasture land in Sauchy-Cauchy; and three houses in Douai.[4]

A century later, things had changed little. Only seven of the twelve (58 percent) of the échevins who served in 1498 appear to have been large landowners, and few of them were overwhelmingly invested in land. Let us look at the three recorded marriages of Anthoine Saingler, one of the senior échevins of the 1498 bench. When Saingler first married, in 1458, he bought 400 écus in merchandise plus 7 rasières 2 couppres of land,

---

3. Even 150 years later, this was still a common pattern in Lille. See, for example, Robert Duplessis, *Lille and the Dutch Revolt* (Cambridge: Cambridge University Press, 1991), 76–77.
    4. AMD, FF 599/1165 (17 January 1401).

along with a city house where his mother lived and where he stored his "marchandise."[5] The bride in his second marriage brought life rents totaling 32 livres per year (secured by urban real estate), 300 livres (in goods); two houses in Douai; a one-fifth claim on her former father-in-law's estate; a house in Sailly, which would go, at their marriage, to the sons of her first marriage; and her "chambre, habits, et joyaux."[6] Saingler's bride in his third marriage, negotiated in 1483 (just two years after his previous marriage), was also endowed with real estate and rents, most of it in Lille, whence she apparently came. She brought one-half of three houses in Lille; one-half of a rent on the city of Dixmuide paying 14 livres 8 sous per year; one-half of another rent in Lille paying 9 livres 7 sous; one-half of a rent on a house in Lille paying 109 sous 4 deniers per year, and one-half of another large collection of rents and due bills, all held on property in Lille.[7]

By the mid–sixteenth century, however, change had come. The échevins who served in 1547 were almost all significant landowners. Ten of the eleven who left records lived almost entirely from land and land rents (91 percent). Some of these men seem to have been extraordinarily land rich— rich in a way fifteenth-century Douaisiens had not dreamed of being. Boudouin Lallart, who married in 1535, had a portement consisting of one-sixth of a house and lands at Rieulay; 2 rasières 2 couppres of land outside the Porte Morel; his "share" of 9 rasières 2 couppres of land outside the Porte D'Esquerchin; 3 rasières 2 couppres of land in Beaumont; 1 rasière of land in Noyelles-Godault; 1,200 livres parisis in cash (or goods); some plate worth 100 livres; his wedding costume; one-fourth of 115 rasières of land in Brebières and Lambres, with a house; one-fourth of 11 rasières 2 couppres of land "près de la justice du Raquet"; one-third of 12 rasières of wheat; one-third of 9½ bonniers of land and a house in Sailly; one-third of 1,741 verges (? verges carrées) of land in Laventie; one-third of a perpetual rent of 6 livres; one-third of 360 verges (? verges carrées) of land, also in Laventie; one-third of 4 livres of rent; one-third of a field and of "divers" rents in Béthune.[8]

This shift to landholding reflects not just an intensification of social hierarchy in Douai, but a change in the general economic climate. In the sixteenth century, things were decidedly better for merchants and land-

5. AMD, FF 622/2923 (28 December 1458).
6. AMD, FF 634/3868 (10 December 1481).
7. AMD, FF 634/3917 (22 October 1483).
8. AMD, FF 652/5380 (29 June 1535).

owners than they had been during the previous two centuries. Demand for foodstuffs was up, as the population finally began to grow again, and grain prices were up as well. Wages did not rise as quickly, however, so that people who owned or traded grain and luxury goods did very well. The Douaisien merchant class obviously benefited from these changes, especially since they were in a position to control much of the grain trade between Artois and Picardy and the region to the North and East. It is no accident that in the sixteenth century so many of Douai's merchants called themselves "marchand de grain" or "marchand de blé" rather than "marchand de laine" or "marchand de drap" as they had more frequently been styled in earlier years, and no accident, surely, that so many acquired rural properties in this age.[9]

The shift to land was not, however, the principal method of redefining assets as "immovable" in these years, although it was surely the most obvious. The majority of Douaisiens, after all—even most who wrote marriage contracts and wills—did not own land, not even in the sixteenth century, and most would never be in a position to purchase such assets. For them, and to a certain extent for their land-rich neighbors as well, the shift in the nature of their assets—a shift from "movable" goods designated for production to "immovable" goods designated for hoarding—took place in imaginative rather than strictly economic terms. People simply began to treat their properties—whether in fact immovable or not—as though they were immovable, as though they were unchangeable through time, as though they bore specific social identities that could be bequeathed to their next possessors.

The process is especially visible in marriage contracts, one of the principal vehicles for the articulation of these ideas of patrimonial inheritance. In one manifestation of these ideas, brides and grooms began assiduously

---

9. The sixteenth-century expansion and the so-called price revolution that accompanied it are well known to historians. For a general overview, see Peter Kriedte, *Peasants, Landlords and Merchant Capitalists* (Lemington Spa, Warwickshire: Berg, 1983). Duplessis's *Lille and the Dutch Revolt* provides a convenient English-language summary of the situation in a nearby urban setting and a reliable guide to the literature; also see M. Rouche and Pierre Demolon, eds., *Histoire de Douai*, vol. 9 of *Collection histoire des villes du Nord/Pas-de-Calais*, ed. Y. M. Hilaire (Dunkirk: Westhoek-Editions, 1985). For the importance of the grain trade in Douai, see, in particular, J. Godart, "Contribution à l'étude de l'histoire du commerce des grains à Douai, du XIVe au XVIIe siècle," *Revue du Nord* 27 (1944): 171–205, and Alain Derville, "Le grenier des Pays-Bas médiévaux," *Revue du Nord* 69, no. 273 (1987): 267–80. In private conversations with me, Herman Van der Wee has pointed out that land was a better investment in the sixteenth century than it was in the fourteenth or fifteenth because grain prices were higher.

to label the origin of their marriage gifts, as they had seldom done in the past. For example, Marguerite Le Raoul, bride of a draper in 1553, specified that the fief, the land, and the land rent in her portement had come from her grandfather; a cash rent had come from her father, along with another, small piece of land; another cash rent had come, however, from her deceased sister via her father's will; 200 livres parisis were from her mother.[10] Entirely expected as it might seem to us to find someone labeling a fief, even cash rents as "family" properties in this way, this had not always been the practice in Douai. Even the fabulously rich Jehene De Bourlon, who married Jehan De Warmoust in 1376, surrounded by eight avoués and laden with land, rents, jewels, houses, furnishings, clothing, and cash, showed little concern with her property's provenance. Only one small holding of 6 rasières and 1 couppre of land was identified as the gift of an aunt. The rest (including 19 rasières of land, a barn, and a mill; another 7-plus rasières elsewhere; a rent of 5 rasières of wheat; a cash rent of 5 sous parisis; another of 8 livres 3 sous; 11 mencaudées of land; and another 9 livres of cash rents) were not so labeled.[11]

In even greater contrast to earlier times, less wealthy men or women of the sixteenth century also came to express the same sense of property's heritage. When Franchoise Gauduin married in the 1550s, for example, she explained that the 200 livres parisis in her portement was a gift from her mother, as was her clothing.[12] Magdelaine Rozel identified the 1,000 florins carolus she would receive as a legacy left in the will of her parents, and she identified another 100 livres as a gift from her grandfather, which he had earmarked for clothing and jewelry.[13] Vaast Hennicque said that he had received the half share in the house he brought to his marriage from the estate of his father, his tools from his stepmother, and his wedding clothes from an unspecified donor.[14]

Less anecdotal evidence displays the same pattern. The forty-one contracts surviving from a sample taken in the 1390s, for example, included less than half a dozen attributions of this kind, while a comparably large sample from the 1520s or 1550s, in contrast, included only one or two contracts that omitted such information. To be sure, this "language of lineage" was not just a matter of rhetoric and the social imaginary; it was

10. AMD, FF 655/5552 (6 March 1554).
11. AMD, FF 586/250 (27 January 1376).
12. AMD, FF 655/5556 (30 January 1555).
13. AMD, FF 655/5546 (26 July 1553).
14. AMD, FF 655/5570 (10 June 1559).

also a reflection of newly dominant inheritance practices in Douai, practices that gave children devolutionary rights. This had not, let us remember, been the rule under custom. Then, parents would do what they wished with their property before death, and their estate was divided equally among their children at death only if the parents had not made prior provisions by means of a will or other legal instrument. During their lives parents could endow a child generously at marriage but still allow the child to collect an equal share of the parents' remaining estate; alternatively, they could endow a child at marriage, but leave the child nothing in the will. Theoretically, they could even deny a child both a marriage gift and an inheritance, although few if any parents did so—and it is hard to imagine how any child could have married without such support. Nevertheless, the decision was in law the parents', and their choice depended on what they thought was best for the child, for other children, or perhaps for the future earning power of the property—not on how custom's rules about equal partibility might have operated in the absence of a will or other legal instruments.

By the late fifteenth century, however, children had implicitly acquired firmer inheritance rights. No longer did parents seem to feel that they could manage their estate as they saw fit; now parents not only felt obliged both to hold their estate for their children and to pass it on to them at specified moments in the life cycle, they felt obliged to demonstrate their compliance with these rules. Hence, beginning in the fifteenth century, if not earlier, most propertied Douaisiens formally calculated marriage gifts as advances on inheritances in a way they had seldom done a century earlier. They did so by specifying that the portements they gave were part of the future inheritance; some contracts went on to specify that, in accepting their marriage gifts, the new couple was relinquishing a future claim on the estate. These provisions thus accomplished two goals: children were assured a "fair" portion of their parents' estates, and parents were assured that they would be seen as having taken care of their children properly.

Thus, when Franchoise Le Quien's marriage contract, written in 1521, laboriously explained that her "lit, couverture, et deux pair de lincheulx" came from her father, that the 400 livres parisis in cash that she listed in her portement was from her grandmother's estate, which her father had held in trust for her, and that three of her landholdings were from her grandfather's estate, while one had come from her grandmother's, we may presume that the object was in part to demonstrate compliance with previously issued wills or other legal instruments, to acknowledge that she had been given her due. A similar motive prompted Catherine Wallers, who in the same year recognized the 400 livres parisis she took into marriage as a "don de son pere," given by way of his will.[15] Marie Du Mont's marriage contract explicitly related her marriage gift to her inheritance, for when she took 300 livres parisis as her portement, she agreed to make no further claim on her father's estate.[16] Marye Le Gentil was equally clear, for she agreed that when she married she would take either 1,500 florins carolus at the time of her marriage or wait to receive 2,200 florins when her parents died.[17] Annette De Warenguies acknowledged the 200 livres she received in her portement as a gift of her father and mother, as was the promise of a share in their "biens" when they died.[18] When Marie Admiral married in 1555, she certified that the 100 livres parisis received from her parents was an advance on money promised in their will.[19] Margueritte Cresteau, who married in 1566, acknowledged that the land rents she took as portement were her share of her grandfather's estate and that she was to receive them only upon her own father's death.[20] Marie De Gentil, who married in 1551, labeled the 1,200 florins carolus and her wedding clothes that she took as part of her portement as her share in the estate of her parents.[21]

It was not brides alone who made such agreements with parents. The marriage gifts given sons were in these days similarly counted as advances on inheritances. It is surely for this reason that so many of the marriage contracts from the late fifteenth and sixteenth centuries included a listing of the groom's portement. The itemization served, of course, no purpose regarding the husband's survivor's rights, as it did for his bride. As survivor of the marriage, he owned the entire conjugal fund, which included all his wife's property except that specifically marked for others in the contract. For him, the listing served only to specify—and thus both to guarantee and to limit—his inheritance.

By labeling and naming pieces of property, their original owners, their proximate donors, their proximate recipients, and their eventual disposi-

---

15. AMD, FF 914 (24 April 1557).
16. AMD, FF 914 (20 January 1557).
17. AMD, FF 914 (13 November 1557).
18. AMD, FF 914 (1557).
19. AMD, FF 655/5560 (11 May 1555).
20. AMD, FF 655/5579 (25 June 1566).
21. AMD, FF 655/5543 (13 November 1551).

tions, Douaisiens did more, however, than settle such legal matters. They also expressed their new ideas about property and its function in social ordering. No longer, they seemed to say, was wealth to be thought of as the earnings generated with the tools, houses, shops, furnishings, and personal property one had been given. Now wealth was the property that one had been bequeathed, the property one held for life, the property that would pass on to lineal descendants or return to the line at death. Of course the *economic* character of these tools and furnishings, clothing and jewelry, shops and inventories had changed not one whit. This was still movable, still infinitely fungible, still precariously ephemeral property.

Nevertheless Douaisiens seemed to be denying that this was so. Even clothing, coin, tools, jewelry, shops, and houses, when labeled in marriage contracts and tracked back to their original owners could, they seemed to say, serve to connect their possessors to the people from whom they had been born or to whom they would give birth. In the process of redefining wealth, Douaisiens were thus creating a new dimension for the circulation of property. This realm was not spatial, as the household had been imagined in old custom, and it was not bounded by a line dividing those who used the property productively from those who did not, as it had been under custom. The realm in which property now circulated was temporal, and its boundaries were set by blood, memory, and imagination, not by residence and use.

The marriage contract, with its laborious tracking of marriage gifts, was an important vehicle of this transformation of property's meaning, but it was arguably not the most powerful one. Rather, it was the testament in which the imaginary was best articulated.[22] Let us look at an early example of this discourse, the testament of Nicaise De La Desous (Dis Dou Pont), written in 1364.[23] The will began, as Douaisien wills of this period usually began, with token gifts to the clergy who would officiate at his death, to

---

22. The Douaisien will, like all wills, was not of course a vehicle for the direct expression of property interests, but a complex construction authored in part by the legal system. For a fuller discussion of Douaisien testamentary practices, see Martha Howell, "Fixing Movables: Gifts by Testament in Late Medieval Douai," *Past and Present* 150 (February 1996): 3–45, and the references cited therein, especially Philippe Godding, "La pratique testamentaire en Flandre au 13e siècle," *Tijdschrift voor Rechtsgeschiedenis* 58 (1990): 281–300.

23. AMD, FF 862 (20 December 1364).

the poor tables, and to the maintenance fund of his parish church. But it then continued with a much longer list of bequests of individual objects to selected relatives:

> To the six children of his brother Jehan De La Desous, and to the two children of his other brother Pierot, he gives 1 rasière of land, to be distributed among them equally;
>
> To the two children of Jacquemart De La Desous and to the daughter of Gillon De La Desous (who is deceased), he leaves 2 couppres of land, to be divided among the three;
>
> To Jaquemart De La Desous, his brother, he leaves a gown, his best ("une reube toute le meilleur que le dis Nichaises ara au jour de son trespas") and two pairs of draperies;
>
> To Jehan De Le Desous, son of Jacquemart, he leaves a featherbed ("une keute"), a pair of linens, and a copper pot;
>
> To his godson, he leaves his best bed "tout estoffe" [fully furnished], but without pillows, one copper pot, and his best bronze frying pan;
>
> To Hanotin Le Ticulier, his cousin, son of Jacquemart Le Ticulier, he leaves his house and holding;
>
> To Esthievenart De La Desous, his nephew, he leaves a featherbed, a pair of linens, his best after those already named;
>
> To Katherine, sister of Esthievenart, he leaves a copper pot and a bronze frying pan with a pair of linens;
>
> To Jehane, sister of Esthievenart, two decorated pillows;
>
> To Katherine, daughter of Jacquemart De La Desous, he leaves a pot with two handles, and to Jehane, daughter of Katherine, a bronze frying pan, the best after that mentioned earlier;
>
> The surplus of his estate he leaves to his executors to distribute to Douai's poor, on behalf of the souls of his relatives named in the will; . . .

De La Desous probably chose to distribute his personal effects so widely in part because he was childless. But he was not alone in so carefully parceling out his movable property in this way. In the same era, Bernard Huquedieu, a tanner, made cash gifts of 200 francs to his son and daughter together (in total, about 330 livres), but also gave his grandchildren his best drinking vessels.[24] Catheline Quoitre, a widow of modest means, gave her house and the "sourplus" of her estate to her son, but she first took pains to distribute treasured personal and household objects to friends and

24. AMD, FF 869 (14 May 1401).

other relatives—for example, a bed, its coverings, pillows, and linens to her niece; the "drapiaux" that she wore daily to her sister; her best "court mantel" (short coat) and "cotte hardie" (cloak) to another sister; a rosary decorated in silver and a reversible cloth to a women friend; and another piece of cloth along with a box decorated in coral to still another woman.[25] Margherite Daire, a widow somewhat richer than Quoitre, made the same kinds of gifts—an onyx cup to a nephew; a book of hours to her nephew's wife; rings to another niece; yards of luxury cloth to a man; silver cups, rosaries, beds and linen, tinware, cooking pots, and kitchenware of all kinds to a niece "for her services"; and similar household goods—a bed with a stitched coverlet, rugs, draperies—to another niece who had rendered special services to her late husband.[26] Marie Le Grand, also a widow, left her best bed equipped with two pair of bedclothes, two pillows, and a serge coverlet; her good "cotte hardie"; her best "cotte à chambre"; her good "plinchon"; a "banquier"; and six of her best cushions to a Jehane De Hainau, stipulating that Jehane's husband, Jehan Bellemer, would get only the bed if his wife were to predecease him. She left similar gifts to nineteen others, including silk purses, rosaries, pots, linens, and fur coats, to friends and relatives.[27]

Common as it was becoming in De La Desous's day to separate objects from land, houses, cash, or an undifferentiated collection of "biens" or "cateux" (chattels) and give them, individually, to friends and relatives, it had not always been so. None of the seventeen testators whose wills survive from the period before 1270 (the earliest Douaisien wills we have) distributed personal effects in this way. Instead, even the richest used the will simply to assure that their principal assets devolved as they wished. Ansel Pererin, for example, wrote a short testament in 1259 that gave his residence and all of his income-producing real estate in Douai, rented or empty, to his son.[28] Marioe Le Paien, a prosperous widow, did little more in the way of elaborating her gifts. She dedicated substantial rents in kind and cash to the church (15 sous parisis to the priest curé of Ste. Ysabiel De Camp Flori, for example), to the poor Beguines (who received thirteen

25. AMD, FF 869 (3 August 1402).
26. AMD, FF 869 (22 May 1403).
27. AMD, FF 869 (13 April 1402).
28. AMD, FF 861 (March 1259), in Monique Mestayer, "Testaments douaisiens antérieurs à 1270," *Nos Patois du Nord* 7 (1962): 64–77, 68–69.

separate rents), and to her granddaughter (who was given 5 rasières of oats, 7 capons, and 40 deniers douaisiens in perpetual rents); to the poor, she gave the furnishings of her house, but she did not bother to enumerate them.[29]

By the early fourteenth century, however, the pattern exemplified by De La Desous's will had begun to emerge, and not just among the richest Douaisiens, those whom we might imagine to have had extra things to give away. Of the forty wills that survive for the period from 1303 to 1329, eleven displayed an impulse to distribute personal property as he would later do. By the second half of the fourteenth century testators even more regularly and more enthusiastically parceled out clothing, jewelry, furniture, and linens in this way. Of twenty-eight wills surviving from 1350 to 1367, nine contained extensive clauses of this kind, and many others made a few such gifts, of drinking vessels, a "houplande" (outer cloak) or a "surcot" (overdress). Jehene Malarde, for example, surpassed De La Desous in her passion to label and distribute objects. She not only bequeathed sumptuous clothing, linens, and draperies to a long list of legatees, she laboriously inventoried her kitchen, her chests, and her public rooms, and she assigned each item to one or another of her many cherished relatives and friends—more than a dozen beneficiaries received countless, and separately itemized, calibrated pots made of tin, kettles, frying pans, bolts of cloth, tablecloths, napkins, pillows and cushions, bedspreads, quilts, draperies, tables, chests, benches, silver hollowware, coats, dresses, purses, belts, hats, and scarves.[30]

Some eighty years later, the practice had, if anything, intensified. Pierre Toulet, a tanner who first registered his will in July 1443 and added two codicils to it in the next few months, for example, left his wife the 300 florins d'or promised in their marriage contract but went on to list dozens of cups, vases, beds, linens, benches, calibrated pots, table linens, and other goods that would be hers and then provided a similarly explicit list of household objects that would go to his son.[31] Jehenne De Cantin's will of January 1455 was less elaborate, but she distributed her goods among a wider circle. Although she bequeathed her children the bulk of the estate (as "sourplus"), she also specifically chose for them six silver spoons each

29. AMD, FF 861 (January 1249), in Mestayer, "Testaments douaisiens," 64–77, 68–69.
30. AMD, FF 862 (26 January 1355).
31. AMD, FF 875 (15 July 1443).

and took from the estate a collection of vases, drinking vessels, fabrics, coats, cloaks, tunics, jackets, vests, beds, and linens, which she passed among female friends, relatives, and servants.[32]

Scholars who have studied wills written elsewhere in late medieval Europe have frequently called attention to bequests like these. From Bruges to Lübeck, from Constance to Avignon to Genoa, it seems, people often laboriously named individual objects in wills and distributed them, piecemeal, among friends and relatives.[33] My point in dwelling on these practices in Douai is not, therefore, to claim that Douaisiens invented a practice unknown elsewhere; rather, it is to argue that these gifts had particular social and cultural meaning in societies like Douai's, a meaning that derived in part from the way the gifts were made and the nature of the goods themselves.

By labeling their objects with such care, by attaching them to their own persons in such specific ways ("my blue dress, the one I wear daily"; "my best cloak, the one with the fur trim"; "six of my goblets, those with silver feet"), and by giving specific goods to specific individuals ("my niece Marie shall have my red satin purse"; "to my goddaughter Jehenne goes my second-best book of hours"), Douaisiens were affecting both the nature of the goods and the nature of the gift.

First, they rendered their goods more than commodities, objects worth more than the economic value they carried. A silver-footed goblet, an illuminated book of hours, a fur-trimmed cloak, a silk dress, even a stack of linens or a soup pot—each placed its owner socially, each resonated with cultural significance, each told a life story. In a paradoxical way, Douaisiens thus made these objects seem more than the money they could buy, seem even to escape commerce. By an alchemy that defies quantifica-

---

32. AMD, FF 875 (29 January 1445).

33. For the southern Low Countries, see, in particular, Godding, "La pratique testamentaire." A 1977 memoir from the University of Liège reported similar practices in thirteenth- and fourteenth-century Huy (A. Gaspard, "Etude sur les testaments de bourgeois et oppidains de Huy de 1263 à 1480" [master's thesis, Université de Liège, 1976–77]).

Also see Paul Baur, *Testament und Bürgerschaft: Alltagsleben und Sachkultur im spätmittelalterlichen Konstanz,* vol. 31 of *Konstanzer Geschichtsund Rechtsquellen* (Sigmaringen: J. Thorbecke, 1989); Steven Epstein, *Wills and Wealth in Medieval Genoa, 1150–1250* (Cambridge: Harvard University Press, 1984); Jacques Chiffoleau, *La comptabilité de l'au-delà: Les hommes, la mort et la religion dans la région d'Avignon à la fin du moyen âge,* vol. 47 of *Collection de l'école française de Rome* (Paris: Diffusion de Boccard, 1980); Ashaver von Brandt, "Mittelalterliche Bürgertestamente: Neuerschlossene Quellen zur Geschichte der materiellen und geistigen Kultur," in *Sitzungsberichte der Heidelberger Akademie der Wissenschaft, philosophisch-historische Klasse* (Heidelberg: C. Winter, 1973), 5–32.

tion, the goods lost imaginative connection with the very world that gave them value.

This was indeed a paradoxical process, for it did not involve the replacement of one kind of value (economic) with another (sociocultural). It involved the addition of sociocultural value to economic. These goblets and cloaks, dresses and soup pots, we have seen, were worth a great deal in the market, in relative terms much more then than now and relatively much more to urbanites of the day than to landed aristocrats, for they made up such a huge portion of urban wealth. So in giving away a dress or a stack of linens, Douaisiens were not simply distributing tokens bearing sentimental value to their near and dear. They were transferring economic capital.

But they were doing more than simply transferring economic capital. They were creating new value, new kinds of capital. When Douaisiens labeled their objects, when they attached them to their persons and to the persons of others in their social network, they seemed to remove their property from the world of movables, of commodities, of mere exchange values. No longer were their dresses, goblets, furs, linens, prayer books and soup pots the "biens" or "cateaux" they had once allowed to pass by custom or had even lumped together in wills of another time. Now these goods were fixed in social space, given precise identities, linked to particular individuals, made special.

Douaisiens were thus employing the products of their commercial world to slow its motion. Rather than letting these objects circulate as commodities, rather than simply calling them "biens" and indiscriminately passing them to others, along with écus or francs, Douaisiens were in a sense denying that they could be transferred into another fungible commodity—a bit of coin, another kind of property, a personal service. By naming their things, by writing them all down, they were, in effect, saving them. Thus, Douaisiens sought to resist the implicit logic of their commercial world. Thus, they imaginatively rendered their wealth "immovable." They were fixing movables.

Second, Douaisiens did more than give property new meanings. They also redefined social relations, for in the process of fixing their movables, Douaisiens were also fixing social relations.[34] By means of their gifts, they

---

34. For a fuller version of this argument, see Howell, "Fixing Movables," and the literature cited therein. In general, on the social nature of exchange, see Marcel Mauss, *The Gift*, (London: Routledge, 1990). For a recent critical assessment, see A. Appadurai, "Introduction: Commodities

were placing themselves alongside, above, or below their beneficiaries in a way that wealth alone did not. Just as a dress, a bed, or a vase acquired new, oddly less ephemeral value by being named and placed with a specific individual, the recipient acquired a fixed relationship to the donor by being given the object. In turn, the donor was himself or herself more securely placed. When Nicaise De La Desous gave his nephew his second-best featherbed and its linens, for example, or chose for his niece a copper pot, a bronze frying pan and a pair of linens, he was saying a great deal about what he considered their needs to be and even more about their relationship to him. When he gave his godson his best bed "fully furnished" (but De La Desous was careful to specify, "without pillows"), a copper pot, and his best frying pan, he was putting spiritual and natal kin in the same sphere, implicitly saying that both were his "parens et amis." His gifts of objects thus elaborated a hierarchical social network and gave it permanence as gifts of anonymous coins or "biens" could not.

Rewriting Gender

The new law had even more profound implications for gender. In contrast to custom, which had put women in charge of property, recognizing them as property's creators (even as it subordinated wives to their husbands) and granting widows of fertile marriages full ownership of the estate, the new law tended to reduce women to carriers of property. Although the will, the marriage contract, and the emerging norms they inscribed did not deny women property rights, they limited women's responsibility for the assets they carried. As we shall see, the law simultaneously articulated new ideas about womanhood itself.

The earliest records of this impulse to define women as carriers of property—to render them simply trustees of wealth for other family members rather than makers of wealth—appear in wills. In his testament dated April 1248, for example, Aleaume Le Cambier left his house—presumably his principal immovable—to his wife, but only so long as she remained a widow; should she remarry, he decreed, the house would pass

---

and the Politics of Value," in *The Social Life of Things: Commodities in Cultural Perspective,* ed. A. Appadurai (Cambridge: Cambridge University Press, 1986).

to their children.[35] In the same year, Bernard De Salar, a merchant or seaman about to venture abroad, wrote a will leaving his house to his wife, but only for her life; he deeded it to his son at her death. He also provided, however, that when (and if) he returned, he would revoke the will and reassume discretionary power over its disposition.[36]

The men who wrote wills during the fourteenth century seem to have been similarly concerned to limit their widows' control over conjugal goods. In 1320, Jehans Li Barbyeres Den Markiet carved 130 livres parisis out of his estate and gave it to his mother and then left the rest to be divided equally between his son and his wife.[37] During the same period Segars De Warlers left his wife only a third of his estate, reserving the remaining two-thirds for their children.[38] Jehans De Bourech took 20 livres parisis from his estate for a daughter who was a nun and, after setting aside some cash for the church and its charities, split the rest—"en dettes, meubles, cateaus, en heritages et en rentes" (in debts, movables, chattels, in héritages and in rents)—between his wife and their remaining children.[39]

The fifteenth-century wills written by prosperous men are the same in this regard.[40] Pierre De Le Bacye, an apothecary, left about 10 livres parisis and a purple fur-trimmed cloak to the church, the tools of his trade to his brother, and all the "heritages" that had come to him from Jehan De Bourben to his wife, but only in usufruct; they would then pass to his sister. To his wife, he also gave the surplus but only on the condition that she did not remarry. If she did, she was to get only a fief containing about

35. AMD, FF 861 (April 1248), in Mestayer, "Testaments douaisiens," 64.

36. AMD, FF 861 (July 1248), in Mestayer, "Testaments douaisiens," 64.

37. AMD, FF 862 (August 1320).

38. AMD, FF 862 (16 March 1311).

39. AMD, FF 862 (December 1313). Not all men seemed so intent on restricting their widows. Some even wrote joint testaments with their wives to assure the mutual donation custom would normally provide only in fertile marriage (AMD, FF 862, Jehan De Bacheret et Chatelins De Tillay [September 1312]). Others wrote joint wills to establish just what religious and charitable donations each spouse could grant from their joint estate and to set aside a portion of it for relatives to whom they felt obligated (AMD, FF 861, Jakemon De France et Hejars De Ghesnaing). Some men who wrote wills were not married; a few were widowers (most of them seem to have been childless); a great many were clerics. In general, such men used the will to distribute their property further and wider than custom would have done, especially to the church and to charities. Jehans De Brebiere, a priest, for example, left his property—apparently all in movables—to his parish clergy, abbeys, the mendicant orders, charities, and to a long list of nieces, nephews, and godchildren (AMD, FF 862 [June 1313]).

40. The wills cited in this paragraph are not in chirographe, but registre. See chapter 3 for an explanation of the differences between these collections.

12 couppres of land plus the 400 livres parisis from her portement.[41] Jac-quemart Le Libert, whom we met in chapter 3, made a deathbed testa-ment leaving all his property to his wife on the condition that she not remarry; if she did remarry, she was to pass the children's share on to them.[42]

Important as the will was in re-gendering property rights, the marriage contract soon displaced it as the principal vehicle for the realignment. As we have seen, contracts typically gave women little authority even to man-age the property they carried. That capacity now lodged with the various men who oversaw their activities throughout each of a woman's life stages. As a daughter, a woman was supervised by her father and, in his absence, by a group of male relatives. As a wife, she was jointly supervised by her avoués and her husband; as a widow, a woman was subject to avoués, her children, and (male) relatives. Only as a childless widow, it seems, did a woman regain full control over the property that was technically hers. But the property she then owned was only a part of what had constituted the conjugal hoard.

The Douaisien marriage contract accomplished this supervision as did all dotal marital regimes, by marking the chief assets in the portement and directing their disposition after death. The contract for the marriage of Ysabel Le Dent and Jean De Temple, written in 1441, was typical.[43] The document began (after the usual formulas) with the statement of Le Dent's portement:

> The said Ysabel Le Dent brings to the marriage, as a gift of her father, for one part, 200 salus d'or or the equivalent in cash, which her father is obli-gated to pay, that is to say: 100 salus in ready cash and the other 100 salus within the year before Easter 1442. And, for the other part of her porte-ment, the said Ysabel brings, as a gift from her father, 28 mencaudées of tillable land or thereabouts, in the boundaries of Vaulz in Artois. And with this a manor and holding in the said city of Vaulz, abutting the holding of Ondart de Uumleville, this 28 mencaudées of land and the said manor,

41. AMD, FF 448, fols. 72v–24r (May 1439). Such provisions were common elsewhere as well. See, for example, von Brandt, "Mittelalterliche Bürgertestamente," and Epstein, *Wills and Wealth in Medieval Genoa*.

42. AMD, FF 448, fols. 29v–30r (23 June 1439). She did remarry, and did so rather quickly. But she had her adult children witness the new marriage contract to confirm that she had obeyed her first husband's orders: see AMD, FF 617/2410 (31 May 1444). Le Libert had written his will in 1439, apparently on his deathbed.

43. AMD, FF 616/2321 (23 April 1441).

which itself contains about 2 mencaudées of land, will be in the possession of the said married couple and their heirs or representatives forever, but only after the death of Jean Le Dent [Ysabel's father]; with it comes the obligation to pay perpetual rents due on the holding to the extent they exist.

These assets, along with any additional properties Le Dent would inherit from her lez et coste during the marriage, were to be returned to her when widowed (her reprise). In addition, she would receive an increase (the douaire or the douaire, assene, et amendement). As a childless widow, Le Dent had absolute rights only to this reprise and douaire, although she was thereby free of the claims of her deceased husband's creditors and could take her reprise and douaire from the estate even before the creditors.

If it happens that after the marriage Jean De Temple dies before Ysabel without a living heir in existence or expected on the day of his death, the said Ysabel will have and can freely take, without obligation of any kind, all the heritages she brought to the marriage and all that came to her in its course, whether by gift, succession, inheritance, or any other way if it was from her natal kin, with the rents and revenues well and sufficiently attached. And she takes without obligation as her portement in money and as douaire, assene, et amendement of the marriage the sum of 500 francs, at 33 Flemish gros for the franc.

To assure Le Dent her douaire, her groom pledged to secure it in real property:

which 500 francs the said Jehan De Temple has promised and is obligated to convert into land or rents situated in the city or territory of Douai within a year, for the security of the said Ysabel.

It was not Le Dent alone, however, who looked over De Temple's shoulder to see that he kept her property safe; she was assisted by her avoués:

And all this with the counsel and advice of Ysabel's advouez named below, with the requirement that the héritages or rents bought by Jean De Temple may not be sold, given away, transferred, or alienated without the permission of Ysabel and her "advouez." If they are sold or [the rents] repurchased, the revenues therefrom must be reinvested in similar héritages or rent, as already required, for the profit of Ysabel.

This contract did not specify Le Dent's rights in the event children were born of the marriage and seemed to give her rights to the reprise and douaire (increase) only if she was childless. Other contracts of the period did, however, spell out what this contract seemed to assume—that a widow who had born a child inherited all the estate but was obligated to hold it for children born of the marriage.[44] Some contracts, especially those written in the later fifteenth and sixteenth centuries, explicitly gave all widows (childless or not) a choice between the douaire coutumier, that is, usufruct on the whole estate, and her reprise and douaire.

Widows obviously gained some important rights under this regime. The property they brought to the marriage was more secure than it had been under old custom, for women were now guaranteed, at a minimum, return of that which they had brought to the marriage, something old custom was not able to do. They were also almost always guaranteed an increase on it, as Le Dent was, either in the form of an outright grant of property or as usufruct on part or all of their deceased husbands' estates. Alternatively, they typically could choose to "stay" in their husbands' estates, thereby acquiring usufruct on the couple's combined properties.

It is also true that women did not lose their claims to patrimonial wealth under the new regime. Women married by contract normally received cash, dresses, and jewels as portements, but they were also commonly given furnishings, tools, houses, rents, and land as well.[45] Of the thirty-five marriage contracts that listed the bride's portement in a sample from the mid–sixteenth century, for example, all but eight of the twenty-one women labeled "rentier" or "prosperous" carried rural or urban real estate (almost by definition, "householders" had no such properties). Among the six rentier brides whose grooms also listed their portements, three carried land or land rents—a proportion exactly matched by their six grooms. Among the fifteen "prosperous" marriage contracts in the sample, there were seven that listed the portements of both brides and grooms: in only

---

44. See, for example, AMD, FF 655/557 (7 March 1555).

45. Unlike their contemporaries in other parts of Europe, who typically were given only cash and personal property at marriage, while their grooms were given the land, houses, and tools that made up households, women in Douai were endowed at marriage in approximately the same way as men. See Jean Hilaire, *Le régime des biens entre époux dans la région de Montpellier du début du XIIIe siècle à la fin du XVIe siècle: Contribution aux études d'histoire du droit écrit* (Montpellier: Causse, Graille and Castelnau, 1957), 55–64, for the constrast; also see Diane Owen Hughes, "From Brideprice to Dowry in Mediterranean Europe," *Journal of Family History* 3 (Fall 1978): 262–96; and Jack Goody, "The Development of the Family and Marriage in Europe" (Cambridge: Cambridge University Press), App. 2.

four did the bride carry no land, land rents, or urban real estate, a number just about matched by the three grooms who were similarly endowed only with movables.[46] These figures differ hardly at all from similar measures taken almost two hundred years earlier, in the 1390s, long before the new ideas about marriage and gender were dominant; in that sample, there were seven rentier brides, five of whose grooms listed their portements; brides and grooms in this sample were exactly equally endowed with land and land rents. Among the "prosperous" brides, there were four grooms who listed their portements and, again, there was little difference between male and female portements in these marriages.[47]

Hence, the new marital property regime did not significantly alter the nature of the assets entrusted to women. The issue here is not, however, the nature of wealth passed to women or their financial security; it is financial control—the right to manage and use property. It was in this regard that the new regime was profoundly different from the old. A woman in this regime had very limited power over the property she took into and out of the marriage. As wife, her portement was managed by her husband, subject only to restrictions on named assets that were supervised by the wife's avoués or other male kin. As widow, she only exceptionally had the power automatically granted the customary widow. Her reprise and douaire would be returned to her, to be sure, but the héritages in these funds were marked for others after her death—children, natal kin, or even the widower should she predecease him. The contract for Gillette Cardron and Andrieu Dapvril, written in 1549, was in this way typical.[48] It provided that the house and holding that the bride had brought to the marriage, along with an orchard, would pass to her plus prochains at her death if no children of the marriage had survived; if there were children, her widower would hold the property for life, but it would pass to their children after his death. Should she survive her husband, the contract implied, she would hold the assets for any children of the marriage. The Douaisien woman thus lost her traditional status as creator and (potential) manager of wealth. Now she was wealth's passive carrier: its creators were the lez et coste; its managers, the men in her life; its owners, her children.

46. AMD, FF 655.
47. See pp. 106–7 above.
48. AMD, FF 654/5542 (2 May 1549).

Living with the New

So profound a redefinition of property, social place, and gender could not have come easily. No wonder, then, that Douaisiens took many long decades, even centuries, before they fully adopted the new rules. No wonder, too, that the transition created the kind of confusion illustrated by the *Le Libert v. Rohard* case. Douaisiens' hesitation in moving from old custom to the new marital property regime was not, however, solely the result of the magnitude of the changes involved. It also reflected, surely, Douaisiens' uncertainty about the suitability of the new, for in certain ways the new marital property regime served gender and social order little better than the old.

The Complications of Multiple Ownership

The new law's most obvious disadvantage lay in its capacity to complicate asset management. As we have seen, the new regime implicitly or explicitly assigned assets to individuals or categories of individuals outside the conjugal household or junior within it, granting them ownership rights equal to those of the heads of household. Guillemete Le Regnier's contract, written in 1522, was in this respect typical. The goods she brought to the marriage—1,200 livres parisis, partly in goods from her father's business, along with a rental income of 60 rasières of wheat, 24 rasières of land held in fief, the livery for a male servant, and personal property—were effectively reserved for her natal kin. Her husband, although he was titular manager of the property during marriage, in fact had little real authority over the property, for he had to be ready to deliver all her "heritages, biens, et meubles" that had come from her "lez et coste" to her "plus prochains" at her death.[1] Thus bound to future owners, Le Regnier's husband was hardly the "baron," or "seigneur et maitre" of the household, as he was often styled; instead, he was reduced to caretaker of assets guaranteed to others. He had no independent authority to exchange these properties for other kinds of wealth or even to borrow against them. He could indeed manage her wealth, but he was accountable to her kin on how well he had done it, especially with respect to the named héritages or other biens labeled in her contract.

It was exactly these limitations that old custom had seemed so determined to avoid. Under custom, decisions about whether to make wool cloth or silk, whether to put cash into grain or real estate, whether to train sons for commerce, the law, or royal service, all were in principle made solely by the head of household. During his life, this was the husband; after his death, it was his widow. In this way, decisions could be made quickly, and, in theory at least, made by the person who knew most about textile markets, grain prices, real estate investments, and the employment prospects in the trades or professions, since the person making the decision was in the business or close to people who were. The new marital property regime sacrificed such efficiency. Because ownership of assets was divorced from management of them, business decisions were more difficult to make. On balance, surely, they were made less well.

Another disadvantage of the new law lay, somewhat paradoxically, in its capacity to disrupt kin relations. Although the system intensified kinship bonds by making kin joint property owners, the new law simultaneously increased the possibility for friction among relatives because it confused their respective property interests. The *Le Libert v. Rohard* case exemplifies one common pattern: stepparents (and stepchildren) vie with children for control of property left by their common relative.

Another, from 1440, was similar in structure but seems to have been considerably more acrimonious than the Le Libert dispute. When Jehan De Quiercy married, some years before the case, he was promised that if his father were to predecease him, he would be heir to half of a rent of 11 couronnes d'or that had long before been purchased on their joint lives.[2]

---

1. AMD, FF 649/5146 (11 June 1522).
2. AMD, FF 292, fols. 68–71 (26 September 1440). The marriage contract has not survived; the dispute, however, was not about the terms of the contract, but about its execution.

By the time the suit was brought, the annuity had long since been re-purchased by its obligor (a privilege commonly granted sellers of annuities in this period), at 8 deniers, that is, at 92 livres 8 sous parisis for the half interest. When De Quiercy's father died, some years after De Quiercy's wedding, his widow (De Quiercy's stepmother) had chosen to "stay" in her husband's estate, and the son claimed in this suit that she had kept the 92 livres 8 sous that had come to the estate when the obligor had repurchased his annuity. De Quiercy sued for that amount, plus about 10 livres for a "drap" that he said his father's sister had given to his own wife but had been left in his father's house. In addition, he claimed the payment due the executors of his father's estate (40 sous) plus his own expenses, at 24 sous per day, for three days. His stepmother countered that De Quiercy had already received 20 livres 18 sous from his father in 1429 and that she and her stepson had made an agreement in 1438 (presumably right after the father's death) that had settled any additional outstanding claims to the annuity. The court apparently judged the latter agreement invalid (or perhaps the widow did not have written proof of it), and the son won the 92 livres 8 sous representing his portion of the annuity's principal. He lost, however, his claim to the cloth and the expenses.

Whatever the legal merits of the son's claim—and he seems to have had the law only partly on his side—his suit's significance for us lies not in the judgment, but in the social and cultural meanings being constructed in the testimony. The son not only intimated that his stepmother had secreted away his money, but also that she had stolen a valuable cloth left for his wife. The charge did not entirely stick, but De Quiercy was able to show that the widow had kept the annuity meant for him. She was thus by implication, suspect as widow—as the "deputy husband" she seemed to aspire to be—and she was instead aligned with the *marâtre*, the mistrusted and despised stepmother of fairy tales.

Another case from the same period bears as eloquent witness to the ways this marital property regime created tensions between in-laws. In 1435, a father tried to regain property he had given his son-in-law and his deceased daughter during their marriage on the grounds that it was not part of the portement promised by the marriage contract and thus should be returned to him, not kept by the widower as part of the wife's estate (to which husbands married under contract typically were heir).[3] The properties in question were 24 livres parisis that the father admitted

---

3. AMD, FF 289 fols. 182–83v (28 May 1435). The marriage contract has not survived.

having given to his son-in-law "to aid him in the expansion of his drapery business"; he also acknowledged that he had given his daughter numerous household items, including "a featherbed with its furnishings . . . worth 10 livres monnaie de flandre, a rabbit throw for bathing children, worth 6 livres monnaie de flandre, a screen worth 20 gros," but these were gifts made personally to her, he said, not to the conjugal fund. In addition, he had gratuitously provided housing and lodging to the married pair for three years.[4]

The son-in-law replied that many of these furnishings had, in fact, been due as portement and that the rest had come, not from the father, but from other relatives: "a bed and many jewels and [other] goods" from a grandmother's will, a silver-decorated belt from her mother, along with other jewels and clothing plus 16 "escus d'or." He also denied that he and his wife had lived with their in-laws ("they had continuously maintained their own household and had provided for themselves and had paid their household expenses themselves, never with the goods of the plaintiff," he protested) although he acknowledged that "on holy days and feast days" they had often dined at the in-laws. He further denied his business debt to his father-in-law. In the end, the échevins ruled that the business loan had in fact been made and that it had to be repaid, but that the rest of the properties claimed were not to be returned to the father; they belonged to the "sourplus" of the daughter's estate and, as such, were the son-in-law's rightful property.

One of the issues at the heart of this case was the definition of the portement, property that in theory went to the husband after his wife's death unless it had been specifically marked for return to her kin. In this case, the problem was that the portement—being made up of movable and hence constantly mutating goods such as clothing and linens—could not easily be distinguished from other properties the bride might have been given as hers alone. In practice, all were part of the "household," each like any other.

Still more significant was the question of where the lines between the conjugal pair and the "lineage" were to be drawn. The newly married couple had not lived with their in-laws, but they were accused of having done so, and the son-in-law admitted they often had dined with their in-laws "on holy days and feast days." The young couple had also taken substantial

4. AMD, FF 289, fol. 183.

favors from them, even financial help for their businesses. Thus, the boundaries between conjugality and kinship had been eroded. When the marriage ended, however, the conjugal unit was dissolved, and it was necessary to redistribute the household's assets and liabilities, giving to the bride's kin what was originally theirs and the husband's (in this case, the husband himself), what was theirs. Under old custom, no such dissolution could have occurred: all property in the conjugal fund—whether originally from a marriage gift, from earnings, or from services, cash, or goods delivered in the course of the marriage—would have gone to the survivor of the marriage, for the conjugal unit would have survived the marriage. Under this new regime, however, every écu, every fur rug, every bed, every necklace was subject to dispute.[5]

The Complications of Gender

More destabilizing still was the new regime's effect on gender. Like old custom, the new law positioned women to subvert the gender order just as it positioned them to enact a particular version of gender hierarchy. Because the terms of gender hierarchy were not the same in this regime as they were in custom, however, so too were the instabilities produced by the regime different from the old. Under this system it was not the powerful widow or the "dumb" wife turned "speaking" widow who was the potential source of tension, as it had been under custom. Under this regime, it was the protected woman, the woman so perfectly protected that, paradoxically, she was perfectly free to wreak havoc.

Let us look, by way of example, at a case brought by Simon Gabriel, widower of a woman to whom household goods worth about 100 livres had been bequeathed by her late sister.[6] Gabriel brought his suit against George Harpin, widower of the sister who had made the gift. Harpin countered that his late wife had had no power to promise these goods. Her marriage contract with Harpin had provided that she could grant only 40 livres in testamentary bequests, not the 100 livres she had in fact

---

5. Marianne Danneel provides abundant examples of how these conflicts arose in late medieval Ghent, as widows squabbled over how to distribute the community goods in the estate (movables), which were to be divided between the widow and lineal heirs: Danneel, *Weduwen en wezen in het laat-middeleeuwse Gent* (Leuven and Apeldoorn: Garant, 1995), 264–92.

6. AMD, FF 292, fols. 38–40v (ca. 1440).

left her sister. Gabriel had tricked her into making the illegal gift, Harpin continued, for Gabriel had come to her seeking the bequest while Harpin was out of town and when she was suffering from a "a very serious illness" and in no position to make sound decisions.

Harpin was on firm legal grounds (for his marriage contract had not given his wife the power to make gifts of 100 livres), and he won. What is interesting here, however, are the gender definitions that underlie Harpin's narrative, not the legal ruling itself. Harpin portrayed his late wife as in need of constant protection—unable even to know the terms of her own marriage contract, so ignorant that she could be tricked into believing what was patently not so. It was her husband who "knew." As the one who "knew," he functioned as her protector. When he was out of town, away from her side, she was vulnerable; by implication, she was safe—and others were safe from her errors—only when he was there.

Another common variation on the theme of the woman in need of protection appears in cases concerning widows who had married by contract and had chosen to stay in their husband's estate, thus relinquishing the protections provided by the contract. To judge from the lawsuits that frequently followed, these women often failed to realize that the estate they enjoyed was burdened by debts for which they were liable. Thus, for example, we find Marie Hourdain, widow of Honnere Emery, who vigorously professed ignorance when she was brought to court by the ministers of the Church of St. Pierre in 1442.[7] The ministers charged that Hourdain owed rental payments on a house her husband had bought from them in 1423, which was now part of the estate Hourdain had claimed. Hourdain countered that her husband had managed the purchase and that she knew nothing about any rents due on it ("se ladite rent avoit este vendu par decre ou aultrement elle en savoit riens" [if the said rent was sold by decree or otherwise she has no knowledge of it]). She lost, for as holder of the douaire coutumier, she was responsible to her husband's creditors. No matter that she may well have been truly ignorant of her husband's dealings, no matter that she may well have been the shielded wife the marriage contract assumed women to be; no matter that the creditors may have been lying about the past debt. By choosing the douaire coutumier, Hourdain had lost the protection of contract—and with it, her ability to claim ignorance.

---

7. AMD, FF 292, fols. 177–78v (22 June 1442).

It will surely not have escaped readers that both the *Gabriel v. Harpin* and the *Ministers v. Hourdain* cases resemble the kinds of lawsuits produced by old custom in that they too feature wives who were fully contained by their husbands. There is, however, a difference between the two. The women who had married under contract were contained because they required protection; the women who had married under custom were contained because their economic powers—and all their property rights—were delegated to their husbands, the heads of household. The shift then, was not so much in what women could or could not do as wives (in either case they could not do much with any property in the marriage, no matter its source) but in the definition of womanhood implied by the legal regime; although subtle, the shift was real. Women of custom were imagined to be competent to manage property, to create it, not just to carry it; they were denied the right to exercise their competence during marriage because the smooth functioning of the household required it. In widowhood, their powers were fully restored, however, because then the household had need of them. Women of contract enjoyed no such transformation. Protected in marriage, they were protected as widows as well. Never did they assume the powers the woman of custom was granted. Although they were never dispossessed of property and never fully denied managerial rights to some degree, they were always in some way supervised—by fathers, avoués, husbands, sons. In effect, they were imagined to be better carriers of property than managers of it, better passive trustees for the assets of men than contributors to the assets of men.

The new legal regime thus resolved the contradiction of custom that made wives their husbands' full dependents, people without property rights of their own, but made widows fully independent, suddenly and magnificently able to exercise full rights over the property over which their husbands had been lords. But the new law did not thereby eliminate widows as a threat to social and gender order; it simply created new sources of tension. The case of Jehanne Buisson, daughter-in-law of the Marie Hourdain whom we just met, nicely illustrates the dangers inherent in this new conception of wifehood, widowhood, and the gender relations constructed by marriage.

Buisson had been married in 1433 under a contract that provided that she could exit her husband's estate with half of all the goods, movables, chattels, and héritages they had owned, along with her "bed and its furnishings, cloths, clothing, jewels, and the 'furnishings for her body' ('aournemens pour son corps')," plus life use of the couple's residence. The other half, "burdened with expenses . . . and debts," would go to his "plus pro-chains."[8] Buisson's parents-in-law owned a dry-goods business, and they had contributed the house in which the couple lived, their son's wedding clothes, and 400 écus in merchandise to their son's own dry-goods business. When the groom died, in 1435, less than two years after his wedding, he had incurred huge debts to wholesalers, and immediately after his death the creditors descended. Buisson, no fool, simultaneously filed for her reprise and douaire and sought to exit the estate, leaving the creditors to fight over the meager remains. Hourdain, her mother-in-law, was customary heir of these remains and thus liable for the debts; in an effort to cover the losses, she sued Buisson to force her to stay in the estate.[9]

Buisson won the case, as a strict reading of the law required. In exercising her legal rights, however, Buisson trespassed on what others considered their rights. She abandoned her deceased husband, she blackened his family name in the business world, and she left her mother-in-law, an aged widow, stuck with huge debts. With her half of the household goods firmly in hand—and free of any obligations whatsoever—she remarried within the year. The protection afforded her by contract thus allowed Buisson to escape the debts her late husband had incurred, to attract a new husband, and to take all her personal property out of the old marital estate. The new marital property thus made the women whom it protected dangerous, for it freed them from obligations to their former spouse, to their late husband's kin, and to the households that old custom had once so unequivocally assigned to the widow's safekeeping.

To be sure, the new law did limit the dangers posed by these widows. Widows who took only their reprise and douaire out of their marriage had little of their deceased husbands' wealth—thus little from a former spouse's property to offer a new spouse. Once the meaning of the douaire coutumier had been clarified (surely by the end of the fifteenth century, if not before) those widows who chose to stay in their deceased husbands' estates rather than take their reprise and douaire had only the use of the marital estate, not ownership of it, and they had to hold it for lineal heirs of their deceased husbands. We have every right to suspect that Douaisien men who chose to marry with a contract did so precisely in order to prevent such property transfers, to assure that most of their assets remained in their line if they should die before their wives.

8. AMD, FF 612/1934 (1433).
9. AMD, FF 290, fols. 164–65 (1436); FF 291, fol. 81v (1436).

Still, these men did not succeed in preventing their widows from remarrying. Women widowed by contract regularly remarried, perhaps as regularly as "customary" widows, and they were able to do so precisely because they were, like the widows of custom, well propertied. Of the twenty-six widows who married by contract in 1441–43, for example, ten had already married under contract once before, and *at least* eight of the eighty-three women in this sample would again marry by contract. Anecdotal evidence is as telling. Jehenne Hordain, a widow with four children, married Hue De Lestree by contract in 1436; by 1440, she had borne him two additional children, but a few years later she married a third time, again by contract.[10] Jehenne Du Mont married Colart De Quiery, a widower, in 1435; he died in 1440, and in 1441, Du Mont remarried.[11] Marie Du Bosquiel married a widowed butcher, Colart Belot, in 1430. He died in 1435, and she remarried in April 1436.[12] Jehene Le Fevre was married in 1424; she was widowed in June 1434, and she remarried in May 1435. In 1457, she remarried yet again.[13]

Contract widows were thus able to walk away from their previous lives (as widows of custom never could) and jettison all their past loyalties, previous debts, and old ties. However ardently the new law thus sought to subordinate women during marriage and rein them in afterward—and no matter how well it succeeded in this task—the constraints thus provided women a liberty that could undermine the gender order as insidiously as old custom's contradictory notions about female agency ever had done. There was, it seems, no perfect way both to harness women's labor and their property and, simultaneously, to reserve them for the single purposes of men.

The Gender of Givers/The Gender of Gifts

Douaisien women thus had an ambiguous relationship to property. This was true whether old custom governed their inheritances and marriages

10. AMD, FF 613/2069 (ca. 1436); FF 292 fols., 62–64; 117–18v.

11. AMD, FF 613/2072 (18 January 1436); FF 616/2347 (26 November 1441); FF 292, fols. 68–71 (26 September 1440).

12. AMD, FF 610/1860 (17 January 1429); FF 613/2082 (27 April 1437); FF 289 fols. 86–86v, 98, 112verso, 122 (ca. 1435).

13. AMD, FF 395, fols. 177v–78v (24 July 1424); FF 289, fol. 32 (19 July 1434); FF 613/2034 (3 May 1435); FF 622/2844 (11 January 1457).

or the new ideas expressed by the wills and marriage contracts held sway for them. In either case, these women enjoyed significant property rights, but in both cases their rights were checked in some important ways. Women married under custom spent their married years without any formal property rights at all, but as widows assumed full powers over their own and their husbands' assets; women married under contract were never entirely dispossessed of property, but they were never fully in charge either, not as wives and not as widows.

Given the ambiguities of their position as property holders, we would expect to find that Douaisien women handled their property differently from men—that they made different decisions about how to use their property, when and what to buy and sell or give away, whom to sell or give it to. The archives in Douai have left only one source that allows a systematic investigation of such matters, but it is a telling source: the will. Even a cursory examination of the testaments left in Douai's medieval archive leaves little doubt that women in Douai had a different relationship to property than men did.[14] They tended to treat property less as economic capital than as cultural or social capital. In doing so, I want to suggest, they helped elaborate the portrait of womanhood that was being simultaneously constructed by the marriage contract: women were different from men in their relationship to property; they did not fully understand economic wealth and its management; they were in some sense less than rational; they needed supervision.

Let us turn to the wills themselves. Two interesting features are immediately apparent. First, a huge proportion of Douaisien wills—about half of all my samples—were written by women.[15] Evidently, women in Douai

14. Samuel K. Cohn, Jr., *Death and Property in Siena, 1205–1800: Strategies for the Afterlife* (Baltimore: Johns Hopkins University Press, 1988), provides a detailed study of the differences between women's and men's testamentary practices; although he concentrates on pious bequests, his general point that women had different social and cultural references parallels my own.

15. In contrast, only about 20 percent of fourteenth-century Lübeck's testators were female (Ashaver von Brandt, "Mittelalterliche Bürgertestamente: Neuerschlossene Quellen zur Geschichte der materiellen und geistigen Kultur," in *Sitzungsberichte der Heidelberger Akademie der Wissenschaft, philosophisch-historische Klasse*, 5–32 [Heidelberg: C. Winter, 1973]), only about 18 percent of Freiburg's 15 percent of Ravensburg's, and 33 percent of fourteenth-century Constance's (Paul Baur, *Testament und Bürgerschaft: Alltagsleben und Sachkultur im spätmittelalterlichen Konstanz*, vol. 31 of *Konstanzer Geschichts- und Rechtsquellen* [Sigmaringen: J. Thorbecke, 1989], 60). In Avignon, about 35 percent of testators were female (Jacques Chiffoleau, *La comptabilité de l'au-delà: Les hommes, la mort et la religion dans la région d'Avignon à la fin du moyen âge*, vol. 47 of *Collection de l'école française de Rome* [Paris: Diffusion de Boccard, 1980], 50), and in Cologne about 53 percent (Baur, *Testament und Bürgerschaft*, 64). In Douai, about two-thirds of all testators

not only retained meaningful property rights, they had a lively sense of their rights and were aggressive about using Douai's legal sytem to ensure that their property went where they wanted it to go. Second, women testators were in different life stages than male testators, and they had testamentary control over less property than men did.

The second characteristic is a direct product of legal norms, for law very much disabled women testators in comparison with men. No married woman whose husband lived, no matter whether she had married by custom or contract, had full testamentary control over any property. A woman who had married by custom could write no will at all; a woman who had married by contract could write a will covering only that property specified in her marriage contract. Men, in contrast, had much more testamentary control over their property. If a man had married by custom, *all* property in the marriage, including the property provided by his wife, was subject to this testamentary control; if he had married by contract, he could not will away his wife's reprise and douaire, but he was often free to do what he wanted with the rest.[16] Once widowed, a woman who had married under custom had the full powers her husband had once enjoyed, but he might well have already disposed of a great deal of conjugal property, whether by testament, by gifts *inter vivos,* or by sales. A widow who had married under contract would be free to write a will covering her own property, but only if she had exited her husband's estate; if she stayed on as dowager, she was obligated to hold the estate for lineal heirs.[17] Thus, the demographics of will writing in Douai were clearly marked by gender dimorphism: married will writers were overwhelmingly male; widowed and single will writers were overwhelmingly female (see table 4). In total, between 49 and 52 of the 54 to 57 married testators sampled in five periods

---

were widows, while only about 36 percent of Constance's were widows (Baur, *Testament und Bürgerschaft,* 61, 65).

16. Many marriage contracts restricted the husband's testamentary rights, limiting him (as it limited his wife) to small bequests.

17. Not only were most female testators widows, but most of the women who wrote wills after about 1350 had been married by contract, so even as widows they did not have full control of the conjugal estate. Even those who had never married—and there were a good number of single testators—may have had only limited control of their assets, for their fathers could well have written wills of otherwise denied them their customary portion of his estate. Many female testators in Douai who had married by custom were constrained by wills their late husbands had written or by other special arrangements their husbands had made during their life, so they too were hardly ever able to write wills covering significant amounts of marital property.

Table 4
Testators by Sex and Marital Status

Sampled Dates	Single and Widowed			Married			Total		
	Male	Female	Total	Male	Female	Total	Male	Female	Total
Pre-1270	2–5	4	6–9	7–10	1	8–11	12	5	17
Early 1300s	2	21	23	13	—	13	15	21	36
1350–67	7	12	19	9	—	9	16	12	38
Early 1400s	3	11	14	8	3	11	11	14	25
Mid-1400s	4	11	15	12	1	13	16	12	28
Totals	18–21	59	77–80	49–52	5	54–57	70	74	144
%	23–26%	74–77%	100%	91%	9%	100%	49%	51%	100%

Note: Figures exclude testaments coauthored by husbands and wives and exclude as well men in major orders (3 men).

over two centuries were men (91 percent); 59 of the 77 to 80 widowed or single testators sampled were women (74–77 percent).

Let us look at one woman's will, written in 1406 by Marie Narrette Dit De Sandemont, a prosperous spinster. After the conventional pious opening and gifts to religious and the poor, Narrette goes on to list elaborate and separately itemized gifts of sumptuous clothing and household goods, each made to separate friends and relatives:

> To Jeanne De Bourech, widow of Jehan Gascoing, her best long "drap" in bright blue, which is lined with fur from the backs of squirrels, and 4 rasières of wheat, with the charge that she pray for her;
>
> *Item*, to Jehan De Haricourt De Durr the Elder, with the same request, she gives one vase in marbled wood with silver feet; he can pick the one he likes;
>
> *Item*, to Jehan De Haricourt Dit Le Petit who lives in Darr, with the same request, one franc;
>
> *Item*, to Tassart De Haricourt, with the same request, one franc;
>
> *Item*, to Maroie De Haricourt, the daughter of Jakemon . . . her best cloak ("cotte hardie") in black fur-lined cloth;
>
> *Item*, to Gillotte, wife of the said Jehan De Haricourt Le Petit, with the same request, her best cloak ("plinchon") lined in rabbit;
>
> *Item*, to Hannette Birchard, daughter of Jakemon, her best silk belt decorated in silver, with the same request;
>
> *Item*, to Marguerite, wife of Jakemon Birchard, mother of Jehanete, with the same plea, her best amber rosary, with silver scarabs;
>
> *Item*, to Marie, widow of the deceased Jehan De Cantin, one vase of marbled wood and 2 rasières of wheat, with the same request;
>
> *Item*, to Hanette Baillet, daughter of Nusart Baillet, with the same request, a cloak ("cotte hardie") of brown cloth, trimmed with feathers;
>
> *Item*, to Caterine, wife of Michel Agace, her lesser cloak ("plinchon") lined in rabbit;
>
> To Marguerite, wife of Jehan Boiscel, her dress ("coritel") with jasper-colored sleeves, the least one;
>
> To sire Robert De Haricourt, priest, at present *curé* at Escehaing, with the same request, 2 francs;
>
> *Item*, to Sebile, wife of Jehan Du Buisson, citizen of Douay, who is her godmother, with the same request to pray for her, the

testator, her best book of hours, the one with nine psalms and
nine lessons;

Item, to Hannette Cressoniere, daughter of Pierre, her
goddaughter, her other book of hours, the best after that
already bequeathed, with the same request;

Item, to Marrette De Fevre, daughter of the deceased Jakemon,
her goddaughter, with the same request, 1 franc;

Item, to Marguerite De Hennin, widow of Jehan Le Fevre, who
lives at the hospital of St. Mahieu in Arras, her best short
overdress ("surcot") trimmed in squirrel, with the same request;

Item, to Agnes Turpine, the Beguine at Camp Flouay, her coat
made of reversible cloth ("son mantel de drap mellé double"),
the least one, with the same request;

Item, to Jacque Le Caudreliere, a red cloak ("cotte hardie") made
of red silk and lined (or trimmed) with feathers, with the
request to pray to God for her;

Item, to Marie De Haricourt, wife of Jehan De Haricourt de
Druy, one dress ("coritel") with sleeves of jasper and one crêpe
kerchief, both the best;

Item, to Marie, wife of Jehan Willate, two couppres of wheat;

Item, to Cede Dartois, a poor woman living near the house of
Colart Beugart in the street of Jehan Le Goy, her best cloth of
coarse, undyed wool ("blanquette");

Item, to Ysabele De Warnpont, to Caterine, wife of Andrieu
Alongerrille, and to Christpenne Doubliere, to each, one night-
kerchief, with the request to pray to God for her;

To Marguerite Des Plangues, one lined hood made of red cloth
("drap") and one night-kerchief, with the same request;

Item, to Laurence De Merles, one red hood with scarlet trim.

In important ways, Narrette's will resembles Nicaise De La Desous's,
the male testator introduced in chapter 5. But Narrette's is even more
devoted to making gifts of individual objects than his was, and it is this
quality above all that makes her will "female." Ten of the eleven early
fourteenth-century wills in which personal property was itemized and distributed in the fashion adopted by both De La Desous and Narrette were
written by women, while only half of the testators in this sample were
female; 66 percent of the "object givers" in the 1350–67 sample were female, while only 43 percent of the testators were women; 75 percent of
those writing such wills in register were female, while only 37 percent of
the entire group were female. The only sample not so skewed is the early
fifteenth-century one from which Narrette's will was taken; 50 percent of

those who distributed property in this way were women, a sex distribution exactly matched in the group from which the wills came.

These distinctive patterns were in part a function of the legal system, which, as we have seen, determined who wrote wills and when they wrote them. No doubt, women devoted so much attention to distributing personal property because the wills and marriage contracts that governed so many women's property rights in this age gave women free access only to such goods, while reserving land, houses, and rents for patrilineal heirs. The legal system authored this pattern in another way as well, however, for by guaranteeing that the typical female testator was a widow or a spinster, it also guaranteed that she would have many people to remember in her will. The typical widow was aged, and she had grown children, grandchildren, and hordes of nieces, nephews, and godchildren. She might also have a circle of female friends from her neighborhood. If she was a spinster her intimates were perhaps more numerous—if less closely related—than those of a mother and widow. The typical male testator, in contrast, headed a household; he was usually a younger, married father whose concerns were his household and his children's and wife's futures. He had little interest in marking and elaborating a wide social circle; his impulse was to claim and protect his own.

The intensity with which women attached themselves to personal effects and attached themselves to others through these goods had, of course, deep cultural roots as well. It had long been and would long remain the practice in Europe for women to have preferential access to personal property.[18] The typical Douaisien marriage contract often stated, in fact, that widows were expected to take the clothes and jewels they regularly wore ("a son corps") when their husband died, even before they filed for their reprise or the douaire coutumier, thereby honoring the venerable European tradition that made these goods always a woman's own.[19] But

18. For a fuller discussion of this issue, see Martha Howell, "Fixing Movables: Gifts by Testament in Late Medieval Douai," *Past and Present* 150 (February 1996): 3–45. In general, also see N. Bulst, "Zum Problem städtischer und teritorialer Kleider-, Aufwands- und Luxusgesetzgebung in Deutschland, 13.–Mitte 16. Jahrhundert," in *Renaissance du pouvoir législatif et genèse de l'état,* ed. A. Gouron and A. Rigaudière (Montpellier: Publications de la Société d'Histoire du Droit et des Institutions des Anciens Pays de Droit Ecrit, 1988), and, for a somewhat different interpretation based largely on Italian evidence, Hughes, "Regulating Women's Fashions," and "Sumptuary Law and Social Relations in Renaissance Italy," in *Disputes and Settlements: Law and Human Relations in the West* (Cambridge: Cambridge University Press, 1983)

19. See, for example, the contract for Jehanne Buisson: AMD, FF 612/1934, in which she was promised, before the estate was split between her and her husband's lineal heirs, "sa chambre

it would be too simple to attribute women's testamentary practices in fifteenth- and sixteenth-century Douai to a simple equation between women and personal effects such as clothing and jewels. Custom, after all, made widows full heirs of their husbands and made daughters equal heirs of intestate parents. Even marriage contracts did not entirely dispossess women of immovable goods or less personal assets, for, as we have seen, women married under contract were regularly granted houses, shops, land, and tools in their portements and took these goods with them as reprises when they exited the estate.

There can be no doubt, however, that women named personal property, particularly clothing and jewels, in their wills more often than men did. Evidently, women disproportionately invested in such goods and chose these among all their possessions to distribute individually. Still, these choices do not necessarily reflect the frivolous passion for finery that European moralists and writers of the day often attributed to women.[20] The

---

estoffe, draps, habis, joyaulx et aronemens pour son corps" (a furnished bedroom, cloths, clothing, jewels, and personal ornaments). This was, however, a right not automatically accorded Douaisien women. If these personal goods were not specifically named as part of the reprise or guaranteed in a separate clause, as they were for Buisson, they were considered under both custom and contract as part of the conjugal estate. This was also the rule in Ghent, as it was by the logic of most community property regimes: Danneel, *Weduwen en wezen*, 272–74. The custom of late medieval Genoa, in contrast, always assumed such goods were women's (as *parapherna*) and that they were returned to widows along with their dowry and *antefactum* (*donatio propter nuptias*). But there too, widows' claims to these goods were precarious. Husbands regularly mentioned these items in wills as though they were legacies left at their discretion, not property due to the woman as her right; in a sense, men were thus marking their sense of proprietorship over these goods, claiming what was technically the women's own. In keeping with this tradition that linked women to personal goods, Genoese men also often gave their widows household possessions—clothes, cookware, and the bed—(the *massaricia*) as legacies, in addition to the dowry and *antefactum* proper: see Epstein, *Wills and Wealth in Medieval Genoa, 1150–1250* (Cambridge: Harvard University Press, 1984).

20. Moralists, writers of advice books, and satirists of the day all charged women with an inordinate lust for finery. The sumptuary legislation of the period reiterated the theme, especially that of Italy: see, for some recent studies of the legal rhetoric, Ronald Rainey, "Dressing Down the Dressed Up: Reproving Feminine Attire in Renaissance Florence" in *Renaissance Culture and Society: Essays in Honor of Eugene F. Rice, Jr.*, ed. J. Monfasani and R. G. Musto (New York: Italica Press, 1991), 217-39, and Diane Owen Hughes, " Regulating Women's Fashions" in *History of Women in the West*, ed. C. Klapisch-Zuber (Cambridge: Belknap Press, Harvard University Press, 1992). Sumptuary legislation in the North was less specifically concerned with women's attachment to clothes, jewels, and make-up, but the theme appears often in the comic literature of the region. See, for example, Chaucer's "The Shipman's Tale" or *The Fifteen Joys of Marriage (Quinze Joies du Mariage)*, ed. Jean Rycher (Geneva: Droz, 1967).

More generally, see Suzanne W. Hull, *Women According to Men: The World of Tudor-Stuart Women* (Walnut Creek, Calif.: AltaMira Press, 1996), Ruth Kelso, *Doctrine for the Lady of the*

dresses, purses, rosaries, books, even the linens and pots, that Narrette listed in her will were, we have seen, worth a small fortune, and it was goods such as these that made up the bulk of her household's assets, just as they did for most other Douaisiens of the age. Given the economic importance of such movable property in the Douaisien household, it makes complete sense that women would have eagerly claimed such goods. And it is surely a mark of women's property rights in Douai, both under old custom and the new law that emerged, that they could claim such valuables as their own.

But there may have been even more to it, another, even better, reason why women would have been wise to content themselves with personal, as opposed to immovable, property. This reason lay in the realities of day-to-day life in urban households, for in these households it was much easier for women to mark personal property as their own. Although the conjugal fund created by marriage was, in Douai, as it was everywhere, under the husband's titular control, wives inevitably had some discretionary power over the movables in this fund, for it was they who made small outlays for the pantry or the linen shelf, who paid tradesmen, who doled out wages to servants.[21] The structural tensions inherent in such systems are obvious: all property was under the husband's control, but in practice the wife had significant responsibilities to manage it. In many places, formal legal mechanisms were devised to reduce the tensions that inevitably resulted. The practices of establishing separate spousal properties in addition to the conjugal fund was of course common to most customary legal systems of northern Europe, and the marriage contracts written in Douai obviously had this as one of their objectives. But even when marital properties were divided into "his," "hers," and "theirs," into héritages or into goods due the plus prochains, tensions about who had day-to-day control over these goods were not eliminated, and many localities devised other strategies for resolving these tensions. In certain German areas, for example, a convention called *Schlüsselgewalt* was adopted to put a ceiling on

---

Renaissance (Urbana: University of Illinois Press, 1956), and R. M. Bell *How To Do It* (forthcoming).

21. If the marriage had been made under custom, the conjugal fund included all property, no matter its kind or origin. If the marriage had been made by contract, the marital property consisted of three parts—"hers" (the reprise and douaire, assene, et amendement); his (any property he specifically marked as "his"); theirs (the rest). The husband had full control during marriage over all that was "theirs" or "his," and he had full managerial control over "hers," limited only by any specific clauses in the marriage contract treating particular properties.

the amount of money a wife could spend out of the conjugal fund without her husband's explicit consent, in performing her duties as housewife.[22] The better-known convention of *feme sole* (*femme marchande publique* or *Kauffrau*) came at the problem from another direction. Recognizing that many wives had separate business lives, it provided that a woman could be declared "feme sole" in order to protect her husband and the conjugal fund for which he was responsible from the debts she might incur when acting on her own.[23]

Yet, however ingenious the legal mechanisms created to lessen these structural tensions, the practicalities of everyday household management derailed the quest for clarity and order. Property brought to a marriage might technically belong to one spouse or another, and the conjugal fund might be carefully divided into "discretionary" and "nondiscretionary" accounts, but in reality bushels of grain, vats of dye, piles of bedcovers, chests of coin, flocks of geese, wagons, looms, or wall hangings could not be kept fully separate. If locked away, they were useless, and most of them depreciated rapidly if unused. Once consumed, they were gone. Once sold, they had become something else—a piece of coin, a rental income, an I.O.U. And the income such an asset earned—the goslings the goose bore, the profits made from the loom or the dye vats, or the cartage fees earned from the wagon—could not easily be held apart. Nor could the losses an object incurred—the wear and tear on the wagon, the death of the goose, the fall in cloth prices. In practice, there could have been no stable, fully separate accounts—his, hers, theirs.

As the subordinate in the marriage, as the ward of her "baron," as the Douaisien texts of the period called the husband, a wife's claim to any of this property was precarious, for goods so nondurable could not easily be tracked. As a widow, she might find it even harder to collect the property due her—whether it was technically hers, her share of common property, or a part of her husband's estate. If she had been married under custom or had been party to a ravestissement par lettre, all the marital estate was hers, but she was thereby liable to all her husband's creditors; and having no certain way of knowing what liabilities her husband had incurred, she

22. For a description, see G. K. Schmelzeisen, *Die Rechtsstellung der Frau in der deutschen Stadtwirtschaft*, vol. 10 of *Arbeiten zur deutschen Rechts- und Verfassungsgeschichte* (Stuttgart: W. Kohlhammer, 1935); he cites Georg Schmitt, *Die Schlüsselgewalt der Ehefrau nach deutschen Recht* (1893).

23. See Schmelzeisen, *Die Rechtsstellung,* 89 ff.

had no sure protections against nasty creditors. A widow who had been married under contract, in contrast, had a constituted right to the reprise of her portement and to the douaire (depending upon the precise terms of the contract, her husband's authority to manage the wealth due her as reprise and douaire would have been to some extent limited), but she had no straightforward accounting that would allow her to separate these assets from an estate likely to be composed of interchangeable and constantly mutating properties.[24]

In these conditions, all wives would have seen the logic of preserving and perhaps even stretching traditions that made a woman's most personal property—her clothing and jewels—fully her own. They would also have had every reason to mark other goods as their own as well, to label them so unambiguously theirs that when the marriage ended, neither the widow nor her heirs would have trouble identifying and claiming what was hers. What better goods to choose than the linens and pots that she had used daily, the books and rosaries with which she had prayed, and the bed where she had slept, made love, and given birth? How better to assure that the money a wife earned at the loom or from her cheese, that the assets tied up in the brewery her father had left her, that the rents she and her husband had perhaps purchased together, were securely hers? Thus, while Douai's legal culture worked to restrict women's control over marital property, it also created opportunities for women. By exploiting tradition and law alike, women could win more certain control of specific movables, especially those associated with their bodies and their domestic spheres.

It is no wonder that Douaisien women collected such movables with devotion seldom displayed by men. In giving their goods away, women distinguished themselves just as clearly. The beneficiaries men chose in their wills were made up almost entirely of lineal relations—male and female—and men made gifts to these people as though to reinforce lineal ties. Their bequests, usually made to sons, daughters, wives, and to other

---

24. All marriage contracts assumed that the husband was manager of all marital property, whether provided by bride or groom, whether movable or immovable, whether originally brought to the marriage or acquired thereafter. In this respect, contracts were like custom, and their texts often referred to the husband as "baron" or "seigneur et maître," the same term used by legal documents describing custom. Many contracts, however, named certain properties—usually héritages—that the husband could not sell or mortgage, and all contracts placed implicit restrictions on the husband by requiring that the reprise and douaire (sometimes made up of specifically named properties) be returned to his widow.

kin and business associates, consisted of mixed collections of cash, land, houses, tools, and movable goods and seemed designed to demonstrate wealth, claim kinship, and preserve craft identity rather than to mark friendship or favor. Jehans Hans De Cuer, for example, gave several cash gifts to his parish, the city's mendicant friars, and hospitals; he left 30 livres to his sister; he released his godson from a debt; he gave each of his godson's sons "a loom for weaving long draperies, along with the associated equipment"; to the table of St. Nicholas he gave his best "robe" and to each of his executors, he gave one "hanap" (drinking cup); the surplus went to his heirs.[25] Jakemes Painmoulliet gave to Sarem Den Broel, his wife, all his "gold jewelry, his hollowware of silver and onyx, all his household furnishings, his equipment, and his looms, large and small," along with all his houses in den Broel, one-half of his house and fullery, all his heritages and rents in Douai (the disposition of which he would control after her death); she was also left 400 livres parisis, her "draperies, knitwear, and tailored costumes," plus "all equipment, household furniture, and hollowware of silver and onyx" and "all rents" that were due to him from the city of Douai.[26] A generous will, but one apparently made in observance of a prior marriage contract, and one that expressed its gifts in summary language, without the elaboration of objects and their specific destinations that so distinguished Narrette's will.

Women, in contrast, made their gifts individually, parceling out a dress to one person, a pot to another, a rosary to a third. They chose women over men as beneficiaries and in general seem to have been identifying the members of their social network and specifying their relationships both to the testator and, implicitly, to one another. Marie Narrette's will was in these ways typical. It included twenty-three female and four male beneficiaries. All the men bore the family name Haricourt; all may have been related to her as well as to each other, although Narrette does not tell us that. Four of the women were wives or daughters of Haricourt men. Another woman was Narrette's godmother, a sixth was a goddaughter, a seventh was one of Narrette's poor neighbors. Four other women were related to another beneficiary (a mother and daughter, an aunt by marriage and the niece). We know nothing about the relationships of the remaining thirteen women. This was a large and diverse group of beneficiaries, some kin to Narrette, many kin to one another, but still more were simply Nar-

25. AMD, FF 862 (May 1327).
26. AMD, FF 862 (October 1315).

rette's friends and neighbors. Each received a different gift—one a prayer book, another an elegant fur coat, a third a kerchief, a fourth a bolt of coarse cloth. Marie Le Grand's will is similar: twenty beneficiaries, a few of them named as kin of one another, most of them female, only one clearly a relative of Le Grand; none of them obviously related to any of the three husbands Le Grand had outlived. Again, Le Grand made clear distinctions among her recipients. The bed with all its linens and draperies, which would go to Jehane De Hainau, would not in their entirety pass to De Hainau's husband (who was her heir). Margherite Daire used her will to thank a niece for personal "services" and to acknowledge the loyalty another had shown her husband.

Women thus bestowed their personal possessions with an apparent delight, a taste for serendipity, and a rare abandon. When giving away beds, jewelry, and furs; cooking pots, wash basins, and measuring cups; or linens, pillows, and benches, women played God. They chose their gifts and their recipients according to rules of their own devising. They gave property unequally to sons and daughters, nieces and neighbors; they settled personal debts, they acknowledged prior service, they rewarded loyalty, they showed love. The man who behaved in this way was the exception; the woman the rule.

Yet women did not act with this freedom when they passed on the family's chief immovables. When bequeathing rents, houses, or land, women normally followed all the conventions; they gave this property where they ought to have, usually intact, in the form it had come to them, as though dutifully serving as the conduits of patrimonial assets they were expected to be. In her will of 1406, for example, Climence Moutonne, the survivor of two husbands, perfectly fulfilled maternal obligations by passing to her children the house she had brought to her first marriage twenty-four years earlier, although she distributed her movables far and wide.[27] Even when women were in a position to make selections among possible heirs, they tended to respect the norms of custom. Peronne Bonnier, twice a widow and apparently childless when she made her will, left lavish gifts of cash and objects to the church, charities, and friends, but

---

27. Moutonne's first marriage (AMD, FF 589/470 [26 July 1382]) had left her half of the marital estate (in which her house was included) plus her "lit, chambre, draps, linge cousus et taillez, joyaulx" (bed, bedroom furnishings, cloths, linens, garments, and tailor-made clothing, jewels); in her second marriage contract (AMD, FF 600/1247 [9 December 1401]), she protected these assets. And in her will she gave them to her children (AMD, FF 869 [16 December 1406]).

she gave her surplus in equal parts to her niece and a female cousin, stipulating that the house go to her niece alone.[28] Jehanne Brigrade, a widow with a son, left clothing and household goods to friends, but ordered that the surplus go to her son; if he were to die before his marriage or his majority, the goods would go to the next in line, her brother and sister; only if these two had predeceased her, would her properties exit the lineage, then going in equal parts to the parish, to the parish poor, and to priests who would say masses for her soul.[29]

Whatever their devotion to the rules of patrimonial inheritance of immovables, women were, however, mistresses of the practice of bequeathing movables far and wide. We have seen that much in tradition, social practice, and law combined to link women to such goods and to encourage such gift giving. There might have been other reasons as well, however, reasons that derived from the ambiguous place they held in commerce. Women were, of course, indisputably in the commercial world. They bought and sold goods daily, they manufactured commodities for long-distance trade, they brokered deals with traveling merchants, they ran inns on their own, and they managed the shops attached to their husbands' *ateliers*. They also avidly collected the products—the dresses and jewels, the linens and furnishings—that circulated through this world. But women were not leading actors here; they were marginal figures, and as the new marital property regime was instantiated, they became ever more marginal. Men, not women, officially managed commerce; men dominated the skilled trades; men sat on the aldermen's bench. Men were increasingly given sole credit for the wealth derived from commerce, men were granted authority over household budgets. Thus, while women were in this world of commerce and exchange, they were less fully "of" it. Bound by gender roles and excluded from the fantasies of control that men could enjoy, they were perhaps more eager to hold their goods close to them, to personalize their gifts, to give life stories to their objects and less easy about the wonders of unbridled commerce, less willing to let their material possessions function as mere commodities.

The great paradox here is, of course, that gifts of movables did not, in truth, slow the motion of commerce. They could accelerate it, thereby not only destabilizing the social order but associating women with social disorder. The rosaries and silk bonnets given to friends, neighbors, and

28. AMD, FF 448, fols. 3r–4r (November 1438).
29. AMD, FF 448, fol. 6v (November 1438).

distant kin were not mere memorabilia, tokens of friendship and love. They were valuable assets. By giving them away as Narrette and her friends did—by passing a dress to one friend, a rosary to another, a cloth to a poor neighbor, a bed to a distant relative—women were heightening, not lessening, the inherent instability of the commercial world. They were often moving wealth out of one lineage into another, away from a single locus of accumulation into the hands of a multiplicity of consumers, people who might use it unwisely, fail to honor its lineage, spend it. In some eyes, surely—perhaps especially in the eyes of the men who looked on as women gave objects worth small fortunes to other women, nonkin, the poor—these recipients were unworthy, the gifts they received unwarranted, and the givers irresponsible.

Even worse from this point of view, the gifts might not clearly articulate social rank; they might even confuse it. Narrette's gift of a silk cloak, the one she gave to Jacque Le Caudreliere, was an unmistakable sign of high bourgeois status in the early fifteenth-century urban North; silk was still the clothing of royalty and the cheap woolen imitations that were soon to confuse the links between fabric and social fabric had not yet come off the looms of the Low Countries' weavers.[30] We might safely guess that the woman to whom it was given was of a similar class as Narrette, but we cannot be certain that there was not some difference in station between the two women, that Narrette was not raising up Le Caudreliere in some way by bestowing this gift on her. In the case of the blanket given to the poor woman we can be surer of the implied social meaning: both the act of giving and the nature of the gift marked the difference between the two women. But what about the red hood given to Marguerite Des Plangues; in what way did this gift mark a shared class position or distinguish the social status of the giver and the recipient? And what about the next time the article of clothing was passed? Would it serve to indicate shared status or to measure social distance? And when it was worn by the beneficiary? What then of its capacity to confer rank? And what subtle shifts of meaning occurred when the gift had lost its social place, when a fake red silk cloak could be had even by a simple artisan's daughter? What then of Marie Narrette's gift to Jacque Le Caudreliere?

---

30. For the changes in production processes that made silk imitations possible, see Patrick Chorley, "The 'Draperies légères' of Lille, Arras, Tournai, Valenciennes: New Materials for New Markets?" in *La draperie ancienne des Pays-Bas: Débouchés et stratégies de survie (14e–16e siècles)*, ed. Marc Boone and Walter Prevenier (Leuven and Apeldoorn: Garant, 1993).

The very law that limited women's property rights and defined them as inadequate managers of wealth thus, simultaneously, created new instabilities. The law freed them from responsibility for their husband's financial problems, freed them even from an obligation to be loyal to their deceased husbands; simultaneously, it positioned them to collect, use, and redistribute movable property—property, let us remember, of enormous value in this economy. It is perhaps no wonder that this age so often told and retold stories about frivolous and vain women who spent their husband's money on silly finery, who careened from husband to husband in search of still more finery, who loved things in excess.

Rewriting Marriage

If the new marital property regime helped rewrite gender meanings, it had an even more profound—if equally paradoxical—effect on the meaning of marriage. In some ways, the new law weakened the conjugal bond itself, for by abandoning the ravestissement, Douaisiens also abandoned the idea that husband and wife could be made one through mutual property interests. They replaced it with an utterly different notion of marital economic interests, one based on a partial and limited partnership, on restrictions and withholdings, on boundaries. The result was a considerably less robust vision of the marital bond as constructed by shared wealth. As we shall see, this hardly implied a repudiation of marriage, but it did necessitate a reimagining of the institution.

We can trace this conceptual shift in the language of the marital documents themselves. The original ravestissement par lettre, we have seen, represented the husband and wife as one, even to the point of creating the absurdity of a wife who needed her husband's permission to make gifts to him. The marriage contract saw husband and wife differently, not as one being but as distinct beings, and it saw marriage between them as a complex matter, hard to arrange and harder still to preserve.

The text of the marriage contract itself perfectly expressed this complexity, both in language and form. Unlike the ravestissement, which imposed an austere simplicity on marriage, the marriage contract reveled in recounting the multiplicity of nuptial ties. In contrast to the short and tidy ravestissement par lettre, the contract was long, typically between seven hundred and two thousand words, and although it was formulaic like the ravestissement, its formulas were tortured, its special clauses and unusual provisions abundant. And the ceremony it described was completely unlike the straightforward ritual of writing the ravestissement. While the ravestissement was ostensibly composed by husband and wife alone, in the presence of only two échevins and their clerk, the marriage contract was written by a crowd. Men and women about to be married under contract were taken to the town hall by a group of friends and relatives: always fathers, usually mothers, and very often grandparents, brothers, stepparents, children of first marriages, uncles, sisters, cousins, aunts, and friends. Antoinette De Cantin, for example, was accompanied at the registration of her marriage contract with Ipoitie Berthe in 1570 by her father and mother, her grandfather, her maternal uncle, her granduncle, her aunt, still another uncle, and another aunt. The groom was accompanied by his father, mother, uncle, and two aunts by marriage.[31] In a group of forty-four sampled marriage contracts from the 1560s, twenty-seven specifically named "parens [et] amis" (friends and relatives) who "accompanied" the bride or groom at the signing of the marriage contract, most of them potential or actual heirs of either bride or groom. Seventeen contracts in the sample did not name such "parens et amis" as witnesses, but most of them did name other actors in the contract—fathers and mothers, grandfathers, grandmothers, or aunts or uncles who made the marriage gifts, or brothers and sisters with whom the gifts were shared, for example—and we might well presume that these people witnessed the marriage contract even though their presence at the signing was not specifically recorded.[32] Once assembled, the large company oversaw the listing of the bride's portement, followed by the many clauses specifying the distribution of the estate. Then there was the matter of testamentary bequests made by either spouse and how they were to be honored; then questions about the disposition of special properties such as heritages. As written by such contracts, marriage was thus a pact among many interests—those of husbands and wives, fathers and mothers, children, and even grandparents and plus prochains.

In this way, the new marital property regime made marriage a messy arrangement. Its chief text, the marriage contract, looked less like a pact

31. AMD, FF 655/5586 (20 October 1570).
32. In contrast, in a sample of fifty-nine contracts taken from the 1370s, none specifically named "parens et amis" as accompanists of the bridal pair, although almost all named avoués, who were frequently kin of the bride (although not potential heirs).

between partners in life than an exhaustive list of bargaining points among hostile participants. The rituals surrounding the contract's signing replicated the themes of caution and distrust. "Sides" lined up; "amis" bore witness; "parens" watched suspiciously as the new bride or groom pledged to share assets that were potentially the property of these "sides," "amis," and "parens."

Yet, it is perhaps the greatest paradox of a history filled with paradoxes that the legal texts that rewrote marriage as so precarious a financial union simultaneously rebuilt marriage on new and even more enduring foundations. They did so indirectly, subtly, in ways recognizeable only if placed within the cultural discourse of which they were a part. This was a discourse in which, as scholars have long pointed out, "affective" ties—bonds of romantic love, mutual devotion to children, new emphasis on monogamous heterosexual desire—were being constructed. Historians are most familiar with these tropes from the literary and didactic texts of the late medieval and early modern period—sermons, conduct books, songs, plays, and stories in which contemporaries constructed the ideal of a union between husband and wife, bound together as much by passion as duty, that was, entirely contradictorily, both hierarchical and fully reciprocal. In texts such as William Gouge's *Of Domestical Duties* of the sixteenth century or the anonymous *Le Menagier de Paris,* of the fourteenth, in Franciscan sermons or Protestant homilies, the late medieval and early modern period celebrated marriage as the only legitimate site of erotic love, the crucible of personal development, the foundation of a larger moral order.[33] The legal documents surviving from Douai do not, of course, perfectly reproduce this language, but they nonetheless present a vision of marriage that is not only entirely compatible with its theme but that seems at times even to echo its rhetoric.

One of the parallels between this cultural discourse and the Douaisien legal texts was their emphasis on marriage as partnership. To be sure, the new Douaisien marital property regime was in one sense an attack on the idea of conjugal partnership, for it discarded the notion of economic commensurability at the heart of the ravestissement, replacing it with an

---

33. Lyndal Roper's *The Holy Household* traces these connections in Reformation Augsburg (Oxford: Clarendon Press, 1989). Edmund Leites's "The Duty to Desire: Love, Friendship, and Sexuality in Puritan Theories of Marriage," *Journal of Social History* 15, no. 3 (Spring 1982): 383–408, and William and Malleville Haller, "The Puritan Art of Love," *Huntington Library Quarterly* 5, no. 2 (1942): 235–72, summarize the Puritan literature on the marriage bond, where the notions of affectionate marriage and "unequal" partnership were most clearly articulated.

arrangement in which female and male were never the same and in which male interests always were preferred to female. Yet, like the homilies about marriage as "partnership" that were so popular in this age, the Douaisien marriage contract sought to disguise hierarchy as equality. The contract did so by substituting for the unity of the ravestissement a kind of parity between bride and groom, a parity based on similar claims if not on equality per se. Thus, while it compulsively separated female from male property and female property rights from male, it also implied a quid pro quo between husband and wife, always answered a clause that granted the wife a particular property right with a clause that provided the husband some right. For example, contracts compiled rigorously parallel lists of survivors' rights—the wife's death with heirs; the husband's death with heirs; the wife's death without heirs; the husband's death without heirs—as though the benefits accruing to each spouse were the same in each of their situations, as they had been under the old ravestissement. In fact, of course, they were not the same: what a woman received as a widow was never the same as—never as much as—what a man got as widower; a mother never had the same powers as a father; a wife was not the substitute for her husband.

The impulse to represent parity, to substitute parity for unity, was perhaps most clearly expressed in the practice of listing the groom's portement along with the bride's in marriage contracts. The listing had no practical effect on marital property relations, since the widower's share of the marital estate was never directly tied to his portement as it was to the widow's; its chief significance was symbolic, a measure of the groom's contribution to the marital estate.[34] Yet, if the parity promised was deceptive—if widowers were "more equal" than widows, fathers "more equal" than mothers—the pretense reveals a great deal about the perceived inadequacies of marriage by contract and about the ways Douaisiens addressed their anxieties about these inadequacies.

Marriage contracts recalled another theme of the marriage literature

34. Although marriage contracts had once listed the groom's portement only very rarely, it became increasingly common to do so in the course of the fifteenth century. Twenty-five of the grooms in a sample of forty-five marriage contracts from the 1550s and 1560s (56 percent), for example, listed their portements, while only twenty-three in a sample of seventy-six contracts (30 percent) from the 1440s did so. Still earlier, in the late fourteenth century, only 10–20 percent of grooms listed the assets they brought to the marriage. The listing could also serve to specify groom's inheritance rights (see chapter 4).

that circulated in the wider culture as well. They emphasized the duty of husband and wife not just to have children—procreation had long been considered a principal reason for marriage, probably the chief reason after its function as an antidote to carnal lust—but to care for them properly. Thus, contracts figured children prominently and displayed a measurable concern for their material welfare, often even to the extent of effacing the mother's interests and reducing her to a carrier of her children's property. Franchoise Le Guien, for example, was required to hold all her immovables—a long list of land, real estate, and rents—for her children.[35] When Nicole De Raismes, a tanner and widower with children, married Marguerite De Mailly in 1556, it was agreed that his estate (after De Mailly's reprise and douaire) would go to the children of his first marriage "tete par tete" ("head by head"); in the event there were children of the second marriage, the estate would be split between the two sets of siblings, assuming De Mailly chose the douaire coutumier (if not, by implication, De Mailly's children would get nothing from the estate but would be dependent on her reprise and douaire).[36] The 1437 contract between the widower Collart Tallon, a painter, and Marie Du Bosquiel, widow of Colart Belot, also included elaborate provisions for the children of their previous marriages. The daughter of his first marriage was to receive specified sums from Du Bosquiel when Tallon died, and the provisions were to be adjusted according to her age and marital state. The three children of Du Bosquiel received similar protections, and all four were guaranteed nurturance, housing, and education: "It is provided and agreed among the said parties that each, Collart and Marie, is required at his or her expense to care for and raise their children, to send them to school, to have them learn a trade, to dress them, to give them what they need as drink, food, clothing, and lodging until they marry, are emancipated, or reach the age of eighteen years."[37] The words used in this text to describe the care due children had become, by this time, entirely formulaic, and they reappear regularly in marriage contracts of this period. It is not only in legal texts like these, however, that the litany is intoned. The fourteenth-century *Le Menagier de Paris*, for example, used similar language in describing the inadequacies of stepfathers and stepmothers (by definition, in this text,

35. AMD, FF 914 (16 March 1521).
36. AMD, FF 655/5562 (17 November 1556).
37. AMD, FF 613/2082 (27 April 1437).

bad parents) "who do not think about providing them a bed, giving them drink and food, or shoes, shirts, or other necessities."[38]

The contract between Du Bosquiel and Belot, like most from the period, assigned the tasks of parenting to both husband and wife, but others from the day also added special instructions for the mother, admonishing her that if she should survive her husband, she alone was obligated to care for the children "comme le doit une bonne mere" (as a good mother might). In this clause lies a telling commentary on the ideology of marriage then developing, for it suggests not only that marriage was being equated with parenthood, but that feminine virtue was coming to be associated with certain maternal tasks. Although this was hardly the first—or the last—European text that would link a woman's moral capacities to the quality of the care she gave her children ("comme le doit une bonne mere"), it does help signal the shift in the definition of marriage that was then underway in Douai.[39]

In addition to marital reciprocity and parenthood, the legal texts sometimes even spoke of love. From the 1550s we have, for example, an unusual version of a ravestissement par lettre, written when the notion of ravestissement itself was dying, which attempts to justify what by then must have seemed an odd decision to share property:

> Jean Vallain L'Aisne the elder, bourgeois of Douai, and Marie De Paradis, his wife, who live in Douai, Marie being sufficiently empowered by her husband, which empowerment she has received happily, as she has stated, declared, and warranted, because most other goods, debts, rents, and heritages consist of properties acquired in the course of their marriage through their common labor, industry, and assets, for this reason *and for the conjugal love and affection they hold for one another* . . . these partners, the said woman being empowered as above, wanted and want that, at the death of the first, the survivor has the entire and total enjoyment and use of all the goods, both patrimonial and after-acquired, that belong to them and of which they are the possessors on the day of the said death [emphasis added].[40]

Sentiment ("pour l'amour et affection conjugale") thus joins labor ("par la labeur industrie et biens communs") as rationale for the mutual donation

---

38. Georgine E. Brereton and Jane L. M. Ferrier, eds., *Le Menagier de Paris* (Oxford: Clarendon Press, 1981), bk. 7, sect. 100, ll. 8–10.

39. On the developing ideology of motherhood in the period, see Clarissa W. Atkinson, *The Oldest Vocation: Christian Motherhood in the Middle Ages.* (Ithaca, N.Y.: Cornell University Press, 1991), 194–235.

40. AMD, FF 655/5564 (8 November 1558).

between husbands and wives, seeming to explain why, in an age when the new written marital property law was figuring husband and wives as natural competitors for marital assets, a couple would have explicitly chosen old custom's principles of mutuality. Admittedly, Douaisiens were not the only people in this period who laced their legal texts with talk of love, and they were hardly the first to imagine that marriages were sealed by mutual affection. But it is just as surely not a coincidence that Douaisien marital property agreements increasingly figured marriage as a romantic alliance just when property relations alone could no longer be represented as the fundament of the conjugal bond.

By the 1550s, such talk of love had become the rule. All the ravestissements in a sample of marriage documents from the 1550s and 1560s, for example, explicitly linked romantic love with the promised property exchange. One document spoke of a "bon amour mutuel"; another of "la bonne amour et affection naturelle et conjugalle"; a third attempted more straightforwardly, if somewhat confusedly, to justify the ravestissement, explaining that the couple has chosen this agreement "for the strong love they have for one another and because they have no children of their own . . . and for many other reasons."[41] The contrast with earlier centuries could not be clearer: none of the ravestissements sampled from the fourteenth century and only a small fraction of those sampled from the subsequent hundred years contained such language. It was only after 1500 that Douaisiens thought that "love" could justify a mutual donation of all conjugal property, only then, it seems, that they thought the justification necessary.[42]

41. AMD, FF 655/5551 (5 March 1555); FF 655/5582 (1 February 1567); FF 655/5584 (25 August 1570).

42. As Lawrence Stone put it, summarizing the long history in which the notion of conjugal affection acquired dominance as the "seal" of marriage, "The nuclear family was thus left to stand far more than ever before on its own bottom, with little to hold it together but its own internal cohesion." Lawrence Stone, *The Family, Sex and Marriage in England 1500–1800*, abridged ed. (Harmondsworth: Penguin Books, 1985), 247.

SEVEN

The Weight of Experience

Douaisiens were not coerced into the legal reform that so significantly altered the marital property regime. They chose to issue the wills, marriage contracts, and other legal instruments that undermined custom without, as far as we can tell, pressure from higher courts or political overlords to adopt these or any other revisions to custom. In this respect, Douaisiens were unlike almost all their near neighbors, for, as we shall see in chapter 8, during this age legal reforms of the kind that took place in Douai were elsewhere often the work of political elites or legal experts. Thus, reform elsewhere always came more quickly and more cleanly; it also usually left fewer traces and almost always occurred less voluntarily.

If Douaisiens made this move of their own volition, they did not, however, make it casually. After all, it cost dearly to issue the thousands and thousands of marriage contracts, wills, and contrats divers that served to revise custom, and the many lawsuits that resulted from Douaisiens' efforts to combine the two marital property regimes were undoubtedly unwelcome interruptions of daily life. Furthermore, the changes did not benefit everyone equally, and even those who, on balance, might have come out ahead would have had something to lament about lost privileges or new burdens. Above all these inconveniences, we have seen, lay a more basic difficulty: the move to the new legal system implied a fundamental reordering of social and gender relations. The Douaisiens who adopted the new rules had to learn to use property differently, to place themselves in relation to others according to altered standards, and to think about marriage, women, and men in new ways.

To change law as they did, Douaisiens thus must have had good reasons. Their reasons, I want to argue, lay in the way the new law allowed them to manage property and to regulate gender hierarchy. In the years after 1300, Douaisiens became more interested in securing property and with it, social and gender relations, and they acquired this interest because both property and the personal relations constituted by it were seen as more precarious. During this period Douaisiens came gradually to regard the mobility provided by old custom as a burden, not a benefit.

As I have argued in chapter 3, this does not mean that the legal reform was a direct response to a particular set of fiscal or economic events or the sudden unleashing of repressed desires for patrilineality. Rather, Douaisiens themselves changed as they confronted the challenges of the last 250 years of the Middle Ages. They slowly, hesitatingly came to prefer marital property law and inheritance practices that preserved property in male-defined lines of descent, that made woman carriers of property, and that put sons and sons-in-law under fathers.

Weathering Crisis

At the heart of the difficulties Douaisiens confronted during these centuries was the decline of the traditional luxury drapery, for its troubles put the entire urban economy in peril. As we have seen, traditional historiography, following Georges Espinas's and Henri Pirenne's magisterial studies, has long emphasized the extent and the finality of this decline.[1] Evidence uncovered since their day has, however, significantly undermined this story of unmitigated crises and sociopolitical collapse, not just for Douai, but for all the great textile towns of the region. At least since the well-known debate about the "depression of the Renaissance" (or the "late medieval depression"), historians have recognized that certain groups prospered during this period—the fifteenth century has, let us recall, also

---

1. Georges Espinas, *La draperie dans la Flandre française au moyen-âge*, 2 vols. (Paris: A. Picard et fils, 1923), and idem, *La vie urbaine de Douai au moyen-âge*, 4 vols. (Paris: A. Picard et fils, 1913); Georges Espinas and Henri Pirenne, eds., *Recueil de documents relatifs à l'histoire de l'industrie drapière en Flandre des origines à l'époque Bourguignonne*, 4 vols. (Brussels: P. Imbreghts, 1906); Henri Pirenne, "Stages in the Social History of Capitalism," *American Historical Review* 19 (1914): 494–514; idem, *Histoire de Belgique*, 4 vols. (Brussels: Renaissance du Livre, 1948–52); and idem, *Early Democracies in the Low Countries*, 1963 (reprint, New York: Harper and Row, 1969). For a recent English summary of the literature on the crises in Flanders, see David Nicholas, *Medieval Flanders* (London: Longman, 1992).

been named the "golden age of the artisan" because real industrial wages rose so significantly in the period—and we have long had a rich body of scholarship documenting the vigor of particular economic sectors, trade routes, and cities. While some of this literature has focused on England or the northern Low Countries, whose relative prosperity could be explained by good fortune (their isolation, their timing, or their privileged access to particular resources), more recent studies have presented evidence of economic well being and peace in some of the very centers of trade and industry from which the Pirennean narrative had taken its original material.[2]

Espinas's interpretation about Douai itself has been subjected to even more specific criticism. Alain Derville has, for example, attacked Espinas's claim that the merchants who ran the cloth industry in the thirteenth century were truly capitalists. Rather than organizing production, Derville argued, these men simply played the part of "commercial" capitalists, putting very few of their own assets into production itself and relying on semi-independent small producers to finance inventories and manage pro-

---

2. Ferdinand Seibt and Winfried Eberhard, eds. *Europa 1400: Die Krise des Spätmittelalters* (Stuttgart: Klett-Cotta, 1984). The original debate about the so-called depression of the Renaissance (or the late medieval depression) was aired in the *Economic History Review* 16 (1964). Also see Martha Howell and Marc Boone, "Becoming Early Modern in the Late Medieval Low Countries: Ghent, Douai, and the Late Medieval Crisis," *Urban History* 23, pt. 3 (December 1996): 300–24 .

For the Low Countries in particular, see Herman Van der Wee, "Industrial Dynamics and the Process of Urbanization and De-urbanization in the Low Countries from the Late Middle Ages to the Eighteenth Century: A Synthesis," in *The Rise and Decline of Urban Industries in Italy and the Low Countries: Late Middle Ages and Early Modern Times*, ed. Herman Van der Wee (Leuven: Leuven University Press, 1988), 323–27, and idem, "Structural Changes and Specialization in the Industry of the Southern Netherlands, 1100–1600," *Economic History Review* 28 (1975): 203–21. Also see John H. Munro, "Industrial Transformations in the North-West European Textile Trades, c. 1290–c. 1340: Economic Progress or Economic Crisis?" in *Before the Black Death: Studies in the "Crisis" of the Early Fourteenth Century*, ed. Bruce M. S. Campbell (Manchester: Manchester University Press, 1991); idem, "Anglo-Flemish Competition in the International Cloth Trade, 1350–1500," in *L'Angleterre et les pays bourguignons (XIVe–XVIe siècles): Relations et comparisons (XVe–XVIe s.); Actes du 35 Rencontres du Centre Européen D'études Bourguignonnes, Oxford 1994*, 37–60 (Neuchâtel: Centre Européen D'études Bourguignonnes, 1995); idem, "Medieval Woollens: Textiles, Textile Technology, and Industrial Organization," and "Medieval Woollens: The West European Woollen Industries and Their Struggles for International Markets"; Yoshio Fujii, "Draperie urbaine et draperie rurale dans les Pays-Bas méridionaux au bas moyen âge: Une mise au point des recherches après H. Pirenne," *Journal of Medieval History* 16, no. 1 (1990): 77–97; and Marci Sortor, "Saint-Omer and Its Textile Trades in the Late Middle Ages: A Contribution to the Proto-Industrialization Debate," *American Historical Review* 98, no. 5. (1993): 1475–99.

duction.[3] Others have raised questions about the relative importance of luxury cloth production during the thirteenth and fourteenth centuries, arguing that medium-priced woolens played a bigger role than Espinas allowed and that very cheap cloths—the sayes and other light woolens occasionally mentioned in contemporary sources—were then an important and unjustly neglected part of the city's export trade.[4] Still others have returned to Douai's archive to investigate just how severe the decline in cloth production might have been during the fourteenth century, and they have generally found little support for Espinas's conclusion that the industry had died by 1350 or even 1375.[5]

The archive of marriage contracts, wills, and contrats divers on which this study is based allows us to extend this revisionist story through the 1520s. These sources leave little doubt that during the long years from 1300 until the first half of the sixteenth century Douai's traditional textile industry did not collapse and that it showed much greater continuity with the past than traditional historiography has acknowledged. Let us return, first, to the evidence from marriage agreements. As table 5 summarizes, throughout the fourteenth, fifteenth, and well into the sixteenth century textile producers were prosperous enough to settle both movable and immovable property on marriageable sons and daughters. Textile artisans, as we have seen, were not alone in their ability to survive these difficult centuries (see tables 1–3 in chapter 3), for it was not until well into the sixteenth century that Douai's productive class, as a group, disappeared from the archive of marriage contracts.

To judge from the size of their real estate holdings, a few of these artisans were surprisingly prosperous indeed. Some even held land outside Douai. In 1428, for example, a woman who married a "potier destain" (tinsmith) brought 8 raisières 1 couppre of land, a house, and 80 livres parisis as her portement.[6] A woman who married an "appareilleur de drap" (cloth finisher) in 1441 (whether he was truly an artisan is, of course,

3. Alain Derville, "Les draperies flamandes et artésiennes, vers 1250–1350," *Revue du Nord* 54, no. 215 (1972): 353–70; and idem, "L'héritage des draperies médiévales," *Revue du Nord* 69, no. 275 (1987) : 715–24.

4. Patrick Chorley, "The Cloth Exports of Flanders and Northern France during the Thirteenth Century: A Luxury Trade?" *Economic History Review* 40 (1987): 347–79.

5. Catherine Dhérent, "Histoire social de la bourgeoisie de Douai de 1280 à 1350," Ph.D. diss., Ecole des Chartes, 1981; "Abondance et crises: Douai, ville frontière 1250–1375," 3 vols., Ph.D. diss., Université de Paris, 1993; and "L'assise sur le commerce des draps à Douai en 1304," *Revue du Nord* 65, no. 257 (1983): 369–97.

6. AMD, FF 609/1816 (January 1428).

Table 5
Textile Artisans and Drapers in Marriage Documents

| | Total Marriage Contracts and Ravestissements | | Marriage Contracts only | | Economic Status, Marriage Contracts Only | | | | | | | | |
| | | | | | Status Not Measurable | | Rentier | | Prosperous | | Householder | |
	Number	% of Total	Number	% of Total	Number	% of Total	Number	% of Total	Number	% of Total	Number	% of Total
Fourteenth-century samples												
textile artisans	28	25	20	25	3	15	0	—	12	60	5	25
drapers	2	2	1	1	0	—	1	100	0	—	0	—
Fifteenth-century samples												
textile artisans	44	22	42	23	4	10	3	7	14	33	21	50
drapers	4	2	3	2	0	—	0	—	3	100	0	—
Sixteenth-century samples												
textile artisans	27	20	23	19	0	—	0	—	11	48	12	52
drapers	6	5	5	4	0	—	0	—	4	80	1	20
Post-1550 samples only												
textile artisans	13	15	10	13	0	—	0	—	2	20	8	80
drapers	4	5	3	4	0	—	0	—	2	67	1	33

Source: Data based on tables 1, 2, and 3; see notes to those tables.

debatable) brought goods valued at 150 livres parisis, 5 couppres of land in one holding, and another 3 rasières in another.[7] To her marriage with a tanner in 1443, a woman brought two houses in Douai, 5 rasières of land, and 100 francs.[8] Of course land-owning artisans like these were hardly the norm in Douai, but they were not anomalies, and their presence bears witness to the city's economic viability.

The city's *Registre aux bourgeois* confirms the impression conveyed by these contracts. Until the mid–sixteenth century, when a precipitous decline began, artisans—huge numbers of textile workers among them—joined the citizenry at steady rates. On average, about twenty-eight new citizens registered each year between 1399 and 1506; at least 25 percent of those identified by trade were textile artisans, and at least another 30 percent were artisans working in other sectors of production. No city suffering the collapse Espinas imagined would have attracted immigrants at this rate. In Douai, citizenship was not required for residence or for trade rights, as it was in many cities of the age, but it was required of those who owned real property; to find so many textile workers and other craftsmen on the list of new citizens is thus powerful proof of how fully such people participated in the city's economy.[9]

Documents of other kinds tell us something about the businesses these textile artisans ran during the fourteenth and fifteenth centuries. Some, of course, still made the traditional luxury cloths. In records of purchases by the Duke of Burgundy, for example, we find the scarlets, browns, and blacks on which Douai's fame had long rested.[10] But there is also evidence that many artisans diversified in these centuries. In Hansa records, for example, we find somewhat cheaper textiles named, some of them certainly like the "nouvelles draperies" being made around Courtrai at the time. Judging from this evidence alone, Douaisien producers were not locked into old production routines.[11] To be sure, the evidence of this

7. AMD, FF 616/2326 (15 May 1441).

8. AMD, FF 616/2383 (4 May 1443).

9. For the citizenship registers, see M. Minet, "Les inscriptions du registre aux bourgeois de Douai au XVe siècle, 1399–1506" (master's thesis, Université Catholique de Louvain-la-Neuve, 1973). Also see Martha Howell, "Citizen-clerics in Late Medieval Douai," in *Statuts individuels, statuts corporatifs et statuts judiciaires dans les villes européennes (moyen âge et temps modernes)*, ed. Marc Boone and Maarten Prak (Leuven and Apeldoorn: Garant, 1996)

10. S. Abraham-Thisse, "Achats et consommation de draps de laine par l'hôtel de Bourgogne, 1370–1380," in *Commerce, Finances et Société (XIe–XVIe siècles): Recueil de travaux d'histoire médiévale offert à M. le professeur Henri Dubois*, ed. P. Contamine, T. DuTour, and B. Schnerb (Paris: Presses de l'Université de Paris-Sorbonne, 1993).

11. I am grateful to Simone Abraham-Thisse for this information, which is based on her ongoing studies of Hansa records in the fourteenth and fifteenth centuries.

kind is spotty and the sources from which it comes have not been fully exploited, but it does point to the conclusion that during the late Middle Ages, Douaisiens, like their neighbors, gradually deemphasized cloths "de haute gamme" (of highest quality) made solely of English wool and that they also abandoned the very cheap sayes and other light woolens made of local wools, which had in the thirteenth century supplemented their export trade. In their place, Douaisien artisans added a wider range of products, many of them surely medium-quality fulled cloths made of Spanish and other less fine wool in the "nouvelle" fashion. As John Munro has pointed out, this was a common response both to the political crises of the period (which effectively closed certain distribution routes or made them prohibitively expensive) and to changes in prices, supply routes, and production structures.[12] Producers in this region thus regularly sought out many kinds of markets—at the high end, the extravagant and burgeoning Burgundian court; in the middle range, Eastern and German markets; at the lower end, Antwerp's entrepôt through which light cloths were exported.[13]

All the available evidence indicates that Douai's merchant class supported small, independent cloth producers in their efforts to pursue these markets and experiment with new products. Rich merchants seem even to have acquiesced as the échevins (who were, quite literally, their kin) imposed regulations that protected small producers. Several times in the fifteenth century, for example, the government helped artisans who had complained that certain merchants were seeking control of dyestuffs and similarly essential raw materials, thus threatening ordinary artisans, who could not survive if prices they had to pay were raised or if key raw materials were withheld.[14] The échevins also let lapse the draconian regulations

12. Munro, "Anglo-Flemish competition," and "Medieval Woollens" (both articles by that name). Also see Sorter, "Saint-Omer," and Fujii, "Draperie urbaine," for discussions of more specifically economic evidence from neighboring cities that suggests a similar history. Also see Howell and Boone, "Becoming Early Modern."

13. The information we have about Douai's distribution networks in these centuries is unusually sparse; Douaisien names seldom appear on the lists of dealers in Antwerp, and Douaisien cloth is not regularly listed in the few Hansa accounts of the period that have been systematically investigated. What this implies is, however, consistent with what we know about the interests of Douai's commercial elite: Douai's merchants were not active in the organization of textile production or in its distribution beyond regional luxury markets; hence, most Douai's middle-range textile production was sold through foreign factors who served as middlemen between Douai's small producers and the wholesalers who bought cloth at Bruges and elsewhere.

14. See, for the relevant legislation, AMD, BB 1, fol. 24v (15 April 1469); and BB 1, fol. 38 (21 July 1473).

of the thirteenth century that had restricted textile artisans to a narrow range of products and subjected them to strict supervision. While Espinas and most scholars after him read this lapse as proof of the industry's collapse, it seems more likely that the decline in legislation signalled a change in the production system. Once, artisans had made a product of uniformly high quality to the specifications of merchants who delivered the cloths to select (and probably preselected) markets. After about 1350, however, sales like these became the exception, not the rule. By the fifteenth century, the normal practice was for drapers to purchase various wools from distributors and to make a variety of cloths, some of them intended for small, high-end markets in the Low Countries, but many more for mass export, through entrepôts such as Bruges, to eastern Europe.

However resilient the textile industry in Douai and however beneficent Douai's political elite in helping smaller producers survive in these difficult days, it was not innovation in the textile industry alone that accounts for the unexpected strength of the Douaisien economy in these years.[15] The grain trade provided an additional boost. Douai's location on the Scarpe, which feeds into the Scheldt and thus into the North Sea through Ghent and Antwerp, gave the city privileged access to the profitable trade in grain that came out of the fertile and easily worked land in the surrounding countryside. As early as the fourteenth century, the city had won staple rights for control of the grain trade in the region, and in the fifteenth and sixteenth centuries, Douai was able to maintain, even to expand, its role in collecting and shipping grain from the region to the rich urban markets that lay north of the city.[16]

This commerce undoubtedly did much to shield Douaisiens from the worst effects of the demographic, political, and economic crises that marked the fourteenth and fifteenth centuries. Residents were not only offered grain at good prices, they were guaranteed access to it—no small matter in an age of unreliable transportation, uncertain harvests, and regu-

15. For a fuller discussion of the staple and its role in the Douaisien economy, see Howell and Boone, "Becoming Early Modern."

16. For a general history of the grain trade in Douai, see J. Godart, "Contribution à l'étude de l'histoire du commerce des grains à Douai du XIVe au XVIIe siècle," *Revue du Nord* 27 (1944): 171–205; and Alain Derville "Le grenier des Pays-Bas médiévaux," *Revue du Nord* 69, no. 273 (April–June 1987): 267–80. Also see M.-J. Tits-Dieuaide, "Le grain et le pain dans l'administration des villes de Brabant et de Flandre au moyen-âge," in *Actes du 11e colloque international "L'initiative publique des communes en Belgique": Fondements historiques (Ancien Régime), Spa, 1– 4 September 1982*, no. 65 of *Crédit Communal de Belgique collection d'histoire*, série in 8° (Brussels: Crédit Communal de Belgique, 1984); and Howell and Boone, "Becoming Early Modern."

lar disruptions of trade. The staple also played a key role in bolstering local employment and building individual fortunes. While the grain trade seems in Douai to have provided fewer jobs for ordinary people than did textiles, the commerce surely generated some employment on the docks and on the ships that transported the grain north and east.[17] More importantly, it also assured the prosperity of the elite. Many of Douai's richest citizens and political leaders were grain merchants, and as the fifteenth century gave way to the sixteenth, an even greater proportion of the city's political and economic elite dealt in the commodity.[18]

Managing Change

Rather than suffering from the social disintegration and economic collapse described by Pirenne and Espinas, Douai thus appears to have enjoyed an unexpected degree of economic sufficiency in the fourteenth and fifteenth centuries. The precise terms of the equation that allowed Douaisiens to weather the storms of this traumatic period are obscure, but a general characteristic is clear. Douai's success depended upon a combination of social, economic, and political flexibility, on the one hand, and, on the

17. Boatmen occasionally appear as principal actors in Douai's marriage documents, wills, and contrats divers. It is no accident that the boatmen were among the best organized of Douaisien crafts, although they, like others, never achieved corporative status: see Espinas, *La vie urbaine,* 2:583–628, esp. 596–98.

18. Marriage contracts provide interesting evidence of this development. Contracts from AMD, FF 586/214–305 (1375–77), named the occupations or social positions of forty-eight principal actors, of which only one was a "marchand"; AMD, FF 596/1887–1994 (1393–94), named twenty-eight, of which one was a "marchand de blé"; AMD, FF 609/1770–1832 (1421–27), provided such information for thirty-nine principal actors, of which two were "marchands de drap," one was a "marchand de grain," and two were simply "marchands."

As we move later in time, the percentage of "marchands" and "marchands de blé" (or "de grain") increases. See, for example, the sample of marriage contracts, AMD, FF 649/5126–5176 (1521–23), which gave occupational identifications for thirty-five principal actors, of which four were "marchands" and one was a "marchand de grain"; AMD, FF 655/5543–5586 (1551–70), gave this information for fifty-five principal actors, of which two were "marchands de drap," one was a "marchand de grain," and nine were simply "marchands"; those contracts in AMD, FF 914 (1557) named twenty-eight occupations or social positions, of which eleven were "marchands" and one was a "marchand de drap." Many of those labeled simply "marchand" dealt, of course, in grain. For a description of the sixteenth-century grain trade and relevant statistics, see Alain Lottin, "Grand siècle ou siècle d'ainain?" in M. Rouche and Pierre Demolon, eds., *Histoire de Douai,* vol. 9 of *Collection histoire des villes du Nord/Pas-de-Calais,* ed. Y. M. Hilaire (Dunkirk: Westhoek-Editions, 1985), 121.

other hand, a taste for stricter social ordering, more clearly marked social boundaries, permanent social networks, and an intensified social hierarchy. Paradoxically, one tendency seems to have been the condition of the other.

The process of social ordering occurred perhaps most visibly among Douai's échevins themselves. Having lost their status as "patricians"—men who ruled by right of birth—at the turn of the fourteenth century, Douai's échevins spent the last two centuries of the Middle Ages as a vaguely defined merchant and industrial elite made up both of old patricians and of "new men"—smaller merchants, artisan-entrepreneurs, even simple artisans.[19] During that period, Douai saw, as one scholar has recently put it, "the regular renewal of the political class" achieved by the inclusion of new men in government who were drawn from both the commercial and artisanal ranks.[20] After 1500, however, this group lost its amorphous character, evolving into a closed and more stable sociopolitical group, an urban aristocracy made up of men who lived from large-scale commerce, rents, or office.

The change in the social profile of Douai's échevins as we move from the fourteenth and fifteenth centuries to the sixteenth is clearly revealed in the marriage contracts they wrote. At least eight of the twelve men who served as échevins in 1497–98 described themselves as artisans.[21] Only one of the men, Jacques Caudy, whose father was styled "maistre" and whose passive investments were huge, was not identified by occupation or social role.[22] Eight of the remaining eleven were still clearly linked to Douai's commercial and industrial economy, either by the occupational labels they or close family members bore or by the nature of the assets they carried into marriage and left as dowers—grain inventories, tools of their trades, warehouses in Douai, cash. For example, Jehan Le Wantier Dit Ramage, one of the most senior officers, wrote a marriage contract in 1476 that

---

19. Alain Derville, "Les échevins de Douai (1228–1527)," in *La sociabilité urbaine en Europe du Nord-Ouest du XIVe au XVIIIe siècles: Actes du Colloque 5 février 1983; Mémoires de la Société d'Agriculture, Sciences et Arts de Douai,* 5th ser., vol. 8 (Douai: Lefebvre-L'évêque, 1983).

20. Derville, "Les échevins," 45.

21. While most of these men were surely artisan-merchants, not simple artisans, it is significant that they did not choose to call themselves "marchands," a term commonly used in the sixteenth century (and whose institution marks the increasing distance between production and trade in Douai).

22. His marriage contract is AMD, FF 635/3966 (28 April 1485); two of his sons also left contracts: AMD, FF 644/4800 (14 April 1511); and FF 646/4952 (4 August 1515).

named him "caucheteur" (a kind of cloth finisher).[23] Jacquemart Pollet, son of a "clerc," was an "apparelleur de draps" (cloth finisher), and he married a woman whose father was in the same craft.[24] Jehan De Brebiere, son of an "old" family and probably father to the échevin of the same name who served on the 1497–98 bench, wrote a marriage contract in 1449 that placed him among Douai's most prosperous citizens, but emphatically not among its rentiers.[25] Others, to be sure, were members of a leisured rentier class, but they were the exception. Men like Alixandre Le Libert, a brewer who served at least six terms in the mid–fifteenth century, were almost as common as the true rentiers. To judge from his 1438 marriage contract, he was rich (or at least he married a rich woman), but he was by no means a man of leisure. He seems to have owned and operated a prosperous brewery and to have come, on both his mother's and father's sides, from a long line of butchers.[26]

By 1550 at the latest, however, this "open" business elite no longer ruled, for by then the échevinage was made up of men belonging to a new sort of urban aristocracy. These men were measurably less involved in industry, less mobile socially and economically, and considerably more distant from the ordinary citizenry than their predecessors of the previous two centuries. These échevins were, for example, more often labeled "merchant," "lawyer," or "knight" than "clothmaker," "finisher," or "brewer." Specifically, only one of the twelve échevins who served in 1547–48 called himself an artisan (Antoine Mollart, "tanner"). Two described themselves only by social label (Franchois Polle, "trained in law," and Andrieu le Willame, "knight")—thus implicitly denying their ancestors' roots in trade—and the brother of a fourth named his office as one of Douai's "Huit Hommes" (an honorary board of advisors to the échevins) in the portement he brought to his marriage in 1539. A fifth and sixth, who apparently lived from land rents, were given no labels of social or occupa-

---

23. AMD, FF 631/3690 (29 March 1476); his portement consisted of two pieces of land in gardens, pasture, woods, and fields that were valued at 400 francs of 32 gros each; his bride brought 700 livres parisis in cash and goods, as well as use of a house for life.

24. AMD, FF 627/3300 (11 June 1468); his portement consisted of 500 livres parisis; his bride's totaled 700 livres parisis, made up of cash and goods.

25. AMD, FF 618/2517 (23 April 1449); his portement consisted of 200 francs and life use of one-half of a house.

26. Alixandre Le Libert was the son of Franchoise Rohard, second wife of Jehan Le Libert, a butcher. Three of Alixandre's half brothers were butchers, as was his grandfather, Willaume Le Libert. Alixandre married Catherine Du Bos in 1438 (AMD, FF 614/2159 [10 November 1438]).

tional position. All the rest—five very rich men—were called "marchands" and only two of them left marital documents betraying any links to the world of active commerce and production.[27] The rest may have financed or brokered trade in grain, wool, cloth, horses, or dyestuffs, but they probably seldom touched these things.

Although in many ways like the patrician regime of old days, this new aristocracy was not, however, a patriciate, at least not in the usual meaning of the term. This group was less defined by blood than the old patriciate had been, and it was, in constrast, better defined by social roles.[28] To belong to this aristocracy was to govern, to hold office, to attend university; it was, increasingly, to own land, to buy country residences, to marry children into the nobility. It was also, as it had been for the last two centuries, to trade. But it was no longer to make goods for trade or to claim to do so.

Thus, over the course of a long two-century period, long after the destruction of the old patrician monopoly in Douai, the social identity of Douai's political elite was slowly recast. Men who had once defined themselves as traders who frequently took part in production itself, sometimes even as artisans, were now more often professionals in the service of the crown, true rentiers who had withdrawn from business to pursue the arts of government and leisure or financiers whose links to industry were less and less direct.[29] This redefinition of social position extended far beyond

27. Pierre De Doucourt, who listed 3,000 livres parisis in grain and other merchandise in his portement, and Jehan Grenet, "hôtelier" (and "marchand"), whose son was accompanied at this wedding by a "hugier" (carpenter or woodworker) and whose daughter married an apothecary.

28. The municipal archives of Douai contain only two marriage contracts left by échevins who served in 1390–91 (another period sampled), alongside three ravestissements, but several of these échevins had close family members who did write contracts. All the men who appear in the contracts were prosperous, most were truly rich, and the majority had extensive passive investments in land and rents. Not all these men, however, had left trade, and not all were in a position to do so. The appellation "marchand" was still rare in this period, and those who actively engaged in commerce seem to have identified themselves with sales of industrial goods rather than with commerce qua commerce.

29. Douai's sixteenth-century elite was thus classic in form. For a summary description of the urban bourgeoisie in this age, especially in France, see George Huppert, *Les bourgeois gentilhommes* (Chicago: University of Chicago Press, 1977), or idem, *After the Black Death* (Bloomington: University of Indiana Press, 1986) or, for German cities, Gerald Lymon Soliday, *A Community in Conflict: Frankfurt Society in the Seventeenth and Early Eighteenth Centuries* (Hanover, N. H.: University Press of New England, 1974). Also see Robert Darton, "A Bourgeois Orders His World," in *The Great Cat Massacre and Other Episodes in French Cultural History* (Harmondsworth: Penguin, 1985), and Roland Mousnier, *Les hiérarchies sociales de 1450 à nos jours* (Paris: Presses universitaires de France, 1969).

the échevinage itself, well into the ranks of Douai's ordinary rich. By about 1550, to judge from the archive of marriage contracts surviving from this period, Douai's elite had distinctly separated itself from the rest of the city's propertied classes in a way that had not characterized the earlier centuries. This new elite was more numerous, richer, and more exclusive than the old. By the 1550s, just over 50 percent of all those whose marriage contracts have survived in Douai's archive were labeled either merchants, officeholders, or nobles, as compared to only 11 percent of those in the late fourteenth-century sample.[30] The shift reflects in part the disappearance of artisans from the archive, but there is also no doubt that absolutely more rich people wrote marriage contracts in this period—indirect evidence that there were absolutely more such rich people in Douai—and that more of them were members of a growing financial and rentier class. A sample of 67 marriage contracts from the mid-1550s, for example, named 78 occupations among the principal actors; 26 were "marchands," and only 35 were artisans or retailers.[31]

One of the paradoxes in this story of social change among the elite is that it seems to have occurred without destruction of the city's artisanal class. To be sure, as the elite grew richer, the economic and social distance between artisan and elite grew as well. The process did not, however, erode artisanal culture. On the contrary. It was, in fact, exactly during the fourteenth and fifteenth centuries, when the "grande draperie" was in decline and this new urban aristocracy in formation that the city's artisans finally managed to form craft associations. From both 1371 and 1403, for example, we have hints that weavers' associations had been formed around parish confraternities.[32] Another document of 1403 suggests that weavers were then permitted to demand membership fees from all practitioners of the trade, a right that, while hardly implying strong corporative organization, does seem to mark the emergence of formal trade identity. The "tondeurs" (shearers), long recognized as Douai's premier artisans thanks

30. See tables 1–3 and Martha Howell, "Weathering Crisis, Managing Change: The Emergence of a New Socioeconomic Order in Douai at the End of the Middle Ages," in *La draperie ancienne des Pays-Bas: Débouchés et stratégies de survie (14e–16e siècles),* ed. Marc Boone and Walter Prevenier (Leuven and Apeldoorn: Garant, 1993), for details.

31. For these figures, see the material in Howell, "Weathering Crisis." The 1521–22 sample of forty-three contracts named forty-five occupations, eight of them merchants and thirty-three artisans. The 1441–43 sample of seventy-five contracts named fifty-eight occupations, two of them merchants and forty-two of them artisans.

32. Espinas and Pirenne, *Recueil de documents* 2, docs. 354 and 384.

to their role in the all-important cloth finishing process, seem at the same time also to have won restricted craft rights.[33]

A few nontextile crafts successfully organized as well. A 1392 ordinance mentioned the "porteurs de blé" (wheat transporters), if only to discipline them.[34] Boatmen and millers have also left some indications that they possessed corporative rights, although they seem never really to have governed themselves. Leatherworkers similarly enjoyed a kind of craft status, although they derived their authority from the duke, not from the commune. Of all Douai's producers, however, only the butchers seem to have controlled membership. They benefited from a rule, similar to those in force in other cities, that provided that the market stalls for meat be passed through families. The practice did not guarantee trade rights for family members, but it assured that certain families—such as the Le Liberts— would be "butcher" families.

These organizations were politically weak; none sought, as far as we know, and none won, true guild status in that none controlled membership, the labor process, or production. Nonetheless, such organizations seem to have become increasingly important markers of social place during the late Middle Ages. To wit, as early as the fourteenth century, we find that Douaisiens regularly named their fellow craftsmen in wills, usually requesting that they carry their bier, and testators sometimes also left small bequests for the religious brotherhoods around which the crafts were frequently organized. In a recent study of such bequests, Jean-Pierre Deregnaucourt has counted thirty-four such institutions to which testators made special bequests, ranging from the "arbalétriers" (crossbowmen) (first named in a 1351 testament) and "drapiers" (first named in 1360) to the "porteurs de charbon" (charcoal transporters) (1480) and "tripiers" (makers of light cloth) (1480).[35]

Even better known to historians are the roles brotherhoods such as these played in the public ceremonies and celebrations that marked civic life in this age throughout urbanized Europe. Douai boasts the Low

---

33. Espinas and Pirenne, *Recueil de documents,* 2, doc. 372: a chirographe (AMD, FF 694 [4 January 1391]), acknowledged receipt of 20 florins by two wardens and six other "tondeurs"— "ou nom et pour tout le corps du dit mestier des tendeurs" (in the name of and on behalf of the entire body of the trade of shearers).

34. For this, see Espinas, *La vie urbaine* 2:583 ff. The men were forbidden any "congregation ne assamblee" (congregation or assembly).

35. Jean-Pierre Deregnaucourt, "Autour de la mort à Douai: Attitudes, pratiques et croyances, 1250–1500" (Ph.D. diss., Université Catholique de Lille, 1993), 254.

Countries' earliest record of a shooting confraternity, the "arbalétriers," (crossbowmen), first mentioned in municipal administrative sources during the thirteenth century and again in evidence in the fourteenth, when they were accompanied by the "archiers" (archers).[36] During the fifteenth century, we also know, the Douaisien shooting confraternities always joined in the interurban competitions and performances that were regularly held throughout the Burgundian Netherlands. It is from the later Burgundian period as well that most of our evidence comes of festivals, parades, theater, and other forms of public cultural life, the same period that yields the most abundant references to religious confraternities attached to crafts and even to embryonic craft associations.[37]

Despite Douai's artisans' ability to survive as independent producers and to develop an unexpectedly vigorous form of associational life, they were not, however, a politically autonomous class. Instead, they seem more like members of a society of estates, men who preserved their socioeconomic independence but depended upon the patronage of their social betters and passively submitted to their political control. Even the craft associations and public rituals in which they took part seem less vehicles for the articulation of independent political voices than agents of their subordination. Certainly, the public processions that punctuated daily life in Douai in this age were crowded with craftsmen, who typically carried torches or banners along with the shrines of their patron saints, and these events were often, moreover, formally organized by the "sociétés" that craftsmen themselves had founded. Still, the performances should not necessarily be read as expressions of preexisting corporative mentality or evidence that civic space was universally shared.

In fact, all the records we have about these festivals suggest that the celebrations were as much creations of the elite as they were of artisans themselves. As reported in town accounts from 1451, for example, the échevins probably organized, certainly authorized, and actually presided

---

36. See Espinas, *La vie urbaine,* 2:584–87.

37. Peter Arnade has offered especially telling social analyses of these kinds of public rituals in the Low Countries, labeling them episodes in the "state theater" that was emerging around the Burgundian Court. He emphasizes as well, however, that the rituals were contests among the urban social orders for control of political discourse. See his *Realms of Ritual: Burgundian Ceremony and Civic Life in Late Medieval Ghent* (Ithaca, N.Y.: Cornell University Press, 1996) and "City, State and Public Ritual in the Late Medieval Burgundian Netherlands," in *Comparative Studies in Society and History* (forthcoming).

over the annual "fête des Anes," a festival of inversion (a festival in which participants reverse social roles, e.g., women play men, ordinary people rule, students act as professors) that took place at the New Year, ostensibly designed to call all authority into question, theirs included. As a contemporary account had it, the échevins sat with honored visitors and distinguished fellow Douaisiens—"knights and gentlemen and notables, in particular the officers of the Duke of Burgundy," to "view and see the games and contests of persons that are named the 'Asne,' which are played in this city during both day and evening, as it is the custom to do each year . . . [and] to dine both during and after this evening and day of the 'Asne' on bread, wine, spices, and other things, while looking at the games."[38] An account of 1513 listed those "sociétés," crafts, even the clergy, scheduled to parade before the body of dignitaries: the "Bon Enfants, la Compagnie des Sayetteurs, celles de L'Estrille, ou de Minchemont, des Clercqs. de Malduisson, des Aventureux, ou d'ailleurs comme le Prêvot des Cocquins de Cambrai." One from 1519 listed a similar mélange of societies dedicated to folly on the one hand, religious and secular brotherhood, on the other: "le Prince d'Amour et sa compagnie, sayeteurs, le Recteur des Bons Enfants, la Compagnie de l'Estrille, celles des bouchers et des porteurs au sac, les procuerurs et clercs de la ville." To conclude this day of parade and games, the account tells us, the assembled participants dined together on roast swan, which was provided by the city.[39]

In addition to presiding over the annual rites of inversion, the échevins organized countless public displays that specifically elaborated their own authority. Public receptions for visiting dignitaries were especially frequent; during 1479, for example, Douai feted such luminaries as the captain of Antwerp's militia; the procureur of the city of Tournai; Philippe, bastard son of the Duke; and Philippe de Clèves. The échevins also publicly celebrated their own elections and the beginnings of their administrative year with sumptuous dinners to which they invited, for example, the duke's bailiff, his lieutenant, the clerk of the "Gouvernance" [the chief administrative office of the district of Lille-Douai-Orchies], and the pro-

---

38. Cited in Monique Mestayer, "Les fêtes et cérémonies à Douai 1450–1550," in *La sociabilité urbaine en Europe du Nord-Ouest du XIVe au XVIIIe siècles: Actes du Colloque 5 février 1983; Mémoires de la Société d'Agriculture, Sciences et Arts de Douai*, 5th ser., vol. 8 (Douai: Lefebvre-L'évêque, 1983), 105.

39. Mestayer, "Les fêtes," 105.

cureur of the duke. The échevins even gave dinners, at municipal expense, to celebrate their own marriages and those of their children. They made many of these celebrations public in the sense that they displayed themselves to their citizenry during the festivities, and they often invited representatives of the ordinary citizenry to these parties. But it was they—not the ordinary citizens—who claimed authorship of the celebrations, they who set its terms.

Thus, whatever the civic and social importance of public rituals, festivals, and games, even of Douai's embryonic craft associations and religious confraternities, such activities did not so much reveal the existence of communal culture in the universal sense implied as they helped constitute a society of orders. In fact, I would argue that they served to mark social distance between the urban aristocracy and the ordinary citizen just as powerfully as they gave voice to a common culture. They were statements about the new social contract in Douai, a contract between an elite that monopolized rule and an ordinary citizenry that was granted economic independence in exchange for political quietism.

Marriage, Inheritance, and Trade

The marital property regime that Douaisiens adopted during these centuries seems perfectly to reflect the same social values. It too gave preference to sociopolitical order over sociopolitical change, to security of social rank over the opportunity for social mobility. It did so by helping to keep trade rights and associated assets in family lines so that sons (and daughters) were assured a future at least as good as the one their parents had known.

The chief element in this process was an increased self-consciousness about the link between trade rights and social identity. By the fifteenth century at the latest, Douaisiens regularly used craft or professional labels to identify themselves. At the same time, they began to marry within their occupational group with a frequency that could not have been produced by chance, and they began to pass trade rights more strictly through lineal ties.

The échevins were especially adept at these practices. Of the twelve échevins who served in 1497–98, for example, seven practiced what were clearly "family" trades. Jehan De Marquette, labeled "tisserand de drap" (weaver of drapery) in the contracts for both of his marriages (to the latter he brought his "metier a tisser des draps" [loom for making drapery]), married one of his daughters to another "tisserand de draps."[40] One of his sons married in 1508, bringing "un metier a tisser le draps" as part of his portement.[41] Jehan Le Soif Dit Jacquessin was labeled "mercier" (grocer) in his first marriage contract of 1480.[42] His son was called "apothicaire" (apothecary), a closely related profession, in both of his marriage contracts of 1505 and 1511.[43] Anthoine Saingler was a merchant, and his son married the daughter of a "marchand de grains" in 1497.[44] Amé Pinchon, an "echopier" (shopkeeper), had a son who was a "marchand."[45] Jehan Le Fevre, "appareileur de drap" (cloth finisher), and "caucheteur" (a kind of cloth finisher), had a son who was called a "marchand detailler de drap" (retail merchant of drapery). Pierre Du Pont, "marchand de drap," had a daughter who married a "sayetteur" (maker of light woolens). Jehan Le Wantier Dit Ramage was a "caucheteur," and his niece married a man in the same trade.[46]

It is considerably harder to obtain statistically meaningful evidence about the tendency of ordinary people to pass trades in families by studying their marriage contracts and wills, for these people left many fewer and much less elaborate records. Among the twenty-three married couples who wrote a contrat divers in 1497–98, for example, we find only five who left surviving marriage contracts of their own and only another six who appear in the contracts of close relatives. Just a few of these documents contain useful information about the occupations of these people. Still, even the partial evidence we have is suggestive. Emery De Cantin, goldsmith, for example, was the son of a goldsmith.[47] The brewer to whom Giles Gollet married one of his daughters was the son of a brewer.[48] Giles De Thiery's mother gave him the equipment to set himself up as a finisher when he married the daughter of a draper.[49] Pierre Villam, a brewer who

40. AMD, FF 630/3589 (7 May 1474); FF 636/4048 (3 May 1488); FF 637/4123 (1 May 1490).

41. AMD, FF 644/4705 (24 June 1508).

42. AMD, FF 633/3807 (30 September 1480); in a later contract, he was labeled "marchand."

43. AMD, FF 642/4611 (13 October 1505); FF 644/4794 (16 January 1511).

44. AMD, FF 639/4345 (31 August 1497).

45. AMD, FF 629/3477 (4 August 1471); FF 635/4014 (14 October 1486).

46. AMD, FF 631/3620 (29 March 1476).

47. AMD, FF 639/4349.

48. AMD, FF 633/3797.

49. AMD, FF 639/4349.

married in 1480, was the son of another brewer.[50] Direct samples of marriage contracts themselves tell a similar story. Among the eighty-eight weddings that produced surviving marriage contracts or ravestissements from 1441 to 1443, for example, nineteen involved at least two principal actors or heirs of principal actors (one on either side of a marriage or a generation) whose trades could be identified. Of them, eight, or 42 percent, were cementing craft identity through the marital union.[51]

The *Registre aux bourgeois* (roll of new citizens) repeats the litany. The register for three different years in the fifteenth century (1438–39, 1451–52, and 1474–75) named sixty-one men who had children, and in twenty-three of these cases we know both the father's trade and the trades of his son(s) or son(s)-in-law. Fourteen of the twenty-three children either took up or married into their father's trade (nine of twelve sons and five of eleven daughters): 61 percent![52]

Anecdotal evidence is as telling. Jehan Casier, for example, registered as cloth furnisher in the citizenship rolls of 1438; in 1480, his son, Julien, identified himself as a "parmentier" (maker of specialty trimmings for drapery) when he married.[53] His bride's son (by a previous marriage) later became a cloth finisher.[54] Another family's story—that of the De Lille's— is more complex and harder to trace, but it too betrays similar themes. The story begins with Willame De Lille, a clothmaker, merchant, and

---

50. AMD, FF 633/3797.

51. The principal marriage contracts in the eight cases were AMD, FF 616/2326 (15 May 1441); FF 616/2331 (9 June 1441); FF 616/2335 (2 August 1441); FF 616/2339 (25 September 1441); FF 616/2372 (23 November 1442); FF 616/2379 (24 January 1443); FF 616/2403 (23 November 1443); FF 616/2406 (27 March 1444). In each case, either marriages of principal actors or the marriages of their offspring were traced.

Data suitable for statistically meaningful comparison with the Douaisien is difficult to obtain, but there is little doubt that the rate of trade endogamy in Douai was high. James Farr's similarly designed study of marriage contracts in Dijon showed that in late sixteenth- and early seventeenth-century Dijon, rates were much lower, on average less than 20 percent. Only the butchers achieved rates higher than 50 percent, a difference that can be explained because butchers in Dijon, like those in Douai and many other places, presumably enjoyed special inheritance rights to the meat stalls: James R. Farr, *Hands of Honor: Artisans and Their World in Dijon, 1550–1650* (Ithaca, N.Y.: Cornell University Press, 1988), 136–38. Also see Marianne Danneel, *Weduwen en wezen in het laat-middeleeuwse Gent* (Leuven and Apeldoorn: Garant, 1995), 354; and Barbara Hanawalt, "Remarriage as an Option for Urban and Rural Widows in Late Medieval England," in *Wife and Widow: The Experiences of Women in Medieval England,* ed. S. Walker (Ann Arbor: University of Michigan Press, 1993); in both Ghent and London in this period widows regularly remarried within the trade.

52. AMD, BB 84.

53. AMD, BB 84; FF 633/3800 (21 August 1480).

54. AMD, FF 641/4434 (17 April 1501).

draper, who registered as citizen, along with his wife, Mehault Lienart, and their eleven-month old son, Colart, in 1438.[55] In 1462, when Colart was twenty-five, he married and called himself a draper.[56] Colart had died by 1480, when his daughter by Marie, Jehenne De Lille, married Jacques Pannequin, a tanner and son of a tanner, whose own parents had first joined the bourgeoisie in 1451.

Jehan Bauchet was the progenitor of an even better documented and much more successful story of trade endogamy. He first registered as citizen in 1451; his son, Jean (called Hanotin), called himself a linen weaver in his marriage contract of 1468.[57] Jean (Hanotin) had at least seven children. All five of his known sons stayed in the cloth trade, as draper, saye-maker, or finisher. The two known daughters married finishers.[58]

Few Douaisiens of the age could marry within the trade and pass their craft down through the line as easily as the Bauchets. Nor could they always preserve social place as trade endogamy is meant to do. This was, after all, the fifteenth century, when times were not easy, and Douai was only a medium-sized city encircled by aggressive commercial competitors and encroaching monarchies. Death, famine, and economic hardship combined to wreak havoc even with the best-designed plans for social ordering. Still, whether De Lilles or Bauchets, whether or not spectacularly successful in keeping trade and wealth in family lines, Douaisiens sought to use inheritance and marriage to cement social relations, and all of them treated profession and trade as a chief element of the social bond. Thus, when they could, they married within occupational rank, and they made sure that sons followed their fathers in the trade. Startlingly visible in the Bauchets' case, the pattern also exists, if it is more faintly traced, in the Pannequin and De Lille story. Jacques Pannequin and his son were both tanners; Willame De Lille and his son Colart were both drapers, and the widow of Colart's son remarried a draper.

Such a high degree of trade endogamy and trade inheritance does not occur randomly. People who marry within a trade and who work in family businesses are, by definition, following rules, whether or not they are formally expressed. In Douai, however, unlike any other northern city in

55. AMD, BB 84; FF 627/3283(1468).

56. AMD, FF 624/3089 (21 September 1462).

57. AMD, BB 84; FF 627/3283 (1468).

58. AMD, FF 639/4355 (1497); FF 641/4498 (1502); FF 644/4717 (1508); FF 640/4408 (1500); FF 636/4081 (1489); FF 646/4962 (1515); FF 644/4782 (1510).

which such patterns have been observed, the rules were not imposed by urban authorities or guilds that legislated craft intermarriage and trade devolution but by individuals acting outside formal political institutions.[59] When Douaisiens married, it seems, they chose spouses whose trades matched theirs, their fathers, or their former spouses; and Douaisien children were urged, compelled, or seduced to follow the trade of their father, uncle, or grandfather.[60] Surely the caution that their choices bespeak was justified. The economy was not expanding in these years, competition in cloth markets was tough, and the urban government could not fully protect either craftsmen or merchants. Like others throughout the Low Countries in this age who were aggressively imposing formal rules regarding inheritance of trade rights, Douaisiens had good reason to marry their own, to pass their occupational assets, along with their houses, tools, jewels, and furnishings to family. Unlike most of their neighbors, however, who depended on political institutions to impose these rules of inheritance, Douaisiens did the job by themselves. Without guilds or municipal law to enforce these practices, Douaisiens wrote marriage agreements instead, thereby securing social place by securing property in male-defined lines of descent. And they married their own, thus assuring that trade rights and business connections remained the property of what they now called "lignage."

59. See Espinas, *La vie urbaine*, 2:598–605, and Martha Howell, "Achieving the Guild Effect Without Guilds: Crafts and Craftsmen in Late Medieval Douai," in *Les métiers au moyen âge: Aspects économiques et sociaux*, ed. J.-P. Sosson (Louvain-la-Neuve: Publications de l'Institute d'Etudes Médiévales, 1994), 109–28. The butchers are the exception here, for family members had inheritance rights to the stalls where all meat had to be sold. Hans van Werveke traced the growing importance of inheritance rights in the organized crafts in Flanders and throughout the North during the fourteenth and fifteenth centuries; in all the cases he cites, the protections were legislated by corporate guilds or municipal authorities: *Ambachten en erflijkheid*, vol. 4, no. 1, of *Mededeelingen van de Koninklijke Vlaamsche Academie voor Wetenschappen, Letteren en Schoone Kunsten van België, Klasse der Letteren* (Brussels: Erasmus 1942). James Farr has traced a similar process in Dijon where, as in Douai, formal rules did not impose such practices. See Farr, *Hands of Honor*, 145, where he remarks that "concerns of lineage" rose for master artisans in the sixteenth and seventeenth centuries.

60. The tendency toward intermarital and intergenerational trade endogamy may have become more marked as the fifteenth century progressed; it is at least easier to measure the pattern in those years because documents from the later years identify people by trade more often. Of course, the more frequent identifications may simply reflect bureaucratic convention, for the documents in which they appear are highly formulaic, but they may also reflect a heightened sense of craft identity born of strengthening traditions of intercraft marriage and inheritance.

However marked, the preference for patrilineality so apparent in these stories was not "natural." Propertied people in Douai did not inherently prefer such property arrangements, and, as we have seen, even the richest moved toward them only slowly. They did so because in the difficult socio-economic environment of the age it seemed more important to secure wealth and social position than to position oneself to acquire them. The central event in this history of legal and social change was the decline of the old drapery. Although the Douaisien socioeconomic system did not collapse as a result, the long industrial crisis did force a refashioning of production relations. Douaisiens decentralized production, rendering the small producer more independent but, simultaneously, placing him more precariously in a less certain and less stable market. At the same time, the Douaisien merchant class slowly withdrew from production itself and concentrated first on sales of wool, cloth, and, above all, grain, and then on professional opportunities in royal courts and the learned professions. Some withdrew entirely from trade to pursue the arts of leisure and government.

A social reordering accompanied the reorganization of production so that, by 1550 at the latest, Douai had become a society of orders. At the top stood a newly constituted urban aristocracy. Under it stood a newly visible petite bourgeoisie, the descendants of Douai's artisanal class, who controlled production and enjoyed new legitimacy as members of the urban corporation, but who were increasingly differentiated from the elite by wealth, by the nature of their property, and by their political impotence.

The new marital system nicely complemented and even enabled this new social order. It helped assure that trade and trade rights were passed through families as men and women married (and remarried) within the trade, that fathers passed their occupations on to sons, grandsons, or sons-in-law. It helped secure property for children and grandchildren, slowed the circulation of wealth, and in general reduced both upward and downward mobility. As these effects were felt, old custom, so long the preferred normative system, fell into greater disuse. Unlike the system that replaced it, old custom did not respect lineage; nor did it treat wealth as fixed assets, and it did not preserve individual social place in the way that Douaisiens now thought necessary. For these faults, old custom had to be laid aside.

EIGHT

The Douaisien Reform in Historical Context

There is much that would lead us to believe that the Douaisien reform and its meaning for social and gender order were *sui generis*. Not only did the Douaisien reform take place in a social environment not quite like any other, but it occurred as legal change elsewhere only rarely occurred. Thanks to peculiarities of their custom and the relative sophistication of their municipal institutions, individual Douaisiens were freer than most of their contemporaries to manipulate their marital property regime. They were thus able to preserve custom as their neighbors often were not and, paradoxically, able to preserve it precisely because they could so easily amend it. The choices they made and the record they left in making their choices were thus probably unique for the age.

Still, if we examine the data closely, we find that neither the custom with which Douaisiens began the late Middle Ages nor the regime they devised to replace it was unique to Douai. Nor was legal reform like this unusual in this age; elsewhere in Europe, certainly in the French- and Flemish-speaking regions on which this study focuses, marital property law was often as unstable as the Douaisien, and it was frequently unstable in exactly the same ways as the Douaisien. Hence, the Douaisien legal reform has a significance well beyond Douai, for it is an extraordinarily well documented version of a story that was played out much more obscurely, and surely in slightly different ways, elsewhere in this age.

To understand the significance of the Douaisien legal reform, we must, then, place it in the larger history to which it belongs. Most fundamentally, this means understanding the way western European marital property and succession regimes of this time defined the family and how they positioned individual family members with respect to property and with respect to one another. This also means understanding how changes in law could occur and thus how law was itself institutionalized. Finally, it also means looking more closely at how the Douaisien marital property regimes compared to others of the day and how the Douaisien legal reform resembled—or did not resemble—legal transformations elsewhere.

The Structure of Marital Property and Inheritance Law in Medieval Europe

Historians of premodern Europe have commonly classified what is typically called "family" law according to a binary typology. The first type of regime favored the respective natal families of the spouses, what most historians refer to as the "line" or, in French, the "lignage." In this system, property contributed to a marriage or earned during the course of it was marked for return to the natal line from which it originally came or to which it was attributed. If children were born of the marriage, the property typically passed to them, but at times and in amounts determined by the male heads of household in which it had originated. The other type of regime preferred the household, usually thought of as a "community" of individuals who shared household property, or it preferred a smaller version of the community, the conjugal pair itself. While all scholars have emphasized that no legal system of the day was purely "lineal," just as none was purely "communal" or "conjugal," most authorities have used these or similar categories as a basic tool for analyzing marital property regimes in this age.

A binary typology like this has served not just to expose the structure of law but also to map the history of legal change itself, for scholars have found that for some social groups, "family" law evolved as a transformation from one of these types to the other. In an article titled "From Brideprice to Dowry in Mediterranean Europe," first published in 1978, Diane Owen Hughes argues, for example, that around 1100 southern Europeans from elite social groups abandoned what she called a "brideprice" system in favor of one characterized by dowry, that is, a lineal system. In the former system, the groom made gifts to the wife and her family at marriage, and the widow shared in the property left by her husband. In the latter, the bride brought a premortem inheritance to the marriage, usually as dowry or dot (although it was often called something else), which was typically protected during the marriage and returned to her, sometimes along with an "increase," at widowhood. Many scholars, anthropologists in particular, have objected that the former system was never a true brideprice system (or, as it is usually termed, a bridewealth system) for it was not unilineal as these systems must be—a distinction Hughes recognizes.[1] Most observers have, however, agreed with Hughes that around this time dowry systems became dominant in southern Europe and that the marriage gifts and inheritance rights that had flowed from the groom to the bride and her family in earlier centuries were restricted, if not eliminated, from this period forward.

In an even more influential series of studies, Georges Duby has pursued a similar theme, arguing that the French feudal aristocracy adopted more aggressively "dotal" marital property and inheritance regimes around 1100, abandoning the more "co-lateral" systems of the early Middle Ages, in which the bride's and groom's sides of the marriage had roughly equal property rights. Duby also emphasized that the shift to a dotal system involved an intensification of conjugality, or what he called a shift to the "ménage," the household, proposing as well that the new dotal regimes thus undermined a certain notion of lineality, for they subordinated the interests of the wider kin to those of the ménage and its (patrilineal) descendants. While it may seem contradictory that Duby would not have characterized dotal regimes as lineal, as most historians have done, the apparent confusion is in terminology, not in conceptualization. Duby generally used the term "lineage" to refer to the wider kin group, not the patriline. Most historians, certainly most French historians, Jacob included, have meant the patriline when they employ the term "lineage" (or they have used the term in both ways).[2]

No such neat chronological organization has been developed to chart the history of marital property adopted by ordinary Europeans in the premodern period, but here too a similar binary typology has often been used

1. Jack Goody's *The Development of the Family and Marriage in Europe* (Cambridge: Cambridge University Press, 1983), Appendix 2, provides a detailed discussion of this matter.

2. Georges Duby, *Love and Marriage in the Middle Ages* (Cambridge: Polity Press, 1994); idem, *The Knight, The Lady, and The Priest* (Chicago: University of Chicago Press, 1993); idem, *Medieval Marriage* (Baltimore: Johns Hopkins University Press, 1978). Also see, for evidence that the shift was not as universal or as complete as Duby believed, Theodore Evergates, *Feudal Society in Medieval France* (Philadelphia: University of Pennsylvania Press, 1993); and idem, *Feudal Society in the Baillage of Troyes under the Counts of Champagne, 1152–1284* (Baltimore: Johns Hopkins University Press, 1975).

to categorize the myriad local systems that proliferated in this age.[3] Legal historians, at least those specializing in French- and Flemish-speaking Europe, have usually argued that from the high Middle Ages forward, this area of Europe was roughly divided into two parts.[4] In the South, what is typically referred to as the "pays d'écrit" or the land of written law, marital property regimes were, for ordinary people as for elites, dotal in form. In the North, in contrast, systems were "customary" or unwritten, in that the status of heirs and their property rights were determined by birth, not by fiat. In much of this region of customary law, instead of the dotal systems characteristic of the South, we find systems that were "communal," not "separatist," in spirit. In these regimes, the property a bride brought to the marriage was not held apart as it was in the South but was, instead, contributed to a communal account that was, typically, under the full control of her husband but to which she had rights as widow, sometimes as dowager but in some regimes as full owner.[5]

---

3. These regimes, as practiced by the European peasantry, are surveyed in Jack Goody, Joan Thirsk, and E. P. Thompson, eds., *Family and Inheritance: Rural Society in Western Europe 1200–1800* (Cambridge: Cambridge University Press, 1976). Also see, for a survey not restricted to the peasantry, the collection *La Femme: Recueils de la société de Jean Bodin pour l'histoire comparative des institutions*, vols. 11–13 (Brussels: Editions de la librarie encyclopédique, 1959–62).

4. For this history and the typology, see the summary in Paul Ourliac and Jehan de Malafosse, *Le droit familial*, vol. 3 of *Histoire du droit privé* (Paris: Presses universitaires de France, 1968–71). Jean Yver has modified this typology by dividing the customary systems of the Nord into two groups. Refusing the most general sense of the term "community property law," which refers to collective (and extensive) familial rights, manifested for example by the *laudatio parentum*, the *retrait linager*, and the *réserve héréditaire*, he distinguishes the Picard-Walloon custom, with its ravestissement, from the Flemish custom, with its reciprocal douaire coutumier and community of movable goods (Yver, "Les deux groupes de coutumes du Nord" [*Revue du Nord* 36]). Some parts of the North were not, of course, "communal," even in the most general sense of the term. See Yver's "Les caractères originaux du groupe de coutumes de l'oeust de la France," *Revue historique de droit français et étranger*, 4th ser., no. 30 (1952): 18–79.

Following Yver's *Egalité entre héritiers et exclusion des enfants dotés: Essai de géographie coutumière* (Paris: Editions Sirey, 1966) and taking children's inheritance rights as his point of departure, Le Roy Ladurie divided premodern France into three areas. One, which included the south and areas of Picardy-Wallonia (along with Douai), allowed parents to favor one child at the others' expense. The second demanded equality (the West of France). The third (the Parisian type) was in-between (Emmanuel Le Roy Ladurie, "Family Structure and Inheritance Customs in Sixteenth Century France," in *Family and Inheritance: Rural Society in Western Europe 1200–1800*, ed. Jack Goody, Joan Thirsk, and E. P. Thompson (Cambridge: Cambridge University Press, 1976).

5. In many such regimes, the husband had to acquire his wife's consent to alienations from this account, on the grounds that she was a silent partner in the property. See, for example, Jacob's description of the custom of the Cambrésis in *Les époux*. In many other community property regimes, in Paris, for example, widows had the right to refuse their share of the community

In principle, community property law operates very differently from dotal law. Community property law, in theory, does not recognize individual ownership of household property, not even of the assets that a person brings to it; instead, property is merged into a "community of goods." In most understandings of the term "community property law," the communal property is vested in those family members who reside together, who share the same "manse" or "maison." Husbands and wives in such systems, along with those who automatically succeed to the property after their deaths, are thus treated as joint owners of the property. It is the parents' control of the household, not their biological parentage per se, that gives the conjugal pair rights to the patrimony, sometimes even rights to decide about its succession (as in the Douaisien case), and it is their residence in the household that gives children the status of heirs. In their purest form, these systems imagine the household (and its property) as an indissoluble unit, one independent of the people who reside there. A member can leave the household, either at marriage or death, but he or she does not thereby decrease the patrimony, the community of goods. The wealth of the "maison" survives its occupiers because it is conceived of as an immortal, organic, whole, not as an assemblage of parts. In their purest form, then, communal households can be very large; they might encompass several generations or even several siblings and their spouses, as well as parents, even grandparents.

Although there were surely isolated regions of the medieval North where communal practices of this kind were the norm, we do not have good records of them. By their nature, of course, customary regions leave few records, and the customary regimes that mandated so expansive a definition of the community seem to have prospered before about 1300, the earliest date from which we have any reliable evidence about social practices among ordinary people of the North. By the late Middle Ages, when we can first look carefully, community property law did not exist in anything like this pure form anywhere in Europe. By then, people—

---

property account (thus avoiding obligations for debts due on it) on the grounds that they had had no say in the management of the account. For a description of this practice, see Philippe Godding, *Le droit privé dans les Pays-Bas meridinionaux du 12e au 18e siècle,* in *Mémoires de la Classe des Lettres, Collection in 4°,* 2d ser., pt. 1 (Brussels: Académie royale de Belgique, 1987), and Ourliac and Malafosse, *Le droit familial.* Under Douaisien custom, where wives were not considered creditors to the marital fund but residual owners of it, no such protections were offered widows; they were full owners of the estate and were fully responsible for its debts, although they too had had no say in the management of the marital fund during their husbands' lives.

especially urban people—normally formed new households when they married, simultaneously forming a new community of goods, headed by the new conjugal couple. Thus, the marital property laws of this age, although often communal in spirit and still bearing traces of their heritage, were in practice more often conjugal, for it was the "ménage," the nuclear couple itself, that constituted the "maison." Moreover, almost all community property laws of the late medieval period were neither purely communal nor conjugal in practice; that which most legal historians call the "lignage" or "famille" had extensive claims to the assets of the "ménage" everywhere. There is even good evidence—although understandably less of it—that this was true before 1300 as it was afterward, that no local system had ever been fully communal, that in only a few places had the principles of unity and perfect communalism ever been realized.

Nevertheless, no matter how attenuated in actuality, traces of communal practices did survive in the northern marital property regimes after 1300, although they were interpreted differently from place to place. In the area around Paris, for example, children who had left the household to marry were traditionally excluded from a share of the property that would be passed down at the death of the parents; the patrimony was divided only among those children who had stayed home—boys and girls alike. No matter how much or how little those who had left had taken with them (usually in the form of marriage gifts), they had no claim to the property rights lodged in the household because they were no longer members of the community.[6] In much of Flanders, where an even more stringent form of community property law dominated, such situations were handled quite differently, but decisions here also displayed a similar loyalty to the "manse." Here, the adult children who had received gifts prior to the parents' deaths were typically obligated to return them to the estate, and the children then shared equally in the now enhanced estate.[7] Next door, in Picardy-Wallonia, as we have seen, a different but related legacy prevailed. The Picard-Walloon customs were not at all egalitarian in this way, of course, but they expressed another aspect of the communal principles—one dramatically more conjugal in tone—by making the surviving spouse of a fertile marriage the absolute heir of communal property.

6. See Fr. Olivier-Martin, *Histoire de la coutume de la prevoté et vicomté de Paris*, 2 vols., 1922–30 (reprint, Paris: Editions Cujas, 1972). By the late Middle Ages, this practice had changed, so that children who had left could participate in the distribution of the estate.

7. In general, see Godding, *Le droit privé*.

Although the Douaisien custom differed in important ways from most of its neighbors, it was nonetheless a recognizable member of this "community property" group. To be sure, the Douaisien version had some unusual features: it treated *all* property as community property, no matter its origin or form (legal scholars call this form of community property law "universal"); it reduced the community of owners to the conjugal unit and its survivor; it guaranteed children no specific inheritance rights, on the grounds that conjugal rights superseded devolutionary privileges. Nevertheless, Douai was not the only place to have so privileged conjugality and not the only place to have developed such traditions out of the principles of "community property" that were hegemonic in much of the North.

The Malleability of Marital Property Law

Douai's custom did not survive the Middle Ages intact, however. It was always subject to emendation, and over time it was replaced by a marital property regime much more lineal in emphasis, one that marked off, as we have seen, the most important properties for lineal kin, that protected children's inheritance rights as old custom did not, and that positioned women very differently. Still, the new marital property regime in Douai was by no means extreme in its preference for the line over the conjugal unit, and in many respects, it closely resembled the regimes then dominant in nearby areas of the North.

Its structure also shared much with the dotal regimes typical of southern Europe. As Robert Jacob has pointed out, for example, the Douaisien reprise and douaire did not grant dower rights as did its neighboring Parisian regime, but instead simply returned a reserved amount of property to the widow, as did the typical dotal regime.[8]

Whether Douaisiens stayed within the traditions of community property law or, as Jacob proposes, broke regional norms when they wrote marriage contracts is of little importance here. For our purposes, it is enough to know that Douaisiens remained well within European-wide

---

8. For Robert Jacob's argument, see *Les époux, le seigneur et la cité: Coutume et pratiques matrimoniales des bourgeois et paysans de France du Nord au Moyen Age* (Brussels: Publications des Facultés Universitaires Saint-Louis 1, 1990), 207–15. The Douaisien douaire coutumier (the option to the reprise and douaire) was, however, like the Parisien.

legal traditions throughout their long oddessy. They began with a version of community property law (although it was a rather idiosyncratic one, it was not unique), and they gradually changed it to conform much more closely with the spirit of regimes both nearby and distant. What is exceptional about the Douaisien story is the way legal change occurred and the record it left, not the range within which Douaisiens moved.

Nor was Douaisiens' apparent indecision about their preferences exceptional. All European marital property regimes of the day, whether technically classified as communal or dotal, belonged, after all, to a more general category of marital property and inheritance law, in which both the groom's and the bride's side of the marriage have property rights in their union. These regimes are what anthropologists have called "diverging devolutionary" because in all of them property goes to both sons and daughters ("diverges") as it descends ("devolves").[9] Thus, whether we are in Picardy or Paris, Genoa or Ghent, we find accommodations to both the line and to the couple, to both the household and the larger family, to both father and mother, to both widow and widower, to both parents and children. And in all these places, recent legal scholarship has amply demonstrated, legal practice regularly fluctuated between these two poles. Everywhere, it seems, law was hybrid and unstable.

The instability of marital property law in this age had, undoubtedly, several origins. In part, it was a result of the weakness of legal institutions. In part, it resulted from the contradictions inherent in legal regimes that tried to accommodate the competing property rights of conjugal pair and lineage, husband and wife, widow and widower, parents and children. In part, it was the consequence of social and economic changes of the day that revalued property, altered the nature of wealth itself, repositioned the household, and reorganized labor relations.

Let us look first at law. Law in medieval culture, "family" law above all, was not yet institutionalized as it would gradually be from about 1500 on. During this epoch, laws of marital property relations and succession could be manipulated by individuals, reformed by common use, altered by sovereigns, and reinterpreted by lawyers with an ease that seems almost incompatible with the notion of "law." One of the reasons for law's mallea-

---

9. For an explanation of this terminology, see, in particular, Jack Goody, *Production and Reproduction: A Comparative Study of the Domestic Domain* (Cambridge: Cambridge University Press, 1976).

bility in these centuries, in the North at least, is that it was for all intents and purposes unwritten. Memories are short, circumstances change, errors occur; if law is not written down, it cannot be held stable. Even the scattered written customs of the late twelfth and thirteenth centuries—the magisterial compilation by Beaumanoir for the Beauvaisis is surely the best known—carry little of the weight we usually attribute to written law.[10] Neither authorized nor enforced by political sovereigns, these editions were mere reports that were drawn up by men with only vaguely defined official roles, and their editions had influence only to the extent that constituted authorities chose to make them influential and were powerful enough to enforce their will.[11] Although the customs written in the sixteenth century under the pressure of edicts issued by French and Hapsburg sovereigns would achieve greater standardization of individual customs, in origin they too were simply compilations of local norms. Even in the South, where law was thought of as "written" because it derived from written principles of Roman law, none of the texts these people relied upon had the authority a written legal text would later have, as we shall see, and none of their compilations of law achieved the standardization of practice we associate with legal codes.

But it was not merely the technical fact that "family" law was unwritten (or if written, then not codified) that gave marital property regimes of this age their flexibility, their mobility. By its very nature, such law was malleable. "The people make law" was the operative principle in this day, especially in the North, and as a product of the local community, law was considered legitimate precisely because it reflected local norms. To be sure, this did not mean that practices were infinitely flexible, that local norms were achieved through a fully consensual process, or that every individual in a community was equally able to adapt law as he or she saw fit. It simply meant that matters of "private" law, as it is still called today, were of little direct concern to public authorities.

---

10. Philippe de Beaumanoir, *Coutumes de Beauvaisis*, ed. A. Salmon, 3 vols., 1899–1900 (reprint, Paris: A. Picard et fils 1970–74). For a general guide to medieval French custumals, see Ourliac and Malafosse, *Le droit familial*, 22–28.

11. On the nature of customary law, see Paul Ourliac and Jean-Louis Gazzaniga, *Histoire du droit privé français de l'an mil au Code civil* (Paris: A. Michel, 1985); Ourliac and Malafosse, *Le droit familial*; G. Lepointe, *La famille dans l'ancien droit*, 2d ed. (Paris: Editions Domat-Montchrestien, 1947); and Manlio Bellomo, *The Common Legal Past of Europe, 1000–1800*, trans. Lydia G. Cochrane, vol. 4 of *Studies in Medieval and Early Modern Canon Law* (Washington, D.C.: The Catholic University of America Press, 1995).

Hence, in the reasoning of contemporaries, law naturally differed from place to place and from time to time; it naturally changed as people changed, evolved as conditions evolved. It was for this reason, above all, that the written customs of the late medieval and early modern period, Douai's included, only gradually acquired legitimacy even as guides to practice, much less as standards of behavior. It was for this reason too that until the eighteenth century, Europeans did not seriously entertain the notion that such law should be both uniform and stable and that only after the French Revolution was any continental state in a position to enforce this idea. Whatever order scholars might be able to impose on law in this period—whether the jurists of those days or the legal historians and anthropologists of today—the law itself was not a direct reflection of principle or an application of codified rules. It was, as Pierre Bourdieu has insisted, merely a description of practices born of a shifting mix of tradition, social norms, and cultural expectations, what he calls "habitus." These are not the same as abstract rules of law. And they cannot be deduced from abstractions.[12]

Douai and Its Neighbors in the North

Given the inherent malleability of a law so weakly institutionalized and given as well the presumptions of a culture that considered private law a local matter, it is no wonder that marital property and inheritance law changed as it did in this age. But there was more to this law's instability than institutional matters of this kind. Marital property and inheritance law was unstable because it tried to reconcile what were essentially incompatible property interests. By its nature, diverging devolutionary marital property law acknowledges the property rights of a potentially very extended family that includes the married couple as a pair, the husband and wife as individuals, widows and widowers, children, parents, and other kin as well. Such law thus seeks to impose order where there is potentially chaos. Order is, however, never perfectly achieved, for the claimants are too many and their needs too great. Hence, a marital property and inheritance regime of this kind is always insecure, always subject to revision as its authors reconsider their options and as competitors for the property

---

12. See, in particular, Pierre Bourdieu, "Normes et déviances: Les stratégies matrimoniales dans le système de reproduction," *Annales E.S.C.* 27 (1972): 1105–25.

realign themselves. Because socioeconomic tension was itself high in this age, marital property and inheritance laws were doubly unstable. It is, thus, no wonder that so much of the change in marital property law in this epoch took place in cities, for it was especially in cities that property itself changed form and meaning with unprecedented speed, especially in cities that the links between property and social place were most easily forged and most easily broken.

Both the tensions inherent in marital property law of the diverging devolutionary kind and those arising from the particularities of socioeconomic conditions of the age are, however, very hard to expose, for the sources needed to pursue such studies are scarce. Douai is one of the few places, possibly the only place in the late medieval urban North, that permits us to witness how people struggled to accommodate the competing claims of kin, spouses, and children and to refashion the way they structured property relations among one another as the socioeconomic environment changed. It is not, however, the only place to have left records of legal change itself. In fact, the last generation of legal scholars has made clear that legal reformation structurally like the Douaisien regularly occurred in late medieval Europe. It seems, in fact, that such reforms occurred just about everywhere historians have been able to look.

Unsurprisingly, it is in the Picard-Walloon region itself that the story of legal change most resembled the Douaisien. Robert Jacob has argued not just that law in this region was unstable, but that it followed a trajectory much like the Douaisien—that over time it tended, as the Douaisien tended, to abandon a preference for conjugality and to give greater weight to the lignage. In Jacob's words, "The constant principle of family law in the Nord in the late Middle Age [was] the retreat of the couple in the face of strengthened ties of lineage" and the "accentuation of the masculine bias of family law."[13] To make his case, Jacob dug deeply into the sources left throughout the region, in village and city, in municipal and ducal courts, providing many individual examples of legal reform resembling the Douaisien. Here let me review just two of his examples.

The original custom of Hesdin (a small city just west of Arras) seems to have been exactly like the Douaisien in that it provided the surviving spouse the same succession rights. In the words of a thirteenth-century

---

13. Jacob, *Les époux*, 319, and passim.

charter, "The survivor possessed [under custom], as his or her own property, the héritages of the deceased such that they never returned to the
heirs of the deceased after the death of the surviving spouse, but stayed
with the heir of the surviving spouse, just as is done elsewhere with respect
to after-acquired properties."[14] As early as the mid–thirteenth century,
however, this feature of custom was abolished by fiat, and Hesdin thereafter required that all héritages return to the natal family of the deceased.
Hesdin, thus, moved abruptly and early to a marital property regime that
Douaisiens would adapt only piecemeal, but the trajectory this city followed paralleled Douai's.

The example from Lille was even more like the Douaisien, although
both the record in Lille and the direction of change it charted are considerably more confused than the Douaisien. Nevertheless, it is clear that marital property law here, as in Douai, was uncomfortably poised between a
preference for conjugal and lineal rights and that it shifted, in fits and
starts, toward lineal rights as the medieval period gave way to early modern. The original custom of Lille and the surrounding area, which is described in a mid–thirteenth century written custom called the *Livre Roi-
sin*, was, however, not as much like the Douaisien as it was like norms
in nearby Flemish-speaking areas of Flanders. Custom in Lille established
a marital "community of goods," composed of all movables, all chattels,
and all property acquired during the marriage (except fiefs), but excluding
immovables brought to the marriage. Husband and wife were considered
joint managers of the fund, and the surviving spouse split the community
goods with the heirs of the deceased. Immovables brought into the marriage never joined the community of goods (as they did in Douai), however, but were returned to natal kin at the end of the marriage. But Lillois
were not confined to custom. At this time, they, like Douaisiens, could
write ravestissements par lettre, and their ravestissements were just like
the Douaisien in that they provided surviving spouses full ownership rights
of all property.

This all would change for residents of Lille itself by the sixteenth century, when the second written custom was issued (and probably before,

---

14. Cited in Jacob, *Les époux,* 242; see also Robert Jacob, "La Charte d'Hesdin (1243) et
la vocation successorale du conjoint survivant dans les pays picard et wallon," *Tijdschrift voor
Rechtsgeschiedenis* 50 (1982): 351–70; the full text of the charter rescinding this custom is edited
there and is reproduced as well in Appendix 1, pp. 419–20, of *Les époux.*

to judge from some surviving records). This document denied wives the rights they had once enjoyed as joint owners of community goods and put this property under the sole control of the husband. At the same time, custom redefined urban real estate as movables, a move that effectively enchanced the survivor's rights: "All houses and land rights in the city and échevinage of Lille are to be considered movable."[15] This was an extremely important expansion for these city dwellers, since most of the assets owned by bourgeois were urban rents, urban real estate, inventories, cash, and other movables, just as in Douai. To judge from this evidence alone, Lillois had moved closer to Douai. They had expanded the definition of the community of goods, thereby increasing the property rights of the surviving spouse, whether male or female. They had also vested managerial rights more exclusively in husbands, denying wives the joint managerial powers they had once enjoyed.

During the same period, however, Lillois had made another move that dramatically undermined the preference for conjugal rights: Lille's courts had very much restricted the scope of the written ravestissement. By the sixteenth century, these documents were interpreted to apply only to "meubles" (although the definition of movables was, we have seen, more generous than it had once been). Marriage contracts issued from the fifteenth century on even more emphatically weakened conjugal claims; they explicitly denied contract writers the ability to write ravestissements on property not covered by contract, and they superseded custom's generous definition of immovables by excluding all urban real estate from the community of goods.

In sum, then, Lillois had very much reduced conjugal rights and increased those of kin. The tensions involved in this move are, however, visible. Lillois did not unequivocally chose the line over the couple, the "famille" over the "ménage." They clumsily and contradictorily made accommodations to both.

The tensions between communal and conjugal interests on the one hand and lineal or patrilineal interests on the other was played out elsewhere in northern Europe as well, in cities more distant from Douai than either Hesdin or Lille. In what is now approximately Belgian Flanders, for example, rules that separated lineal assets from conjugal and that subordinated female property interests to male were combined with an inheri-

15. Cited in G. Lepointe, "L'évolution de la communauté entre époux dans la ville de Lille," *Revue historique de droit français et étranger*, 4th ser., 8 (1929): 524–68.

tance system rigidly communal in spirit. They did so, as was the widespread practice in the region of "community property law," by dividing the marital property into two parts. "Community goods" were defined as movables and after-acquired properties; the surviving spouse of an infertile marriage took only half this fund plus usufruct on the half credited to the deceased spouse. *Propres,* the property either spouse had brought to the marriage, were handled differently. They were held apart from this fund and returned to the surviving spouse at the end of the marriage. The rest of the marital estate (the deceased's propres and his or her half of the community goods) passed to lineal kin. Had the marriage been fertile, however, the community of goods was in some places effectively redefined to include *all* property that had either been brought to or acquired during the marriage ("universal" community). Still, the survivor got only one-half this amount, with the other half going to the children, on which the surviving spouse had only usufruct. The children were, in addition, the presumptive heirs of all that the surviving spouse acquired.[16]

Throughout this region, indeed throughout the southern Low Countries, we thus find hybridity similar to that which characterized the Picard-Walloon regimes. We can also find instances of radical instability not unlike those in Douai, Hesdin, or Lille. In Ghent, in eastern Flanders, for example, the definition of movables was expanded during the late Middle Ages, as houses in the city (but not their building sites) came to be considered movable property and thus were included in the community property account, a modification that dramatically increased the value of the properties that passed to the surviving spouse.[17] Almost next door, in Antwerp (located in the Province of Brabant), a similar move also strengthened conjugal rights. During the fifteenth and sixteenth centuries, the definition of community goods was broadened as, first, land along the Scheldt, Antwerp's great river, was counted as movable property and,

---

16. In some areas of Flanders, law was more generous to the surviving spouse. Bruges and Ypres were among several places that granted the survivor of infertile marriages half the entire estate, just as most customs in the region provided survivors of fertile marriages. Even in these two cities, however, the principle of conjugality recognized by this provision was undercut by another, for the survivor was denied usufruct on the portion of the estate that passed to "heirs."

17. The system created massive confusion, since the building lot itself was not counted as a movable; after several marriages, a house could have one set of owners, its lot another. In the sixteenth century, the custom was changed so that the lot on which a house stood could be treated as a movable; rents, however, retained their status as immovables: see Godding, *Le droit privé,* 273–74.

second, houses along with their building lots were added to the fund. In addition, it became customary to allow the proceeds of sales of propres to be invested in new properties that were treated as "after-acquired" properties. Hence, citizens of Antwerp could in effect reduce the value of propres and increase that of community of goods during the course of the marriage, thereby improving survivors' rights and reducing the claims of kin.[18]

But it was not these regional versions of community property law that would set the French standard. That was established by the laws of the "Centre," the region of Paris, Orléans, and environs, where what was called "le loi commun" reigned. Customs in this area were the basis for the sixteenth-century codifications—that of Paris being the most influential—which would, much later, themselves serve as the basis for the Code Civil. Like the customs of the southern Low Countries, these rules were, however, still very much in flux in the late Middle Ages. They too had been born in a concept of community as immortal organism, but by this period that spirit of community had to a great extent been effaced. If the occasional pre-1300 marriage contract, the odd piece of legislation, the rare court record all indicate that people in this region had once formed universal communities, even joint households, when they married, they no longer did so by about 1300.[19]

By then, the custom recognized two distinct marital property funds, rather as in the southern Low Countries. One was the community of goods, composed of movables and after-acquired properties. As in most community property regimes throughout the North, either surviving spouse was considered to have roughly equal rights to this property, although just what these rights were and just how the "community" was defined still varied enormously, depending on the place and the date of the record. Other goods, the propres that either spouse had brought to the marriage, were held apart from the community during the marriage and returned to the natal line from which they had come (according to a principle—"materna maternis, paterna paternis"—which could be used to

---

18. For the southern Low Countries, see, in general, Godding, *Le droit privé*; Yver, "Les deux groupes"; and E. M. Meijers, "Le droit ligurien de succession," *Tijdschrift voor Rechtsgeschiedenis* 5 (1924): 16–32.

19. This history, and the evidence for it, is recounted by Olivier-Martin, *Histoire de la coutume*; also see P. Petot and A. Vandenbossche, "Le statut de la femme dans les pays coutumier français du XIIIe au XVIIe siècle," in *La Femme: Recueils de la Société de Jean Bodin pour l'histoire comparative des institutions*, vol. 12 (Brussels: Editions de la librarie encyclopédique, 1962).

trace goods back several generations). Propres were generally understood to be immovable goods, but the definition was under constant pressure throughout this period, and even well into the early modern period was gradually expanded to include chattels, certain income, and other property once counted as community.[20] The husband, as head of household, managed the communal account. His management rights were absolute with respect to the movables in the account, but until the fourteenth century he could not alienate the after-acquired immovables in the fund without the express consent of the wife.[21] The husband also managed the propres of both spouses, but he could not alienate his wife's and was obligated to keep his own intact because they formed the basis of his widow's dower.

The defining feature of marital property law in this region was the dower, the *douaire coutumier*. Here, widows received not only their share of the community of goods (along with its associated debts) and their propres, but also the famous douaire coutumier, rights to the income from a portion of her late husband's propres.[22] Thought to be a legacy of the Frankish *dos ex marito*, the douaire coutumier had once implied full ownership rights but by the late Middle Ages had been reduced to usufruct.[23] In practice, the size of the Parisian douaire was usually fixed by separate marital agreements, and custom itself set no minimum, providing only that if no written contract existed, the douaire equaled one-half the value of the propres the groom had brought to the marriage. This widow's right lapsed at her death, and the properties returned to the heirs of the deceased husband—the children or, in their absence, his natal kin.

20. See, in particular, Ralph E. Giesey, "Rules of Inheritance and Strategies of Mobility in Prerevolutionery France," *American Historical Review* 82, no. 2 (1977): 271–89. Also see Barbara B. Diefendorf, *Paris City Councillors in the Sixteenth Century: The Politics of Patrimony* (Princeton: Princeton University Press, 1983), and Olivier-Martin, *Histoire de la coutume*, vol. 2. As it was generally understood in the late medieval period, the category of *propres* was limited to named assets brought to the marriage; income earned from these properties fell into the community of goods as though it was an after-acquired good. Debts either incurred in the course of the marriage or in existence at its inception were secured by community property (except that debts incurred by the wife were charged against her propres unless the husband had authorized otherwise).

21. Olivier-Martin, *Histoire de la coutume*, 189 ff.

22. Widows here also often had the right to renounce their share of the community goods on the theory that they had had no role in managing the account; they were thus shielded from the ruin that could come to them from debts incurred by the husband. By the fourteenth century, Parisien widows had the right to renounce their claim to both the movable and after-acquired property, since both funds could be encumbered at the husband's volition during the marriage. In the course of the fifteenth century, this right was restricted to noblewomen.

23. On the douaire in the southern Low Countries, see Godding, *Le droit privé*, 262 ff.

The *Pays d'Ecrit*

Although the community property law of the North, the *pays coutumier*, was hardly homogeneous, never fully communal, more conjugal than communal in practice, and less widely honored in 1400, say, than it had been in 1200, the term serves to signal that in structure law in this region was different from that in the late medieval South, the *pays d'écrit*. In the latter region, decisions about marital property relations and succession were made in rough accordance with principles of law derived from the Roman, and the rules were written down, commented upon, and authorized by legal scholars, judges, and magistrates. In this system, custom did not govern inheritance as it theoretically did in the North. Individuals had choices about how their property was used and transferred, and those people deemed owners of family assets were given much more leeway than Northerners in making these decisions. In theory, it was possible for fathers to endow children differently at marriage, for husbands to deny their widows any income from the family property, for parents to favor one child over another in estate distributions. In the North, people did not have such freedom of choice or, if they did have such choices (as Douaisiens did), they owed their freedoms to a peculiar interpretation of "community" rather than to general principles that vested absolute ownership rights in individuals.

The general principles that informed marital property law in the South have long been labeled "separatist" because the property either spouse brought to the marriage was considered distinct, and no conjugal fund was created by wedlock. The wife's dot, her contribution to the marriage, was typically returned to her when she was widowed. Although a widow often received an increase as well or usufruct on a portion of the property her husband owned at his death, she was not guaranteed this property, and it was not designed, when granted, to provide her a share in either the gains or the losses made during the marriage.

Still, the South was itself hardly more uniform than the North and was considerably less devoted to the notion of separatism than this legal typology implies. At least until about 1500, marital property law in the South was like northern communal systems in its hybridity and mobility. It was also highly susceptible to "communal" influences just as northern regimes were susceptible to "lineal" claims, and it too could bend and be bent to the needs of the people who lived under them. After 1500, we also know, the communal practices adopted in the Middle Ages survived among much of the peasantry in this region. Jean Hilaire's studies of Montpellier and its region are perhaps the best known of the recent studies that reveal these patterns. Located in the Languedoc, the heart of the pays d'écrit, where, in theory, principles of Roman law reigned, legal institutions were well developed, and lawyers and their learning wielded enormous influence, Montpellier and its environs was hardly the model of stability and dotality its legal texts promised.[24] The area's traditional dotal regime, described in the first written Custom of 1204 (reedited in 1205 and several times thereafter in the Middle Ages), was in practice regularly amended by means of the very marriage contracts that people in this region regularly used to set the terms of dotal marriage. With them, Montpellieriens and their neighbors utterly transformed, and sometimes entirely erased, the dotal system by imposing upon it rules of community property law.

The forms of community that these people constructed varied widely. Some involved the new marital couple and the parents of one spouse; these communities were usually of limited duration and hierarchical in nature. Others were what the French call *affrèrements,* more egalitarian arrangements between siblings and their spouses, or even between a married pair and a third party. There were also true "universal communities" between spouses; they first appear in fourteenth-century documents, but probably had an older history, and until their gradual disappearance during the late fifteenth century, such universal communities appeared in about a third of the contracts written in the city of Montpellier itself.

The "communitarian spirit" that Hilaire uncovered in the marital property agreements of this region was not always in evidence, however, not across the social spectrum and not through time, for people regularly modified law as they wrote their marriage agreements. In Montpellier such interventions in normative law were especially frequent during the fourteenth and fifteenth centuries, an age of periodic economic crises. Even then, however, communal principles were not adopted by all social groups. Around 1340, when "communal" amendments seem to have been especially frequent, the city's merchant class seems rarely to have issued contracts in this form. In contrast, about one-third of the city's artisan population did so.[25] By the end of the fifteenth century, however, even artisans

---

24. Jean Hilaire, *"Le régime des biens entre époux dans la région de Montpellier du début du XIIIe siècle à la fin du XVIe siècle: Contribution aux études d'histoire du droit écrit* (Montpellier: Causse, Graille and Castelnau, 1957); idem, "Vie en commun: Famille et esprit communautaire," *Nouvelle revue historique de droit française et étranger,* 4th ser., 51 (1973): 8–53.

25. Hilaire, *Le régime des biens,* 278.

had largely reverted to dotal marriage. In the nearby village of Ganges, in contrast, the evidence of communitarian property arrangements, which were in form more extreme than those of the city, mounted throughout the fifteenth century and did not subside until after 1550. In this area, such marital property agreements were made by people who shared both work and residence ("la même maison, le même pain, le même vin"), thus in practice conforming almost perfectly to the social logic of such laws.

Nowhere in Montpellier did the community property movement prosper after the 1500s, however, and by the seventeenth century, the dotal system inscribed in the region's written customs seems to have been everywhere hegemonic. The reasons for the decline are obscure, but Hilaire flatly rejects the standard juridical explanation, which attributes renewed dotality to the "second renaissance" of Roman law dating from the sixteenth century. He argues instead that the revival of interest in Roman law and the legal learning of that culture that occurred in the sixteenth century came after the decline of communitarian agreements was already in progress. On balance, Hilaire opts for "social forces" that produced a kind of "individualism" that dotal property regimes nurture and protect.[26] Until they triumphed, however—that is, until the sixteenth century— marital property law in this region bore little resemblance to the schematic produced by scholars. Until then, in Hilaire's words, "The dotal regime as it was practiced in Languedoc in the Middle Ages had scarcely the character of a separatist marital property regime."[27]

In the border areas that lay between the pays d'écrit and the pays coutumier, the instability or flexibility of law seems to have been even more marked. In the *pays de Vaud*, for example, the Swiss-French region that includes Lausanne, a dotal form of marital property law obtained, although the region is classed as a "customary" region. The dots that wives brought to their marriages were under their husband's absolute managerial control, although the women technically retained full ownership of the dots and claimed them, without encumbrances, in their widowhood. In addition, by custom the wife received an *augmentum* (increase) on her dot, payable in cash and in most marriage contracts set at 50 percent of the dot, a payment that recalls the spirit of the northern regimes. Recalling that spirit even more explicitly, husbands began in the sixteenth century

26. Ibid., 312.
27. Ibid., 212.

to give their wives morning gifts (the *Morgengabe*) as well.[28] The custom also granted widows an option that further recalls the northern systems: they could renounce their dot and augmentum, choosing literally to "stay"—to reside—in their deceased husbands' households, and most widows seem to have done so until they remarried.

Still another insecure compromise between communal and dotal principles was under negotiation in the Bordelais, in southeastern France. Crossroads of several legal systems and home of diverse agricultural and urban economies, this region was the home of a thirteenth-century written custom that described a dotal-like system, one nonetheless heavily inflected by the communitarian spirit of the North. The subsequent written custom, which dates from the sixteenth century, seemed to have suppressed these "northern" influences, for it described an almost purely dotal system, with all the usual appurtenances. Between the two dates, however, written "custom" was in practice ignored as frequently as it was honored. According to a recent study of marriage contracts written throughout the region from about 1450 to 1550, people in the Bordelais amended law in several different ways, sometimes preserving (if only barely) the spirit of the dotal regime described by custom but as often jettisoning it entirely. In total, 76 percent of the marriage contracts registered in Bordeaux and the Bordelais in this century subverted the dotal system by creating at least a limited community of goods.[29] The choice of marital property regime seems to have varied directly with social place. Urbanites married differently from residents of the countryside, rich differently from poor, merchants not the same as landowners or peasants.

The Duchy of Burgundy, which lies right on the border of the pays d'écrit and the pays coutumier, provides a last, particularly telling, example. The first compilation of custom for the region, dated 1459, described a marital property regime very much like the Parisian in that it mixed a dotal-like with a communal regime. It granted widows both half of the community of goods, made up of movables and after-acquired properties

---

28. The augmentum, apparently accepted as customary in the Middle Ages, was in the early modern period awarded only to widows who had marriage contracts that required the payment. Unlike the douaire coutumier in the "Centre" or the usufruct on immovables due widows in Ghent, for example, the augmentum in this area was often paid only if the widow remarried, and in the Middle Ages no restrictions were put on widows who remarried. The morning gift is a payment to the bride by the groom after consummation of the marriage.

29. Jacques Lafon, *Les époux bordelais 1450–1550: Régimes matrimoniaux et mutations sociales* (Paris: S.E.V.P.E.N., 1972), 183 ff.

along with a small douaire coutumier, usufruct on the propres of the deceased husband equal to a third of the bride's dot. In compensation for the fact that she had had no managerial rights over this property during the marriage—that her husband could use, even lose, this property without consulting her—a widow in Burgundy could, just as a widow in Paris, renounce her claim to the community goods in order to protect herself from the creditors her husband may have left behind. In doing so, however, she also lost her claim to the douaire coutumier and kept only the dot she had brought to the marriage, a limitation unknown in Paris and one most commentators have seen as draconian.

Marital property rules in this region were not, however, as settled as this written custom implies. Before 1459, marital property law in this region had fluctuated wildly, from place to place and period to period. Even after this text was issued, the rules of marital property law and succession that it contained were regularly rewritten in practice. Some people adhered to more local norms, which varied in subtle, and not so subtle, ways from the text; some issued marriage contracts or wills that even more forthrightly subverted the written norms. Legal historians have traditionally ascribed this instability to the region's location. Situated as it was in the border of the pays d'écrit and the pays coutumier, Burgundy's law was, they have argued, confused.

In a series of recent studies, however, Georges Chevrier has argued a different case.[30] The county's location where two legal regimes met did not, he contends, produce the instability or the hybrid quality of Burgundian marriage law. Rather, location simply allowed a more open, more visible, and more vigorous display of the tensions that lay at the heart of all European marital property regimes. What was different about Burgundy was not the impotence of law, but law's ability to contain and display contradictions that almost everywhere else were better suppressed. The system inscribed as customary in 1459 was, thus, not a moment in a chaotic legal history but a kind of compromise, "a middle way, more modern and more moderate, which played its part regarding the interests of the wife, at the same time safeguarding the interests of the family."[31]

---

30. See, in particular, G. Chevrier, "Sur quelques caractères de l'histoire du régime matrimonial dans la Bourgogne ducale aux diverse phases de son développement," *Les droits des gens mariés*, vol. 27 of *Mémoires de la Société pour l'Histoire du Droit et des Institutions des anciens pays bourguignons, comtois et romands* (Dijon: Faculté de droit des sciences économiques de Dijon, 1966), 257–85.

31. Ibid., 265.

Rather than as a story of how a diminished form of community law clumsily displaced Roman, as most legal scholars have read it, Chevrier thus sees the Burgundian evidence as testimony to the contradictions inherent in marital property law, which must regulate the interests of lineage and household, male and female, in a social world that is fractured and changing and in a legal culture where rules are not firm and authorities are not well established.

> It is thus that in its historical evolution, from the fourteenth century [forward], the Burgundian marital property regime, despite its tendency toward systematization and its conversion into a particular kind of community property law with the [customary] douaire, never ceased to evidence contradiction. It remained at the center of an incessant struggle between the structure of the small domestic family and that of the large, lineal family. Its variations do not reflect just the ups and downs of the economy, the rise of Roman law or the transformations of moral life. They reflect the permanent oscillation of family rights between a conception favorable to the financial interests of the couple and its household . . . and a tendency toward a reinforcement of the patrimonial prerogatives of the lineage.[32]

Law's Social Meanings

So much, we might conclude, for the sanctity of law. The more important lesson to draw from these examples—or the lesson that is more pertinent here—is, however, that people in late medieval Europe, at least in the Flemish- and French-speaking world, did not manage marital property relations according to unchanging rules, whether written or unwritten, whether based on ancient codes or long use. They took every opportunity to adjust and readjust the norms they had inherited, the principles their lawyers divined, the rules their magistrates handed down. And they did so without major opposition from kin, lawyers, or governors. Of course, this is not to say that institutional histories did not matter, that political circumstances did not help determine the range of choices any individual had when negotiating a marriage or arranging an estate. It is, however, to point out that late medieval people in this part of Europe were considerably less attached to legal abstractions than their historians have usually been.

32. Ibid., 283–84.

Hard questions remain, however. Why were late medieval Europeans inclined to intervene in established traditions so energetically, and with what effects? Is it possible that they did so simply when they could, as Chevrier argues, in an unceasing and fruitless effort to establish equity among mutually exclusive interests? Whatever the merits of such an explanation, it cannot be sufficient. It begs the question of why people chose as they did—why for a given person at a given time one set of interests would have seemed more important, one set of needs more pressing. In Douai, I have argued, people chose more lineal marital property regimes when preservation of wealth seemed more urgent than its acquisition, when social place seemed harder to acquire and more difficult to protect, when social mobility felt less like opportunity and more like risk. To move from custom to the new regime required, however, more than a realignment of priorities. It required, we have seen, the suppression of one social and gender imaginary and the elevation of another.

Little from the records that have been left in other places or from the studies that have been done to trace legal histories elsewhere directly address these issues, so we cannot know whether the Douaisien story of legal change and its social implications were like the stories that took place in Dijon or Lille, in Montpellier or Bordeaux. Nevertheless, the Douaisien evidence can teach us much about the possible social meaning of legal change elsewhere, about the ways in which the instability of law in the county of Burgundy, for example, was not simply a measure of tensions inherent in the structure of the law; about what kind of "social forces," to which Hilaire appeals, may have been at work as Montpellierians chose to eliminate community property provisions from their marriage contracts—and about what was not at issue as well. The Douai story can teach us even more about what we need to know to write a satisfactory social history of law in these places.

Let us begin by returning to the structure of law itself. Legal historians have frequently assumed that social meanings are directly reflected in law's structure. In such an argument, regimes like those dominant in northern Europe in this age were not just communal or egalitarian in structure; they bespoke social ethics and practices that were communal or conjugal, collateral, and egalitarian. In contrast, the dotal regimes of the South reflected a social reality that was in spirit lineal, separatist, patrilineal, hierarchical, and patriarchal (i.e., male-dominant). To be sure, we now know that the line between the North and South was less clear than this typology implies and that within each region there was wide variation, but this evidence has served such scholars precisely as proof of their point: that law changed to reflect social circumstances.[33] Thus, for example, when peasants in the Languedoc chose to add communal provisions to their marriage contracts, they were expressing the experiences of a social world in which the "manse" was the place where all residents—men, women, and children—shared "le même pain, le même vin." When merchants in Bordeaux or officeholders in Paris chose to label assets patrilineal, they were seeking to preserve capital (cultural and economic) in economically viable units and to reserve them for the individual males whose social status had to be guaranteed.

Although there is much to recommend this reasoning, in this form the claim assumes too much. It assumes that law is monolithic, that it encodes a single social logic and records a set of social practices that are uniformly experienced. Or it assumes that law is the inscription of the powerful who share and are positioned to impose this single logic. It also assumes that law perfectly captures social meaning, that law, in its structure, is an unmediated reflection of social experience. The evidence from Douai exposes the fallacies in such reasoning.

Let us once again review the Douaisien case. Neither Douai's original law nor its replacement embodied a single, unadulterated social vision. Douai's custom was, to be sure, aggressively conjugal in comparison with others of the day, if by that we mean that it privileged the conjugal pair over natal kin as property owners. In that sense, the reformation of law was, as Jacob put it, "the kin's revenge on the couple."[34] But this does not

---

33. This kind of reasoning is implicit in many of the best legal histories of the period. See, for example, Jean Gilissen, "Le statut de la femme dans l'ancien droit belge," in *La Femme: Recueils de la Société de Jean Bodin pour l'histoire comparative des institutions*, vol. 12 (Brussels: Editions de la librarie encyclopédique, 1962), 256–57: "One of the most remarkable features [of urban marital property law in the southern Low Countries in this age] is certainly the tendency toward equality between the sexes, both within marriage and outside of it." Also see, more generally, Ourliac and Malafosse, *Le droit familial*, and Godding, *Le droit privé*. For an effort to tie legal structure more specifically to concrete social experience, see Charles Donahue, Jr., "What Causes Fundamental Legal Ideas? Marital Property in England and France in the Thirteenth Century," *Michigan Law Review* 78 (1979–80): 59–88.

On the general difficulty of reconciling the work of legal and social historians, especially in medieval French historiography, see Jacques Le Goff, "Histoire médiévale et histoire du droit: Un dialogue difficile," *Storia sociale e dimensione giuridica: Strumenti d'indagine e ipotesi di lavoro; Atti dell'incontro di studio, Firenze, 26–27 aprile 1985* (Milan: Giuffrè, 1986), and Paul Ourliac, "Histoire nouvelle et histoire du droit," *Revue historique de droit français et étranger* 70, no. 3 (1992): 363–71.

34. The phrase appears on p. 238 and passim: Jacob, *Les époux*.

necessarily imply that the Douaisiens who married under custom were hostile to their kin, that they saw parents and children, brothers and sisters, as unworthy competitors for their wealth. Custom was, in fact, not at all hostile to lineality as such. After all, custom guaranteed one-half of all the property in the household of the deceased, no matter its origin or nature, to the lineal kin if the marriage had been infertile. And custom provided living children of a marriage an equal share in the entire estate left by the last surviving spouse. It also allowed fathers (and their widows) unlimited freedom to give conjugal property away during their lives, a privilege that was regularly used to limit custom's capacity to move property away from the line. The system did, admittedly, put some forms of lineality at risk by allowing all children of the deceased to inherit equally, even those born of another marriage, and it recognized only living heirs, not their heirs, thus effectively disinheriting a descendent line established by a deceased heir. But these provisions were not so much a repudiation of the notion of lineality as a particular conception of it.

Nor was the new marital property, in practice, hostile to conjugality. While we have seen that the change in marital property law reimagined the roles of husband and wife, both with respect to conjugal property and to the business of the household, the new system did not treat the conjugal unit or the household it formed as unimportant, even as secondary, to the interests of the natal lineage. On the contrary. I will return to these points in the conclusion; here let me simply point out that to distinguish male property interests from female is not, in itself, to deny the economic, social, or moral importance of the marriage between male and female. It is to reassign their tasks and reconstruct their union, not necessarily to undermine conjugality itself.

Moreover, the old regime was not truly egalitarian unless by that we mean simply that children were equal heirs of their parents in intestate successions. No more was it egalitarian with respect to gender, unless by that we are referring simply to the radical equivalence of widow and widower in intestate successions. We might also profitably pause to ponder what it means to say that male interests were privileged under the new regime. Although the system did provide certain men new advantages, it did so at the price of disempowering others, husbands and childless widowers chief among them. We might even argue that the only true winners in this story were fathers—*some* fathers—not men. In this sense, the new laws were patrilineal, but it is worth noting that not all men were "paters" and that no man was always or exclusively a "pater." "Patrilineal" in this sense implies a positioning of certain males to females that puts specific interests, labeled male, above those labeled female. It does not mean all men can claim that position. Finally, it is not entirely clear that women qua women suffered a net loss under the new marital property regime. Certainly, they lost many of the property and legal rights they had enjoyed as widows, but in return they gained important protections as wives, and as we have seen, as widows they preserved property rights that were far from neglible.

Thus, while the two Douaisien marital property regimes were indeed different, their structural differences cannot be reduced to a contest between a social ethic that was conjugal and one that was lineal, between communal social values and separatist values, or between egalitarian ideals and hierarchical, especially "male-dominant," notions. Neither Douaisien regime, nor the reformation itself, can intelligibly be expressed in these terms, in part because neither regime was entirely one or the other, in part because the terms themselves do not fully capture the complex relations among family members described by either regime.

These terms fail for another reason as well: they describe only structural relations among those with claims to family property and do not take account of the way their meaning depends upon the particular social circumstances. Even if in structure a marital property regime is egalitarian, in that, for example, it provides widow and widower equal succession rights, gives wives an equal voice in management of conjugal assets, or perhaps grants wives veto power over alienations of patrimonial properties, this is not to say that the law is the direct reflection of women's economic power, still less that it is the product of a society in which women are the social equals of men.

Let us look, by way of illustration, at the radically conjugal form of community property law in Douai. In this situation, we can certainly argue, some women (propertied widows above all) would have enjoyed genuine benefits—wealth, of course, but also the authority to manage it and the prestige that came from such power. But these benefits derived not just from the property itself but from the social world in which the assets were located. It was precisely because conjugal pairs in cities such as Douai lived and worked independently, apart from parents and kin, that the female survivor of such a marriage gained independence and authority. As heir to and uncontested manager of the dwellings, inventories, cash, plate, jewels, and rents that constituted the bulk of urban wealth, widows could, like Franchoise Rohard, disperse as they chose wealth that had been their husbands', selecting beneficiaries, even heirs, at will; they could also trade inherited goods for other kinds of wealth; they could change occupation, residence, and social place with relative ease. Even in community property regimes less radically conjugal than the Douaisien—regimes, for example, like those in Flanders proper—widows had powerful rights as managers, if not as owners, of a significant portion of the conjugal estate. There too, if the property was mercantile and movable, widows gained real autonomy.

But community property law in itself does not guarantee these rights, not even a community property law that is conjugally inflected like the Douaisien. Let us consider, for example, how the original Douaisien regime might have operated in the countryside, in a peasant community where the chief asset was land rights, a community like those where the Douaisien system probably originated. In such a place, this legal system would not necessarily give women—or men—the kind of autonomy and authority we associate with property rights. To a peasant, male or female, it would matter little whether the holding was entirely vested in the conjugal pair (or its survivor); in a wider, not coresident, kin group; or in a single male and his male heir. In any of these cases, the head of household would not be "free" to use the manse or to dispose of its wealth in any way other than as required by the general norms of the community and the material realities of the day. Peasant proprietors in this age were, after all, bound to land and effectively rendered socially and geographically immobile because markets for land, labor, and produce were then so undeveloped. Sucession rights might guarantee social place in such societies, but they did not provide modern ownership benefits. Thus, even if the conjugal pair or its survivor technically possessed the manse independently, they effectively had fewer rights than someone in an urban setting, where property was movable and exchangeable. For women, the contrast between city and country would have been greater still. A widow in the countryside whose claim to her husband's estate assumed her continued residence in his household and preservation of his land rights would have gained considerably less autonomy than was granted Franchoise Rohard by the ravestissement for which she fought. Bound to the land she inherited and effectively to her male relatives on whom she depended for labor, technical expertise, and voice in village affairs, such a widow might reasonably have welcomed the limitations—and freedoms—of a dotal system.

Let us consider as well how the effects of a more lineal system might be determined by the particular social setting in which it operated. In certain settings, such separatist marital property regimes undoubtedly worked to contain women as some community property would not have. Christiane Klapisch-Zuber's studies of Renaissance Florence have, for example, laid bare the sternly patriarchal character of the dotal regime as practiced by this city's merchant class. In this city, women were positioned as nothing more than carriers of mercantile property, so dispossessed that they were never granted ownership even of the trousseau that their husbands titularly provided them. As a result, women were rendered mere objects in men's households—as girls, those of their fathers; as wives, those of their husbands; and as widows, those of their brothers. So extreme was male dominance and so confined were women that mothers did not even take chief responsibility for rearing their own children; men managed those matters, often even hiring the nurses who fed and cared for the infants their wives bore.[35]

In early modern France, we also know, as marital property law was steadily rendered more lineal, women lost many of the rights they had once enjoyed both as wives and widows. Barbara Diefendorf has argued that the change in law was made deliberately, to disempower widows, that in Paris during the sixteenth century, men intensified the separatist features of marital property law precisely to assure that their widows had little autonomy even over community goods.[36] Sarah Hanley has similarly characterized the "family-state compact," which began to take shape in northern France at this time, as a defeat for women. According to its terms, men were granted greater control over family property (and family members), in exchange for their submission to state control in other arenas. Although the pact was not specifically designed to control women, women figured centrally in the drama, and many of the tensions that resulted from the shift of power were focused on male-female relations, on the terms of gender hierarchy itself.[37] According to Robert Jacob, the subordination of women was also a leitmotif of the legal change that took place throughout Picardy-Wallonia in this age: "Replacing the formal

---

35. Christine Klapisch-Zuber, *Women, Family and Ritual in Renaissance Italy*, trans. Lydia Cochrane (Chicago: University of Chicago Press, 1985); see, in particular, the articles "The Griselda Complex," "The Cruel Mother," and "Blood Parents, Milk Parents."

36. Diefendorf, *Paris City Councillors*.

37. Sarah Hanley, "Engendering the State: Family Formation and State Building in Early Modern France," *French Historical Studies* 16, no. 1 (Spring 1989): 4–27; idem, "Family and State in Early Modern France: The Marriage Pact,'" in *Connecting Spheres: Women in the Western World, 1500 to the Present*, ed. Marilyn J. Boxer and Jean H. Quataert (New York and Oxford: Oxford University Press, 1987), 53–63.

equality of spouses in succession and of brothers and sisters in inheritance was an asymmetrical system in which sons and husbands were the dynamic element, but daughters and wives were the passive element in the transmission of goods within the family. In effect, lineality ("la parenté") and masculinity progressed together."[38]

As other scholars have pointed out, however, a lineal marital property regime does not, in itself, determine the character of gender relations. Stanley Chojnacki has argued that in Venice, where marital property laws were in structure as patriarchal as the Florentine, husbands and wives regularly cooperated in management of the household and its assets and that they achieved what other scholars have characterized as "affectionate" marriages.[39] Still other observers of the dotal systems characteristic of Italy's merchant elite of this age have argued that even in the abstract, dotal regimes might be "better" for women than community property regimes because they protect wives from the misadventures or ill will of their husbands and give them, as wives, property of their own.[40] Barbara Harris has dissected the workings of the English aristocratic family in this age, showing that even in these classically patriarchal structures, there was room for conjugal love, feminine pleasure, and even a kind of female autonomy.[41] Marianne Danneel has argued that in Ghent, where widows had only usufruct rights on immovables and had to split movables with lineal heirs of their late spouses, widows nonetheless often actively managed business and financial affairs left to them and their children.[42] Even in Douai, where the move from old custom clearly cost women some au-

38. Jacob, *Les époux,* 239.

39. Stanley Chojnaki, "Dowries and Kinsmen in Early Renaissance Venice," *Journal of Interdisciplinary History* 5 (1975): 571–600, and idem, " 'The Most Serious Duty': Motherhood, Gender, and Patrician Culture in Renaissance Venice," in *Refiguring Woman: Perspectives on Gender and the Italian Renaissance,* ed. Marilyn Migiel and Julian Schiesari (Ithaca, N.Y.: Cornell University Press, 1991).

40. See Diane Owen Hughes, "From Brideprice to Dowry in Mediterranean Europe," *Journal of Family History* 3 (Fall 1978): 262–96; also see Thomas Kuehn, "Law, Death and Heirs in the Renaissance: Repudiation of Inheritance in Florence," *Renaissance Quarterly* 45, no. 3 (Autumn 1992): 484–517, and Julius Kirshner, "Wives' Claims Against Insolvent Husbands in Late Medieval Italy," in *Women of the Medieval World,* ed. Julius Kirshner and Suzanne F. Wempel (Oxford: Oxford University Press, 1985).

41. Barbara J. Harris, *Of Noble and Gentle Birth* (Oxford: Oxford University Press, forthcoming).

42. Danneel, *Weduwen en wezen in het laat-middeleeuwse Gent* (Leuven and Apeldoorn: Garant, 1995), esp. 269–70, where she comments that the customary inheritance law "concentrated significant property in the hands of widows." Citing Gilissen, "Le statut de la femme," she remarks on the "egalitarianism" of the gender order thus implied.

thority, there is no doubt that their losses came with some gains.[43] A widow whose husband's estate was heavily encumbered, whose estate was invested in a business she could not manage, whose estate was jointly owned by his kin—such a woman would surely have preferred the guarantees of the Douaisien reprise to the uncertainties of the ravestissement.

In structure, then, legal regimes only set the boundaries of social possibility; they do not determine its content. They do, however, have social meaning, the more so in eras such as the late medieval, when legal institutions allowed extraordinary flexibility. The problem for historians, then, is to learn to use legal sources as entries into social process, rather than as perfect representations of social experience. The evidence from Douai provides one example of how law both mapped and helped shape social practice, but there too, as we have seen, terms such as "egalitarian" and "hierarchical" do not capture the social meaning of either legal regime or of the legal transformation itself. To reveal social meaning, we have had to look for more complex social logics and to develop more situated analyses of the legal transformation.

To uncover law's social meanings elsewhere, we will have to be similarly precise, but there can be no doubt that what we have learned in Douai can help. Let us look, for example, at one of the most distinctive patterns of legal change in this age—the way that urbanites, particularly rich urbanites, preferred lineal over communal marital property regimes. It was they among Europe's commoners, legal historians have told us, who first moved from communal to more lineal regimes, and it was the richest among them who did so first. Similarly, in regions where more lineal regimes had been bequeathed to ordinary people, it was, again, the richest urbanites who appear to have been most eager to preserve them. In late medieval Montpellier, for example, merchants clung to the dotal system prescribed by written custom, while peasants and small artisans made different, more communal arrangements.[44] In the Bordelais, it was also artisans and peasants who added what legal scholars call "community property" provisions to their contracts; urban merchants did not do so, preferring the separatist, more lineal regimes prescribed by written custom.[45] In Paris, where custom automatically provided certain protections

---

43. Jacob acknowledges these gains but concludes that they were the price men paid to secure their new privileges as heads of families.

44. Hilaire, *Le régime des biens.*

45. Lafon, *Les époux bordelais.*

to lineal assets, elites worked assiduously from the sixteenth century on to extend these protections by reducing the widow's control over the goods labeled "community property" and to limit the power a widow had over her dower.[46] In Florence, rich merchants made the strictly dotal regimes prescribed by custom even more patrilineal in practice than they were in form.[47] And, among Europe's landed aristocracy, patrilineally inflected marital property regimes were, of course, the norm. Few went so far as some of the English aristocracy, it seems, but in this age all gave preference to male-defined lineages over the conjugal pair or, even, over co-lateral kin.[48]

The Douaisien evidence has taught us, however, to be cautious with such evidence, for in this city, the rich were not inherently more disposed to prefer lineal regimes: although the richest Douaisiens were disproportionately represented among the writers of marriage contracts and wills, they were accompanied by thousands of artisans and small shopkeepers who similarly chose more lineal regimes. Even more significantly, it was only a portion of the rich who made this choice; most of Douai's merchants, and a great many of its rentiers and professionals, married and passed property under the customary regime until the late fifteenth or early sixteenth century. Whether the elites in other cities of French- and Flemish-speaking Europe were as relatively slow to adopt patrilineal inheritance systems remains to be seen, and some of the evidence we have suggests that they were not, or at least they were not joined by artisans and shopkeepers as they were in Douai; until we have assembled records as rich as the Douaisien, however, we simply cannot know for sure.

What we can be certain of, however, is that a preference for patrilineality was not acquired with wealth itself; the preference had to be learned. Merchants in fifteenth-century Montpellier and Bordeaux may have been as devoted to patrilineally inflected arrangements as they appear to have been, but we shall need to know more about the institutional and social circumstances in which they made their choices in order to explain their preferences. We cannot assume, as has too readily been assumed, that they chose as they did simply because they could and that their choices reflected

---

46. See, in particular, Diefendorf, *Paris City Councillors.*

47. Klapisch-Zuber, *Women, Family and Ritual;* and Anthony Molho, *Marriage Alliance in Late Medieval Florence* (Cambridge: Harvard University Press, 1994).

48. For a general discussion of this pattern, see Henri Bresc, "Europe: Town and Country (Thirteenth–Fifteenth Century)," in *A History of the Family,* vol. 1, ed. André Burguière et al. (Cambridge: Polity and Blackwell, 1996), 430–66.

an inherent taste for lineality, social hierarchy, and male dominance. After all, the "line" is not ignored in communal regimes; hierarchy existed in all the marital property regimes available to Europeans of this age; males were preferred in all of them. To choose a more lineal regime was, then, to choose a certain kind of hierarchy and to privilege certain kinds of gendered behavior. It was not to opt for "hierarchy" over "egalitarianism" or "men" over "women."

Douai's old custom, although born in a rural society because there the need to maintain the "manse" superseded other needs, was assiduously preserved in the city because it so well accorded with the dominant social imaginary there as well. It served to protect a particularly urban kind of household economy, one made up largely of movable goods, most of them conceived of as working assets that had to be attentively managed. In the social logic that underlay custom, the appropriate manager of these goods was the head of household, someone skilled, mature, responsible, and devoted to the tasks at hand. Normally, that was the male head of household. In his absence, it was his wife or widow, his "deputy," but the social logic and the law were perfectly able to accommodate the notion that she would abdicate her responsibilities in favor of a new spouse, who was—in theory—able to assume the tasks she had inherited and better able than she to attend to the household economy.

For all its logic, this system was, however, replete with contradictions about social and gender order. It allowed social mobility—upward and downward—of extraordinary kinds, as new spouses acquired wealth accumulated by former spouses, as children with no "blood" claim to household wealth were granted shares in it, as "blood" children were denied equal rights in family estates. The system also destabilized gender hierarchy, for it positioned widows to own and manage property as no other marital property regime of the day did, while—at the same time—it required wives to relinquish *all* property rights to their husbands.

The legal regime inscribed in marriage contracts, in contrast, imagined a household made up to a significant degree of immovable goods, property that served as investment capital rather than as working assets, property that had not so much to be managed as preserved. Such a system limited social mobility, for it made it possible to tie specific individuals to specific properties, thus assuring them the social place that came with guaranteed possession of a house, a shop, trade rights, jewelry, luxurious clothing, and furnishings. It also resolved a central contradiction of custom concerning gender, for it did not construct the absurdly contradictory woman of custom who was, as wife, without property rights yet, as widow, fully possessed of them. Instead, this regime consistently limited women's access to property, making them more carriers of property than creators of it.

Still, the new regime was hardly tension-free. Even in its "pure" form— a state rarely achieved in late medieval Douai—it did not relinquish everything to the line and did not entirely dispossess women. Moreover, it complicated asset management, multiplied the occasions for disputes among kin, disempowered husbands and childless widowers, and set husband against wife with respect to marital property. The decision to replace one legal regime with another was, thus, a fraught process, a long and never fully completed journey with many detours and dead ends. When made, however, even in the leisurely way it was made in Douai, the legal reform implied changes of enormous import in social and gender imaginaries.

Surely imaginaries like these were at play elsewhere in Europe where people had some opportunities to design their own marital property and inheritance arrangements and where commerce had become a way of life. Surely in Bordeaux or Ghent or Montpellier, when people chose one kind of marital property arrangement over another, it was not just a matter of one legal regime versus another, not even a matter of whether kin should outrank the conjugal pair and whether women should ever have independent property rights. Surely it was a matter of how property would be defined; how people would link themselves to others by means of property; whether they would regard marriage as a vehicle for perpetuating individual status rather than the moment of household formation; whether they would come to see women principally as carriers rather than as creators of property.

Marie, Franchoise, and Their Sisters

The Ministers of Orphans v. Marie Du Bosquiel

In 1434, the same year that Franchoise Rohard was brought to court by her three stepchildren, Marie Du Bosquiel, the widow of Colart Belot, was sued by Douai's Ministers of Orphans, men charged by the city to oversee the financial affairs of minor children who had lost a parent.[1] The ministers were suing Du Bosquiel to prevent her from exiting her husband's estate. Were she to prevail, she would take the reprise and douaire of 100 francs 34 livres, and a life rent of 30 livres per year (plus her clothing, jewels, and "chambre") promised in her marriage contract, which had been written just four years previously.[2] The children would then be sole heirs of their father's (remaining) estate, an estate already heavily in debt and now to be further depleted by the removal of Du Bosquiel's reprise and douaire.

The suit began when, as the law required, Du Bosquiel filed in court to "seize" her husband's property so that she could collect her reprise and douaire. In making their bid to stop her, the ministers argued that she had not complied with a provision of the law demanding that widows planning to exit an estate leave untouched all property in it until they actually had taken their promised douaire and reprise. Du Bosquiel, the ministers asserted, had taken delivery of some horses due her husband

---

1. AMD, FF 289, fols. 86r and v, and 98, 112v (1434). Not all children in Douai had such protectors. Only those who had previously been granted firm inheritance rights, perhaps by a will or their parents' marriage contract, were represented by these officials when one parent died. These children had what children in Douai customarily did not have—devolutionary rights— and it was the job of the ministers to see that these rights were honored.

2. AMD, FF 610/1860 (17 January 1430).

and had allowed a cloak that had been his to be sold or given away. The widow denied the charges. She countered that the horses had been delivered before her husband's death and that the cloak had not been sold but had simply been returned to the woman whose it was, a friend who had left it at the house when she had visited Belot on his deathbed. Du Bosquiel won the argument and was allowed to take her reprise and douaire out of the estate. The children were thus left only Belot's remaining property, and with it came all the debts Belot had owed.

Du Bosquiel thus demanded and won the protections provided by the new marital property regime in Douai. In contrast to Franchoise Rohard, who had so eagerly sought to "stay" in her husband's estate, Du Bosquiel rejected this right. She did so, of course, because the estate her husband had left was burdened by onerous debts, as Le Libert's had not been. The significance of this case here is not, however, that it reveals the ways the new law could advantage widows, but that it exposes the confusions attending the shift from old law to new and the way the new preserved vestiges of the old.

The confusions become evident when we turn to the details of the court testimony itself, for in this document we see that Du Bosquiel herself was not so devoted to the new principles of law as it first appears. In addition to her reprise and douaire, Du Bosquiel also claimed rights to run a fish business that had been conjugal property (but that she may have run alone as "feme sole"). To make this claim, a claim that the right of reprise and douaire patently excluded, Du Bosquiel had to return to custom's principle of conjugal unity. In court she argued that "according to the law and custom of Douai," she was "a citizen by virtue of her husband and that, in demanding execution of her marriage contract [i.e., her reprise and douaire], she did not lose the right of citizenship that allowed her to sell herrings on her own account, just like others, without being held accountable or liable for her deceased husband's debts."[3]

As she exited her husband's estate, free of its debts and with the property promised in her marriage contract intact, Du Bosquiel thus claimed the right to a part of that estate. Had Douai's échevins strictly observed the principles of the new legal regime, her claim would have failed, for the rights to the fish business belonged to her late husband's household, which

3. AMD, FF 289, fol. 86v.

she had expressly chosen to exit. The Du Bosquiel case thus sits uncomfortably—and illogically—between two different conceptions of marital property relations, one that treats husband and wife as a unit and one that treats husband and wife as distinct persons. That Du Bosquiel managed to sustain her odd claim in court is surely evidence of the instability of marital property and inheritance law in mid–fifteenth century Douai, a measure of how vaguely Douaisiens then demarcated old principles from new.

The Ministers of Orphans, however angrily they opposed Du Bosquiel's claim, seem to have been similarly poised between old and new. They brought their suit as trustees for the children of Du Bosquiel and Belot, men charged with the fiduciary responsibility of seeing that the children's property was protected. They were thus positioned as representatives of the husband and his line, against Du Bosquiel, who was positioned as a threat to the children. In structure then, this case perfectly expresses the logic of the new marital property regime: husband and wife are separate beings, representing distinct (and potentially antagonistic) property interests. Yet, in bringing their suit, the ministers invoked old custom's notions of conjugal unity, the idea that a husband and wife were one indivisible economic unit. In fact, they claimed that Du Bosquiel had an obligation to remain in the estate precisely because the estate was in debt.[4]

Du Bosquiel thus exited her husband's estate, leaving the creditors its meager remains and, at least ostensibly, leaving her children paupers. In fact, however, Du Bosquiel did not abandon her children. She took them with her, and she took care of them. When she remarried Collart Tallon about two years later, in 1437, she stipulated in her marriage contract that she and her new husband would support them. "[They] were obligated, at their expense, to support and raise the children, to send them to school,

---

4. There is yet another peculiarity of this case. The ministers bringing this suit were not just trustees for the children but creditors to the estate itself, for it was to them that Belot had owed money, and it was they who would have been paid from the reprise and douaire Bosquiel might have been compelled to leave in the estate. Just how they might have tried to justify their ambiguous position, as both protectors of the children and creditors of the estate, we do not know. They may, however, have seen no contradiction. Yes, they would personally benefit if Bosquiel were forced to stay in the estate, but that did not disqualify them as representatives of the children. If they forced the mother to stay in the estate, they would establish the children in life, just as they were obligated to do.

to see that they learned a trade, to dress and nourish them, to give them food, drink, and clothing and all their necessities, until they were married . . . or reached the age of eighteen years."[5]

In addition, Du Bosquiel left 60 francs to her children, making each of them the heir of the other if there were no children born of her marriage to Tallon. Had Du Bosquiel stayed in her first husband's estate, she would not have been in a position to give her children this financial help. In debt herself, she probably would have neither found a new husband nor had anything left to bequeath her children. The best way to protect her children, she must have reasoned when she left Belot's estate in 1434, would be to protect herself. As it turned out, she was right.

A confusing mixture of old custom's notion about conjugal unity and the new law's ideas about the distinction between a wife's and a husband's property, this case probably would have had another outcome one hundred years later. By then, the échevins would surely have refused the strange logic Du Bosquiel offered in claiming both the fish franchise and her reprise; for their part, the ministers might have known better than even to attempt the case, so clear would have been the principle of law that protected a widow's right to the reprise.

Still, even in the mid–sixteenth century, people in Douai had not entirely jettisoned the norms of old custom and had not entirely resolved the tension between these two different notions of marital property relations. Many people still married by the old rules; a few even wrote ravestissements par lettre. Even the contracts and wills most propertied Douaisiens issued were not extreme in their preference for lineality or for male interests: daughters were not denied lineal goods (héritages) in early modern Douai; wives and widows technically owned property, movable and immovable, in their own names; widows still had the option of staying in their husbands' estates and managing the assets, if only as dowagers. Similarly, the social practices that custom had so closely tracked would not quickly disappear from Douai. Certainly in the sixteenth century, and probably in the seventeenth as well, artisan and merchant households often still functioned as production units, and wives took active roles in them. Just as married women had long done, some wives still bought and sold wool and cloth; they made clothing, foodstuffs, and leathergoods for sale in local and regional markets; and they assumed their husbands' businesses when widowed.

5. AMD, FF 613/2082 (27 April 1437).

There was, however, a subtle, but significant, difference between the early modern and the medieval. By the later period, when the principles of the marriage contract had become hegemonic, women no longer took on such tasks with the full authorization old custom had provided. Over time, the ambiguities of the legal situation made it harder for women to assert rights, harder to seize the legal privileges that had once clearly empowered them to perform these jobs. Hence, gradually if unevenly, both the tasks and the rights associated with them became marginalized. Women were supposed to carry property, to hold it for their children or their natal kin or to provide it for their husbands' use. They were not supposed to actively manage assets—to negotiate marriage settlements for their daughters, as Franchoise Rohard had done; to distribute their husbands' property to long lists of non-kin, as Marie Le Grand had done; or to buy and sell fish, as Marie Du Bosquiel had done. Thus, in the end, it became unusual for women to claim independent businesses or to assert, as Du Bosquiel had asserted, that they derived these rights from their marital status. It even became improper for women of Du Bosquiel's station to manage fish businesses and, for this reason, rare that they did so.

To argue, therefore, that the Douaisien woman who married by contract was figured as a different being than the woman of custom is not to insist that in their social practices Douaisiens crossed over a huge divide sometime during the late Middle Ages, that women suddenly lost independent property rights or an active role in market production. The move from old to new in Douai appears abrupt in law, but that is simply law's illusion. Social change itself came much more slowly and unevenly. But it came.

Gender Lessons

What changed dramatically in the shift from custom to contract in Douai was the gender code itself. The city's old custom inscribed a notion of womanhood that positioned women as creators of property, as essential elements in a conjugal social and economic unit. The new, in contrast, positioned women as carriers of property, as individuals with economic and social interests distinct from their husbands'. The first woman was thus imagined as competent and valued for her skills if feared for her potential power. The second woman was imagined as not fully competent, as in need of help, protection, and supervision. Valued when obedient, she was feared for her weaknesses—perhaps for her propensity to choose beneficiaries unwisely, as Marie Le Grand or Marie Narrette might have been thought to have done; for her willingness to abandon, even turn on, her former in-laws, as Ysabel Cartoy seemed to have done; for her inability to manage even her own small property as the nameless wife of George Harpin was described as having done.

As clear as the differences in these two codes may be, this does not mean that the new marital property regime itself entirely abandoned the old notions of gender. The regime of contract allowed widows to refuse their reprise and douaire and to stay in the estates of their husbands. For many long years, widows could interpret this right as the right of ravestissement, just as Franchoise Rohard managed to do, but even when the right to stay had been more clearly defined only as usufruct (the douaire coutumier), the new marital property regime preserved a memory of the idea of conjugal unity, simply by allowing women to stay and to manage—if not to own—the bulk of the estate.

Douaisiens were not alone in their attachment to the gender code implied by old custom. Elsewhere in Europe, in Paris or Ghent, for example, law was equally indecisive about whether women were creators or carriers of property.[6] In the marital property systems typical of these cities, the contest between the two notions of womanhood was, however, not staged, as it was in Douai, as a battle between two different systems. It was staged

---

6. For Paris, see Fr. Olivier-Martin, *Histoire de la coutume de la prevoté et vicomté de Paris*, 2 vols., 1922–30 (reprint, Paris: Editions Cujas, 1972), and for Ghent, Marianne Danneel, *Weduwen en wezen in het laat-middeleeuwse Gent* (Leuven and Apeldoorn: Garant, 1995). Paris and Ghent were not, of course, the only places to combine elements of both imaginaries in their customary regimes, and theirs were only two of the many solutions attempted in the late medieval urban North. See chapter 8 for further discussion of French-speaking Europe. The problem was not confined, however, to this region. Cologne provides a particularly revealing example. There, the city governors aggressively sought to enforce a vaguely defined "custom" that treated all marital property as "joint," rather as Douai's old custom treated all property as conjugal. Women in Cologne, however, (particularly those from rich families) regularly sought to subvert this rule, by writing contracts and making other agreements that exempted their marriage goods from the joint property and exempted them from complicity in their husbands' business. See, for Cologne, Marian Matrician, Ph.D. diss., Rutgers University, New Brunswick, N.J. (in progress).

The variety and hybridity of marital property law in this age extends well beyond the northern cities. See, by way of convenient example, the contrast between the systems described by Natalie Zemon Davis, *The Return of Martin Guerre* (Cambridge: Harvard University Press, 1983); Carol F. Karlsen, *The Devil in the Shape of a Woman* (New York: Norton, 1987); and John Hine Mundy, *Men and Women of Toulouse in the Age of the Cathars* (Toronto: Pontifical Institute of Mediaeval Studies, 1990).

as a battle within a single regime. Like the women of Douaisien custom, who were full heirs to all property in the marital estate, widows in these regimes were heirs to at least a part of "community property" (usually defined as movables). But, like the Douaisien women of contract, women in these regimes were only carriers of lineal assets (the *propres*) and had only usufruct rights—at best—to a part of their husbands' propres. Thus, like Douaisien women, these women were caught between two different gender imagineries, positioned both as competent and incompetent, as responsible and irresponsible, as trustworthy and untrustworthy. In these and similar cities too, just as in Douai, the late medieval and early modern period saw the first notion of womanhood lose out to the latter, as propres were increased, as the "community property" account was diminished, or as the widow's claim to either account was restricted in various ways. There too, just as in Douai, the effect was to suppress one notion of womanhood and to give new prominence to another.

As profound as the implications of these changes may have been for gender meanings themselves, this does not mean that the effects of the legal reform in Douai or anywhere else can be evaluated as a contest between men and women, that we can draw up a balance sheet toting up the pluses and minuses for either gender. Matters were by no means so clear. Many women in Douai would surely have welcomed the new protection from irresponsible husbands that the marriage contract and its new separatist regime provided. Other women, it is equally certain, would have resented the new constraints imposed by male kin, children, and in-laws. Similarly, there may have been as many women who would have enjoyed the new clarity about what constituted correct femininity as there were those who would have chafed at the restrictions imposed on their widowhoods.

As a group, men might have been equally ambivalent. Those who had daughters needing marriage gifts would surely have been relieved to know that they would retain claims to the property they contributed to the marriage. Men entering marriages, in contrast, might have resented the limits imposed on them in managing family finances. In the eyes of men as husbands, the new marital property regime must have had other disadvantages as well, for it put them under the control of the previous male generation, usually their own fathers and their fathers-in-law. To be sure, these husbands could look forward to the day that they too could keep a son or son-in-law on a short leash, but to the twenty-five-year-old male, that day must have seemed a long way off.

However we might assess the implications of the legal reform for the relative "status" of women and men—and however difficult we might find it to make any such assessment—it is evident that the reform had significant implications for the meaning of marriage itself. In one sense, we have seen, the legal documents from Douai seem to confirm what other historians have long argued: that in the early modern age, European marriages were being more explicitly defined as voluntary bonds between spouses who regarded their unions not just as the vehicles for full membership in the community but as the principal sites of their emotional lives and the exclusive domains of their sexual lives.[7] Certain themes of this discourse, we have seen, recurred repeatedly in the Douaisien marriage contracts and even in the written ravestissements of the age—the notion that husband and wife had a similar, if not identical, investment in the marriage; the emphasis on parental, especially maternal, duty; and the celebration of conjugal love as the principal cement of marriage.

But, we have also seen, there are many ambiguities and contradictions in this story. These expressions of conjugal ties were voiced precisely as the Douaisien marriage pact was being rewritten as a union among kin, not among husband and wife, and when the social and economic, if not the demographic, nuclearity of the household was being eroded. The new marital property agreement, we have also seen, was figured as a contract between a husband and wife whose economic investments and interests were fundamentally different, even opposed, not ever identical. Thus, in the contracts that set forth the new rules about marital property law, the marriage bargain was depicted as a tense arrangement, the product of long negotiations among many people with competing interests—husband and wife, fathers and mothers, sisters and brothers, grandparents, aunts, uncles, and "amis." It was, moreover, an agreement that reified gender difference and gender hierarchy in a way the old notion of marriage as economic pact did not. While this is not to say that marriage as imagined by old custom was egalitarian with respect to gender—*egalitarian* is not the right word for the radical equivalence imagined by custom—it does point out that the new marital property regime imagined women as fundamentally different from men, not as men's substitutes.

Thus, a particularly useful lesson to be learned by examining the shift in gender meanings implied by Douai's legal reform is that a rhetoric about

7. See notes 18–21 of the introduction for references to this literature.

"affectionate" or "companionate" marriage was not born in the nuclear households of people like Franchoise Rohard and Jehan Le Libert, households where husband and wife were the full heirs of one another, not just of wealth but of the powers to manage wealth and the household it supported. It was not these households that produced documents talking of love, maternal devotion, and mutual accord. To judge from the evidence we have from Douai, we would be compelled to argue exactly the opposite, for talk of love and companionship exploded in Douaisien sources precisely when the old notion of marriage as economic unity was breaking down and when the marriage pact had come to seem insecure, fragile, and uneasy because it was no longer based on equivalence, but on difference. "Love" then became the seal of marriage, not because marriage was being newly constructed as a union between a man and a woman who, as "partners" in a household economy voluntarily chose to make a life together, but precisely because marriage was no longer such a union.

Studying the Douaisien legal reformation provides one further lesson as well. It teaches us to see marital property laws not as literal representations of gender but as efforts to inscribe gender codes, codes that were necessarily unstable and fraught with contradiction. This is not, however, to say that the documents were mere legal fictions. Old custom's assumptions about conjugal unity and the equivalency of male and female in marital property succession reflected the practices of a society in which women could and did behave like Franchoise Rohard and Marie Le Grand. Similarly, the contract that so fundamentally rewrote marital property relations, denying women full responsibility for making or competently managing wealth, accurately described the legal possibilities available women like Marie Du Bosquiel or Ysabel Cartoy.

What we do learn from our analysis of these documents is that none of these women—not Du Bosquiel, Cartoy, Rohard, or Le Grand—perfectly enacted the cultural script written for her in law. Franchoise Rohard was not the ideal deputy husband; Marie Le Grand was hardly the steadfast widow; and neither Marie Du Bosquiel nor Ysabel Cartoy was the docile, inept creature imagined by the marriage contract. And we further see that women's capacities to subvert the law's intention as these women did, to disrupt the narrative of social and gender order in which they were cast, was a product, not of their refusal to obey the law, but of the contradictions within the law. The law, after all, permitted Rohard, Le Grand, Du Bosquiel, and Cartoy the powers they claimed; in fact, the law granted them their powers in the same moment that it labeled them deputy husband or steadfast widow or incompetent manager. It was thanks to this legal sleight of hand that Franchoise Rohard could both manage her husband's estate and endow her own daughter at the expense of her stepchildren; that Marie Du Bosquiel could both protect herself but, had she so chosen, abandon her children to creditors. Each gender image contained in the law was thus Janus-faced. Each had its "good" women: the deputy husbands, docile wives, and protected widows of custom and contract; and each had their evil twins as well: women who used their power over male property to subvert male interests, women who escaped male control when they escaped responsibility for male assets.

The legal records in Douai thus belong as much to a cultural history of gender as to legal history. Like the literary texts of the age that they often so eerily echo, these documents betray the instability of gender codes that seek to link gender meanings to property and to construct gender hierarchy through property relations at a time when property's location and meaning were quite unstable. Reading these legal documents as cultural texts, we might thus say that the characters who populated the comic literature of the day—the merry widows, wicked stepmothers, frivolous consumers, and faithless wives of *fabliaux*, popular drama, and fairy tales—were not, then, just characters in tales that might have been told to Douaisiens. They were characters Douaisiens themselves scripted, for as they drafted contracts, ravestissements par lettre, and wills featuring women such as Rohard and Du Bosquiel, Douaisiens were themselves telling such tales.[8]

The Douaisien legal documents were, however, not just cultural texts, for they bore institutional authority of a particular kind. As Douaisiens shifted away from custom, they were not only implicitly aligning Franchoise Rohard with the wicked stepmothers of fiction, suggesting that she was more *marâtre* than *belle-mère.* They were writing documents that ensured that no widow would henceforth wield Rohard's powers, that Douaisien stepchildren and husbands need no longer fear her displeasure quite as they had. Simultaneously, as Douaisiens wrote contracts that surrounded women with avoués, parens, amis, and plus prochains, they were

---

8. For a useful discussion of the way that legal texts might be read as cultural texts, on how they serve to impose "fixed meaning on social experience in the context of a crisis in which meanings have become indeterminate," see Sarah Maza, "Stories in History: Cultural Narratives in Recent Works in European History," *American Historical Review* 101, no. 5 (December 1996): 1493–1515 (quotation from p. 1500).

not only aligning the Marie Du Bosquiels or Marie Le Grands of their age with the widows of comic literature who were too merry, or the female consumers who were too frivolous. They were creating legal mechanisms that guaranteed that such women would be rendered impotent. The great paradox here is that the new marital property regime constructed a woman who seemed incapable of the discipline required to manage property well and simultaneously positioned her to function in a way that fulfilled its expectations.

Thus, the law produced the very gender code it seemed only to inscribe, making it appear natural that women be supervised and protected. Only because we know that Douaisien women had not always been protected in this way, only because we have been able to witness the labored transition from one conception of female property rights to another, only because we encountered Marie, Franchoise, and their sisters in the archive, do we know how artificial this construction was.

APPENDIX A

The Evolution of Douai's *Douaire Coutumier*

Jacob has argued that the douaire coutumier developed as a substitute for what he calls the *ravestissement sous réserve du contrat*, a cumbersome mechanism adopted by many fifteenth-century Douaisiens to mix old custom with new convention. Couples employing this device first wrote a conventional marriage contract and thereafter a ravestissement par lettre. Some of these ravestissements explicitly referred to the previous contract, implying that the new text treated only those properties not named in the contract, but others were silent about the existence of the prior document or about the exact relationship between the two.[1] The exact meaning of these special ravestissements is not certain, and Jacob has acknowledged that they might have meant different things in different circumstances. Some may have applied only to property not named in the contract, some may even have been intended to override the contract. Jacob is inclined to believe, however, that the ravestissement, despite its name, was not really a grant of old custom's rights, but only a provision of usufruct, whether intended to cover all property or only that not covered by the contract.[2]

We have no direct evidence, however, that this was the meaning of these

1. AMD, FF 585/173 (May 1374), a ravestissement written in 1374 between Colars De Mauhille "caucheteur" (a kind of cloth finisher) and Marguerite Dagre acknowledged a marriage contract written in 1369, before an imperial notary. According to Robert Jacob, *Les époux le seigneur et la cité: Coutume et pratiques matrimoniales des bourgeois et paysans de France du Nord au Moyen Âge* (Brussels: Publications des Facultés Universitaires Saint-Louis 1, 1990), 179 (and n. 307), between 15 and 50 percent of the ravestissements par lettre surviving from samples of marriage agreements taken in the late fourteenth and early fifteenth century were actually ravestissements sous réserve du contrat.

2. See Jacob, *Les époux,* 179–91. Jacob concedes that the ravestissement sous réserve du contrat might have had a different import in origin—that it once granted full ownership rights to the remaining estate, just as the term implies. But he concludes that this peculiar form of the ravestissement was an intermediate step to the douaire coutumier and came, therefore, to be understood as providing only usufruct rights.

strange documents, and, as Jacob acknowledged, there is some rather good evidence suggesting a less tidy shift away from the old notions of ravestissement. The finding in the *Le Libert v. Rohard* suit is a particular case in point. In this instance, the échevins recognized Rohard's right to stay in her husband's estate and to give up the property promised by her marriage contract; and they treated her right to stay as the full right to the customary ravestissement. To judge from this case alone, Douaisiens were, as late as 1435, perfectly willing to allow widows who had married under contract to renounce the contract and claim the old ravestissement. Why not, then, allow the residual assets treated by a ravestissement sous réserve du contrat to follow, as its name suggests, the same principles?

Yet, even if Jacob is too quick to conclude that Douaisiens had by the mid-fifteenth century jettisoned the ravestissement as a residual right—as I am inclined to suspect he is—he is almost certainly correct in his claim that the formal clause of douaire coutumier never implied anything more than usufruct. In fact, he is surely correct that the clause was added to contracts in order to clarify precisely this point, to prevent women such as Franchoise Rohard from claiming the ravestissement as her residual right under contract.

Written Custom and Old Custom in Douai

The first written custom began with a recitation of the old rules, presenting them as though they were uncontested. The first article of Section I announced that in Douai "le mort saisit le vif" (death seizes the living), that the closest heir take all the deceased's property, including patrimonial properties (héritages) in the jurisdiction of Douai, as though no succession had occurred and, therefore, with no liability for death duties ("sans que soit requis faire aulcun actuelle apprehention par relief"). The second article provided that if the marriage had been subject to a ravestissement ("quand deux conjoinctz par mariage ont entre advesty l'un l'aultre par sang ou lettres"), the surviving spouse was the full and absolute heir of all property of any kind ("tous et chacuns les biens, moebles, cateulx et héritages") and that any children of the marriage or, in their absence, any other relatives, had no rights whatsoever in the property ("sans que les enffans procedans duddit mariaige ou, en faulte d'enffans, les parens duddit premier morand y puissent avoir droict en quelque sorte que ce soit"). The third spelled out the rights of the surviving spouse in marriages that had not been made subject to a ravestissement: he or she was to make an equal division of all the property in the conjugal estate, along with its debts, with the heirs of the deceased ("heritiers du premier decendant, de quelque lèz et coste qu'ilz viennent et procedent"). Articles 4 through 12 outlined attendant provisions: all children of the deceased inherited equally in intestate successions; *rapport* (the practice by which previous gifts from an estate are returned before division of the estate among heirs) and *représentation* (the principle by which heirs of an heir represent the heir) were denied, and parents were the heirs of their childless and unmarried children.[1]

It was only in Section V that the new rules of marital property relations made an appearance. This section provided that a widow had forty days to decide

---

1. The text is edited by Robert Jacob, *Les époux, le seigneur et la cité: Coutume et pratiques matrimoniales des bourgeois et paysans de France du Nord au Moyen Âge* (Brussels: Publications des Facultés Universitaires Saint-Louis 1, 1990), Appendix 2.3.

whether to take the douaire coutumier or the douaire conventionnel and required that a widow choosing the former come before the échevins to execute her late husband's will. Somewhat unclear in itself, the passage long confused historians because neither the customary douaire coutumier nor the douaire conventionnel of this section seemed to bear any relationship to the widow's rights described in Section 1: there she was simply the survivor, the heir of the conjugal estate (or half of it in infertile marriages). Jacob has, however, solved the puzzle: Section V, he has shown, had no relationship to Section I, but described a widow who had married under contract, not old custom. The douaire coutumier referred to in the passage was the optional right to stay in a marriage arranged by contract; the douaire conventionnel was the douaire, assene, et amendement, or increase, added to the widow's reprise. Thus, this section in the written custom recorded a stage in Douai's move from the traditions of old custom to the rules of the marriage contract.[2]

Douai's first printed custom, of 1627, even more explicitly undermined old custom. The document retained the two kinds of widow's rights so confusingly combined in the sixteenth-century text: the ravestissement, on the one hand, and the choice between the douaire conventionnel and the douaire coutumier, on the other. It otherwise went much further than its unprinted predecessor, however, in overturning old custom: in this edition, children of a first marriage were guaranteed the properties brought to the marriage by the deceased spouse, in case the surviving spouse of the new marriage were to remarry (the beginnings of the right of dévolution); it ended the possibility that goods left by one spouse could be carried into another marriage by the survivor and shared among the children of that marriage, along with the children of the deceased; it introduced the notions of représentation and rapport, which had been explicitly refused in the first written custom. By the late seventeenth century, the journey was all but complete, and the ravestissement effectively disappeared from Douaisien practice.

Thus, via an extraordinarily twisted route, Douaisiens turned the exception into the rule, turned "convention" (the written act) into "custom" (which in its original meaning is unwritten). It was not an easy journey. Not even the written custumals of the sixteenth and seventeenth century managed to complete the odyssey, for they left Douaisiens suspended between two worlds: either they chose to write a marriage contract, which put their marriage under the rules of new "custom," or they married without a written property agreement, which left their marriage subject to old custom.

2. See Jacob, *Les époux,* for this analysis.

augmentum. The "increase" on the **dot,** which in some regions the widow received on the death of her spouse.

avoués. In early Douasien marriage contracts, avoués served as trustees of the properties that would secure the widowhood of the bride. Later, in contrast, they served only as overseers of the financial affairs of the bride, assigned by the marriage contract between the groom and the bride's legal agent.

biens. Goods—including tools, equipment, jewelry, furnishings, clothing, and cash. In general, *biens* refers to movable goods, but in Douai the term could also be used to include immovables such as houses, warehouses, and sheds. (See also **héritages.**)

chirographes. Separate parchments recording individual acts in the archive of Douai. There, chirographes had three parts, each reproducing the text of the legal agreement; each party to the agreement received one section, and the third was kept by the registrars.

contrats divers. A collection of "various contracts" in the Douaisien municipal archive. The collection consist of quitclaims and records of property transfers.

couvenenche de mariage. A term frequently used in Douai for marriage contracts written in the late Middle Ages.

dévolution. The right of children to claim the chief properties of their parents (the patrimony), which would make up the bulk of their eventual inheritance.

dot. In certain marital property regimes, the property contributed to a marriage by the bride's family and, typically, returned to her at widowhood, sometimes with an increase.

douaire, assene, et amendement. In Douai, the increase on the **reprise,** which was added to the the wife's reprise at the death of her husband. The douaire, assene, et amendement was typically expressed in cash, although it could include real estate or usufruct on real estate.

douaire conventionnel. In Douai, the douaire conventionnel meant the **douaire, assene, et amendement** specified in the marriage contract. A widow could choose either this or the **douaire coutumier.**

douaire coutumier. The usufruct that a widow held on all or a portion of the marital estate or (as in the Parisian regime) on a portion of the husband's goods. In Douai, the widow who had married by contract had the right to choose to stay in the estate and take the douaire coutumier or to take the **douaire conventionnel** specified in the marriage contract.

feme sole (also **femme marchande publique** or **Kauffrau**). A legal convention by which the conjugal fund and assets of the husband were protected from the debts of a wife who maintained a separate business life from the husband.

héritages. The immovable assets of a family. In the classic use, héritages were not supposed to be alienated, since they were imagined as belonging to the family line, not to the particular holder at a given moment.

lez et coste. "Side," that is, the natal kin.

lignage. "Lineage"; as used in Douaisien sources and by most French historians, natal kin.

manse. The land to which an enserfed peasant family had heritable use rights. Though ultimate ownership resided with the lord, the right of the peasant and his heirs to the use of the manse could not be alienated. The transfer of the land from one generation to the next could be taxed. (See also **relief.**)

plus prochains. The closest kin, that is, those first in line to inherit.

portement. The goods that each spouse brought to the marriage under contractual marriage in Douai. In Douaisien contracts, the bride's portement formed the basis of what she would take from the marriage on the death of her spouse (the **reprise**), and it was usually specified. The groom's portement was typically unspecified in the fifteenth century, but later it was more often listed in marriage contracts.

propres. The property that each spouse possessed independently of the conjugal fund, which reverted to the lineage if the possessor died without living heirs. This term was used in the Centre of France (the Isle de France and area surrounding Paris, Orleans, and its environs.)

rapport. The practice by which premortem inheritances were returned to the parental estate before division of the estate.

ravestissement. The legal condition under which property rights in the conjugal fund were transferred to the surviving spouse. The *ravestissement par sang,* which occurred when a wife gave birth to a live child, was part of the customary law of Douai. The *ravestissement par lettre* was a separate document that guaranteed absolute property rights to a widow or widower whether or not their union had produced any heirs.

ravestissement sous réserve du contrat. In the fifteenth century, some

Douaisiens mixed custom with new convention by this mechanism, which entailed first writing a marriage contract and then a ravestissement par lettre, which sometimes referred to the marriage contract. See Appendix A for a full discussion.

relief.   A tax claimed by the lord from the heirs of the deceased.

rent viagère.   A life rent.

reprise.   In Douaisien marriage contracts, the property that reverted to the widow at the death of her husband. Often, the reprise was expressed as the portement.

sourplus (also **surplus** or **residual**).   The property left in an estate after specified distributions from it.

usufruct.   The right of a widow or widower to enjoy the use and profits of property that ultimately belonged to the lineage or offspring of the marriage. Thus, absolute ownership and free disposal of an inheritance did not occur until the death of both parents.

These measures are approximate, intended only to give a general idea of the magnitude of landholdings and rental incomes. They represent values during the late medieval and early modern period, approximately from 1200 to 1600.[1]

bonnier (surface): ca. 1.4 hectares (hectare = ca. 100 sq. meters or ca. 2.47 acres).

couppre (surface and volume): ¼ to ⅕ rasière.

quarrau or **carreau** (surface): ca. 30–40 square meters.

mencaudée (surface): normally taken as ¼ bonnier (i.e., 35 square meters), although some sources put it equal to the rasière or even higher.

mencaud (volume): in Cambrai (in wheat), ca. 56 liters; in Arras (in wheat), ca. 86 liters.

mine (surface): ca. 39 square meters.

mine (volume): in Paris (in wheat), ca. 78 liters; in Hesdin (in wheat), ca. 84 liters.

1. Principal sources for this material include Alain Derville, "Les anciennes mesures à blé du Nord et le Pas-de-Calais," *Cahiers de Métrologie* 7 (1989): 31–42; idem, "Les Mesures de l'avoine au Moyen Age dans le Nord et le Pas-de-Calais," *Cahiers de Métrologie* 11–12 (1993–94): 411–20; Horace Doursther, *Dictionnaire universel des poids et mesures anciens et modernes*, 1840 (reprint, Amsterdam: Meridian Publishers, 1965); Frédéric Godefroy, *Lexique de l'ancien Francais* (Paris: H. Welter, Librairie universitaire, francaise et étrangère, 1901); P. L. Lionet, *Manuel du système métrique ou livre de réduction* (Lille: Vanackers, 1820); and Ronald Edward Zupko, *French Weights and Measures before the Revolution: A Dictionary of Provincial and Local Units* (Bloomington: Indiana University Press, 1978).

muid (volume): in Hesdin (in wheat), ca 12 setiers or 24 mines (ca. 1900 liters); in Arras (in wheat), ca. 16 mencauds (ca. 1400 liters).

rasière (surface): ca. 510 square verges (ca. 45 square meters).

rasière (volume): in Douai (in wheat), ca. 87 liters.

setier (volume): in Hesdin (in wheat), ca. 166 liters; elsewhere smaller.

verge (length): ca. 3 meters.

Primary Sources

Archives Municipales de Douai (AMD) (manuscript)
Séries AA: 38 (Copie de la coutume de 1627).
       97 (Le texte de l'ancienne coutume de Douai, 17ème siècle).
Séries BB: 1–2bis (Registres aux consaulx; 1452–1531).
       12 (Registre aux mémoires; 1491–1520).
       83–95 (Registre aux bourgeois).
Séries FF: 8, 13, 14, 15, 19, 21, 22 (Jurisdiction immédiate des rois de France et d'Espagne, des ducs de Bourgogne et des comtes de Flandre).
       287–88 (Justice échevinale: registres des paix, 1400–77; 1441–1616).
       289–93 (Justice échevinale: registres civiles; 1434–37; 1439–46; 1458–60).
       385–88 (Justice échevinale: registres criminels; 1387–97; 1424–31; 1445–55; 1496–1519).
       393–411 (Registres divers: actes et contrats; 1421–28; 1442–47; 1441–1518 [incomplete]).
       444–50 (Testaments en registre; 1419–95 [incomplete]).
       583–656bis (Contrats de mariage en chirographe; 1228–1648).
       657–860 (Actes et contrats en chirographe; 1224–1575).
       861–89 (Testaments en chirographe; 1228–1574).
       913–15 (Actes en papier; contrats de mariage et ravestissements; 1454–1560).
Séries HH: 223–75 (Archives des métiers; various processes; fifteenth and sixteenth century).

Brereton, Georgine E., and Jane L. M. Ferrier, eds. *Le Menagier de Paris.* Oxford: Clarendon Press, 1981.
Coutumes de la ville et eschevinage de Douay: Confirmées et decretées par le Roy nostre

Sire, Comte de Flandres etc. en l'an de grace mil six cents vingt–sept, le 16. de Septembre. Ghent: Pierre de Goesin, 1777.

de Beaumanoir, Philippe. *Coutumes de Beauvaisis.* Edited by A. Salmon. 3 vols. 1899–1900. Reprint, Paris: A. Picard et fils, 1970–74.

Espinas, Georges, and Henri Pirenne, eds. *Recueil de documents relatifs à l'histoire de l'industrie drapière en Flandre des origines à l'époque Bourguignonne.* 4 vols. Brussels: P. Imbreghts, 1906.

Funck-Bretano, Franz, ed. *Annales Gandenses.* Paris: A. Picard, 1896.

de Sagher, H. E., ed. *Recueil de documents relatifs à l'histoire de l'industrie drapière en Flandre: Deuxième partie, le sud-ouest de la Flandre depuis l'époque Bourguignonne.* 2 vols. Brussels: Kiessling, P. Imbreghts, 1951–56.

Rycher, Jean, ed. *Les quinze joies de mariage.* Geneva: Droz, 1967.

Secondary Sources

Abraham-Thisse, S. "Achats et consommation de draps de laine par l'hôtel de Bourgogne, 1370–1380." In *Commerce, Finances et Société (XIe–XVIe siècles): Recueil de travaux d'histoire médiévale offert à M. le professeur Henri Dubois,* edited by P. Contamine, T. DuTour, and B. Schnerb. Paris: Presses de l'Université de Paris-Sorbonne, 1993.

Anderson, Perry. *Lineages of the Absolutist State.* London: Verso, 1979.

Appadurai, A. Introduction to "Commodities and the Politics of Value." In *The Social Life of Things: Commodities in Cultural Perspective,* edited by A. Appadurai. Cambridge: Cambridge University Press, 1986.

Arnade, Peter. "City, State and Public Ritual in the Late Medieval Burgundian Netherlands." *Comparative Studies in Society and History* (forthcoming).

———. *Realms of Ritual: Burgundian Ceremony and Civic Life in Late Medieval Ghent.* Ithaca, N.Y.: Cornell University Press, 1996.

Aston, T. H., and C. H. E. Philpin, eds. *The Brenner Debate: Agrarian Class Structure and Economic Development in Pre-industrial Europe.* Cambridge: Cambridge University Press, 1985.

Atkinson, Clarissa W. *The Oldest Vocation: Christian Motherhood in the Middle Ages.* Ithaca, N.Y.: Cornell University Press, 1991.

Baur, Paul. *Testament und Bürgerschaft: Alltagsleben und Sachkultur im spätmittelalterlichen Konstanz.* Vol. 31 of *Konstanzer Geschichts- und Rechtsquellen.* Sigmaringen: J. Thorbecke, 1989.

Bell, R. M. *How To Do It.* Forthcoming.

Bellomo, Manlio. *The Common Legal Past of Europe, 1000–1800.* Translated by Lydia G. Cochrane. Vol. 4 of *Studies in Medieval and Early Modern Canon Law.* Washington, D.C.: Catholic University of America Press, 1995.

Bideau, Alain. "A Demographic and Social Analysis of Widowhood and Remarriage: The Example of the Castellany of Thoissey-en-Dombes, 1670–1840." *Journal of Family History* 5, no. 1 (Spring 1980): 28–43.

Bigwood, G. "Gand et la circulation des grains en Flandre du XVIe au XVIIe siècle." *Vierteljahrschrift für Sozial- und Wirtschaftsgeschichte* 4 (1906): 397–460.

Bloch, Marc. *Feudal Society.* Translated by L. A. Manyon. Chicago: University of Chicago Press, 1961.

Blockmans, Fr. *Het Gentsche Stadspatricaat tot omstreeks 1302.* Antwerp: de Sikkel, 1938.

Boone, Marc, and Walter Prevenier, eds. *La draperie ancienne des Pays-Bas: Débouchés et stratégies de survie (14e–16e siècle).* Leuven and Apeldoorn: Garant, 1993.

Bourdieu, Pierre. "Normes et déviances: Les stratégies matrimoniales dans le système de reproduction." *Annales E.S.C.* 27 (1972): 1105–25.

Bresc, Henri. "Europe: Town and Country (Thirteenth–Fifteenth Century)." In *A History of the Family,* edited by André Burguière et al., vol. 1, 430–66. Cambridge: Polity and Blackwell, 1996.

Britnell, R. H. *The Commercialization of English Society, 1000–1500.* Cambridge: Cambridge University Press, 1993.

Brundage, James. *Law, Sex, and Christian Society in Medieval Europe.* Chicago: University of Chicago Press, 1987.

Brunner, Otto. *Land and Lordship: Structures of Governance in Medieval Austria.* Translated from the 4th revised edition by Howard Kaminsky and James van Horn Melton. Philadelphia: University of Pennsylvania Press, 1992.

Bulst, N. "Zum Problem städtischer und territorialer Kleider-, Aufwands- und Luxusgesetzgebung in Deutschland, 13.–Mitte 16. Jahrhundert." In *Renaissance du pouvoir législatif et genèse de l'état,* edited by A. Gouron and A. Rigaudière. Montpellier: Publications de la Société d'Histoire du Droit et des Institutions des Anciens Pays de Droit Ecrit, 1988.

Burguière, André, et al., eds. *History of the Family.* 2 vols. Cambridge: Polity and Blackwell, 1996.

Chaytor, Miranda. "Household and Kinship: Ryton in the Late Sixteenth and Seventeenth Centuries." *History Workshop* 10 (1980): 25–60.

Chevrier, G. "Sur quelques caractères de l'histoire du régime matrimonial dans la Bourgogne ducale aux diverse phases de son développement." In *Les droits des gens mariés,* 257–85, vol. 27 of *Mémoires de la Société pour l'Histoire du Droit et des Institutions des anciens pays bourguignons, comtois et romands.* Dijon: Faculté de droit des sciences économiques de Dijon, 1966.

Chiffoleau, Jacques. *La comptabilité de l'au-delà: Les hommes, la mort et la religion dans la région d'Avignon à la fin du moyen âge,* vol. 47 of *Collection de l'école française de Rome.* Paris: Diffusion de Boccard, 1980.

Chojnaki, Stanley. "Dowries and Kinsmen in Early Renaissance Venice." *Journal of Interdisciplinary History* 5 (1975): 571–600.

———. "Marriage Legislation and Patrician Society in Fifteenth Century Venice." In *Law, Custom, and the Social Fabric in Medieval Europe: Essays in Honor of Bryce Lyon,* edited by Bernard S. Bachrach and David Nicholas. Kalamazoo, Mich.: Medieval Institute Publications, 1990.

———. " 'The Most Serious Duty': Motherhood, Gender, and Patrician Culture in Renaissance Venice." In *Refiguring Women: Perspectives on Gender and the Italian Renaissance,* edited by Marilyn Migiel and Julian Schiesari. Ithaca, N.Y.: Cornell University Press, 1991.

———. "The Power of Love: Wives and Husbands in Late Medieval Venice." In *Women and Power in the Middle Ages,* edited by Mary Erler and Maryanne Kowaleski. Athens, Ga.: University of Georgia Press, 1988.

Chorley, Patrick. "The Cloth Exports of Flanders and Northern France during the Thirteenth Century: A Luxury Trade?" *Economic History Review* 40 (1987): 347–79.

———. "The 'Draperies légères' of Lille, Arras, Tournai, Valenciennes: New Materials for New Markets? In *La draperie ancienne des Pays-Bas: Débouchés et stratégies de survie (14e–16e siècles),* edited by Marc Boone and Walter Prevenier. Leuven and Apeldoorn: Garant, 1993.

Cohn, Samuel K., Jr. *Death and Property in Siena, 1205–1800: Strategies for the Afterlife.* Baltimore: Johns Hopkins University Press, 1988.

Comaroff, John, ed. *The Meaning of Marriage Payments.* London: Academic Press, 1980.

Dalle, D. "De bevolking van de stad Veurne in de 17e–18e eeuw." *Handelingen van het Genootschap voor Geschiedenis 'Société d' Emulation' te Brugge* 106 (1969): 49–139.

Danneel, Marianne. *Weduwen en wezen in het laat-middeleeuwse Gent.* Leuven and Apeldoorn: Garant, 1995.

Darton, Robert. "A Bourgeois Orders His World." In *The Great Cat Massacre and Other Episodes in French Cultural History.* Harmondsworth: Penguin, 1985.

Davis, Natalie Zemon, *The Return of Martin Guerre.* Cambridge: Harvard University Press, 1983.

Delumeau, Jean, and Daniel Roche, eds. *Histoires des pères et de la paternité.* Paris: Larousse, 1990.

de Poerck, G. *La draperie médiévale en Flandre et en Artois.* 3 vols., nos. 110–12 of *Werken uitgegeven door de faculteit van de wijsbegeerte en letteren, Rijksuniversiteit te Gent.* Bruges: De Tempel, 1951.

Deregnaucourt, Jean-Pierre. "Autour de la mort à Douai: Attitudes, pratiques et croyances, 1250–1500." Ph.D. diss., Université Catholique de Lille, 1993.

———. "Le dernier voyage: L'ambulation funèbre à Douai aux 14e et 15e siècles." In *La sociabilité urbaine en Europe du Nord-Ouest du XIVe au XVIIIe siècles:*

Actes du Colloque 5 février 1983; Mémoires de la Société d'Agriculture, Sciences et Arts de Douai, 5th ser., vol. 8. Douai: Lefebvre-L'évêque, 1983.

———. "Les derniers voluntés d'un échevin douaisien à la fin du XIVe siècle," *Amis de Douai*, 5th ser., 7 (1977–80): 163–67.

———. "L'élection de sépulture d'après les testaments douaisiens (1295–1500)," *Revue du Nord* 65 (1983): 343–52.

———. "La piété et son décor à Douai du XIVe au XVe siècle." *Amis de Douai*, 5th ser., 8 (1980–83): 175–78.

———. "La symbolique et sa signification dans le discours testamenaire des bourgeois de Douai à la fin du Moyen-Age." *Amis de Douai*, 5th ser., 7 (1977–80): 224–29.

———. "Le testament: Un reflect de la conjoncture sanitaire, individuelle et collective—l'exemple de Douai au bas Moyen-Age." *Revue du terroir* 24 (1985): 117–29.

Derville, Alain. "Les anciennes mesures à blé du Nord et le Pas-de-Calais." *Cahiers de Métrologie* 7 (1989): 31–42.

———. *Douze ètudes d'histoire rurale: Flandre, Artois, Cambrésis au moyen âge*. In *Revue du Nord, Hors Série: Collection Histoire 11*. Lille: Université Charles-de-Gaulle-Lille 3, 1996.

———. "Les draperies flamandes et artésiennes, vers 1250–1350." *Revue du Nord* 54, no. 215 (1972): 353–70.

———. "Les échevins de Douai (1228–1527)." In *La sociabilité urbaine en Europe du Nord-Ouest du XIVe au XVIIIe siècles: Actes du Colloque 5 février 1983; Mémoires de la Société d'Agriculture, Sciences et Arts de Douai*, 5th ser., vol. 8. Douai: Lefebvre-L'évêque, 1983.

———. "Le grenier des Pays-Bas médiévaux." *Revue du Nord* 69, no. 273 (1987): 267–80.

———. "L'héritage des draperies médiévales." *Revue du Nord* 69, no. 275 (1987): 715–24.

———. "Les Mesures de l'avoine au Moyen Age dans le Nord et le Pas-de-Calais." *Cahiers de Métrologie* 11–12 (1993–94): 411–20.

———. "Le nombre d'habitants des villes de l'Artois et de la Flandre Wallonne (1300–1450)." *Revue du Nord* 65, no. 257 (1983): 277–99.

Desquiens, Jean Charles. "Douai, topographie et société de 1224 à 1374, d'après un fonds d'archives particulier ou 'Du parchemin à l'ordinateur.'" 4 vols. Ph.D. diss., Université de Paris, 1994.

Dhérent, Catherine. "Abondance et crises: Douai, ville frontiére 1250–1375." 3 vols. Ph.D. diss., Université de Paris, 1993.

———. "L'assise sur le commerce des draps à Douai en 1304." *Revue du Nord* 65, no. 257 (1983):369–97.

———. "Histoire sociale de la bourgeoisie de Douai de 1280 à 1350." Ph.D. diss., Ecole des Chartes, 1981.

Diefendorf, Barbara B. "Give Us Back Our Children: Patriarchal Authority and Parental Consent to Religious Vocation in Early Counter-Reformation France." *The Journal of Modern History* 68, no. 2 (June 1996): 265–308.

———. *Paris City Councillors in the Sixteenth Century: The Politics of Patrimony.* Princeton: Princeton University Press, 1983.

———. "Widowhood and Remarriage in Sixteenth-Century Paris." *Journal of Family History* 7, no. 4. (Winter 1982): 379–95.

Dirks, Nicholas B., Geoff Eley, and Sherry B. Ortner, eds. *Culture/Power/ History.* Princeton: Princeton University Press, 1993.

Donahue, Charles, Jr. "What Causes Fundamental Legal Ideas? Marital Property in England and France in the Thirteenth Century." *Michigan Law Review* 78 (1979–80): 59–88.

Doursther, Horace. *Dictionnaire universel des poids et mesures anciens et modernes.* 1840. Reprint, Amsterdam: Meridian Publishers, 1965.

Duby, Georges. *The Knight, The Lady, and The Priest.* Chicago: University of Chicago Press, 1993.

———. *Love and Marriage in the Middle Ages.* Cambridge: Polity Press, 1994.

———. *Medieval Marriage.* Baltimore: Johns Hopkins University Press, 1978.

Dulumeau, Jean, and Daniel Roche, eds. *Histoire des pères et de la paternité.* Paris: Larousse, 1990.

Dupâquier, J., E. Hélin, P. Laslett, M. Livi-Bacci, and S. Sogner. *Mariage et remariage dans les populations du passé.* Academic Press: London, 1981.

Duplessis, Robert. *Lille and the Dutch Revolt.* Cambridge: Cambridge University Press, 1991.

Epstein, Steven. *Wills and Wealth in Medieval Genoa, 1150–1250.* Cambridge: Harvard University Press, 1984.

Espinas, Georges. *Les finances de la commune de Douai des origines au XVe siècle.* 2 vols. Paris: A. Picard et fils, 1902.

———. "Jehan Boine Broke: Bourgeois et drapier Douaisien." *Vierteljahrschrift für Sozial- und Wirtschaftsgeschichte* 2 (1904): 382–412.

———. *Les origines du capitalisme.* 4 vols. Lille: E. Raoust, 1933–49.

———. *La vie urbaine de Douai au moyen-âge.* 4 vols. Paris: A. Picard et fils, 1913.

Evergates, Theodore. *Feudal Society in the Baillage of Troyes under the Counts of Champagne, 1152–1284.* Baltimore: Johns Hopkins University Press, 1975.

———. *Feudal Society in Medieval France.* Philadelphia: University of Pennsylvania Press, 1993.

Farr, James R. *Hands of Honor: Artisans and Their World in Dijon, 1550–1650.* Ithaca, N.Y.: Cornell University Press, 1988.

Favarger, Dominique. *Le régime matrimonial dans le comté de Neuchâtel du XVe au XIXe siècle.* Neuchâtel: Editions Ides et Calendes, 1970.

*La Femme: Recueils de la société de Jean Bodin pour l'histoire comparative des institu-
tions.* Vols. 11–13. Brussels: Editions de la librarie encyclopédique, 1959–62.

Flandrin, Jean-Louis. *Familles, parentés, maison, sexualité dans l'ancien société.*
Paris: Hachette, 1976.

Fossier, Robert. "The Feudal Era (Eleventh–Thirteenth Century)." In *A History
of the Family,* edited by André Burguière et al., vol. 1. Cambridge: Polity and
Blackwell, 1996.

Fujii, Yoshio. "Draperie urbaine et draperie rurale dans les Pays-Bas méridionaux
au bas moyen âge: Une mise au point des recherches après H. Pirenne." *Journal
of Medieval History* 16, no. 1 (1990): 77–97.

Gaspard, A. "Etude sur les testaments de bourgeois et oppidains de Huy de 1263
à 1480." Master's thesis, Université de Liège, 1976–77.

Giesey, Ralph E., "Rules of Inheritance and Strategies of Mobility in Prerevolutionery France." *American Historical Review* 82, no. 2 (1977): 271–89.

Gilissen, Jean. "Le statut de la femme dans l'ancien droit belge." In *La Femme,
Recueils de la Société de Jean Bodin pour l'histoire comparative des institutions,*
vol. 12. Brussels: Editions de la librarie encyclopédique, 1962.

Godart, J. "Contribution à l'étude de l'histoire du commerce des grains à Douai
du XIVe au XVIIe siècle." *Revue du Nord* 27 (1944): 171–205.

Godding, Philippe. *Le droit privé dans les Pays-Bas meridinionaux du 12e au 18e
siècle.* In *Mémoires de la Classe des Lettres, Collection in 4°,* 2d ser., pt. 1. Brussels:
Académie royale de Belgique, 1987.

———. "Le droit au service du patrimoine familial: Les Pays Bas méridionaux
(12e–18e siècles)." In *Marriage, Property and Succession,* edited by L. Bonfield,
vol. 10 of *Comparative Studies in Continental and Anglo-American Legal History.*
Berlin: Duncker and Humbolt, 1992.

———. "La pratique testamentaire en Flandre au 13e siècle." *Tijdschrijft voor
Rechtsgeschiedenis* 58 (1990): 281–300.

Godefroy, Frédéric. *Lexique de l'ancien Francais.* Paris: H. Welter, Librairie universitaire, française et étrangère, 1901.

Goldthwaite, Richard A. *Wealth and the Demand for Art in Italy, 1300–1600.*
Baltimore: Johns Hopkins University Press, 1993.

Goody, Jack. *The Development of the Family and Marriage in Europe.* Cambridge:
Cambridge University Press, 1983.

———. *Production and Reproduction: Aa Comparative Study of the Domestic Domain.* Cambridge: Cambridge University Press, 1976.

Goody, Jack, Joan Thirsk, and E. P. Thompson, eds. *Family and Inheritance:
Rural Society in Western Europe 1200–1800.* Cambridge: Cambridge University
Press, 1976.

Greilsammer, Myriam. *L'envers du tableau: Mariage et maternité en Flandre médiévale.* Paris: Armand Colin, 1990.

Hajnal, J. "European Marriage Patterns in Perspective." In *Population in History:*

Essays in Historical Demography, edited by D. V. Glass and D. E. C. Eversley. London: E. Arnold, 1965.

Haller, William, and Malleville Haller. "The Puritan Art of Love." *Huntington Library Quarterly* 5, no. 2 (1941–42): 235–72.

Hanawalt, Barbara. "Remarriage as an Option for Urban and Rural Widows in Late Medieval England." In *Wife and Widow: The Experiences of Women in Medieval England,* edited by S. Walker. Ann Arbor: University of Michigan Press, 1993.

———. *The Ties That Bound: Peasant Families in Medieval England.* Oxford: Oxford University Press, 1986.

———. *Women and Work in Preindustrial Europe.* Bloomington: Indiana University Press, 1986.

Hanley, Sarah. "Engendering the State: Family Formation and State Building in Early Modern France." *French Historical Studies* 16, no. 1 (Spring 1989): 4–27.

———. "Family and State in Early Modern France: 'The Marriage Pact.'" In *Connecting Spheres: Women in the Western World, 1500 to the Present,* edited by Marilyn J. Boxer and Jean H. Quataert, 53–63. New York and Oxford: Oxford University Press, 1987.

Harris, Barbara J. *Of Noble and Gentle Birth.* Oxford: Oxford University Press. Forthcoming.

Harte, Negley, ed. *The New Draperies.* Oxford: Oxford University Press, 1997.

Henry, Louis. "Schémas de nuptialité: Déséquilibre des sexes et age au remariage." *Population* 6 (1969): 1067–1122.

———. "Schémas de nuptialité: Déséquilibre des sexes et célibat." *Population* 3 (1969): 457–86.

Herlihy, David. "Family." *American Historical Review* 96, no. 1 (1991): 1–16.

———. *Medieval Households.* Cambridge: Harvard University Press, 1985.

Hilaire, Jean. *Le régime des biens entre époux dans la région de Montpellier du début du XIIIe siècle à la fin du XVIe siècle: Contribution aux études d'histoire du droit écrit.* Montpellier: Causse, Graille and Castelnau, 1957.

———. "Vie en commun: Famille et esprit communautaire." *Nouvelle Revue historique de droit française et étranger,* 4th ser., 51 (1973): 8–53.

Houlbrooke, Richard. *The English Family 1450–1700.* London: Longman, 1984.

Howell, Martha. "Achieving the Guild Effect Without Guilds: Crafts and Craftsmen in Late Medieval Douai." In *Les métiers au moyen âge: Aspects économiques et sociaux,* edited by J.-P. Sosson, 109–28. Louvain-la-Neuve: Publications de l'Institute d'Etudes Médiévales, 1994.

———. "Citizen-clerics in Late Medieval Douai." In *Statuts individuels, statuts corporatifs et statuts judicaires dans les villes européennes (moyen âge et temps modernes),* edited by Marc Boone and Maarten Prak. Leuven and Apeldoorn: Garant, 1996.

———. "Fixing Movables: Gifts by Testament in Late Medieval Douai." *Past and Present* 150 (February 1996): 3–45.

———. "Weathering Crisis, Managing Change: The Emergence of a New Socioeconomic Order in Douai at the End of the Middle Ages." In *La draperie ancienne des Pays-Bas: Débouchés et stratégies de survie (14e–16e siècles),* edited by Marc Boone and Walter Prevenier. Leuven and Apeldoorn: Garant, 1993.

———. *Women, Production, and Patriarchy in Late Medieval Cities.* Chicago: University of Chicago Press, 1986.

Howell, Martha, and Marc Boone. "Becoming Early Modern in the Late Medieval Low Countries: Ghent, Douai, and the Late Medieval Crisis." *Urban History* 23, pt. 3 (December 1996): 300–24.

Hughes, Diane Owen. "From Brideprice to Dowry in Mediterranean Europe." *Journal of Family History* 3 (Fall 1978): 262–96.

———. "Regulating Women's Fashions." In *History of Women in the West,* edited by C. Klapisch-Zuber. Cambridge: Belknap Press, Harvard University Press, 1992.

———. "Sumptuary Law and Social Relations in Renaissance Italy." In *Disputes and Settlements: Law and Human Relations in the West.* Cambridge: Cambridge University Press, 1983.

Hull, Suzanne W. *Women According to Men: The World of Tudor-Stuart Women.* Walnut Creek, Calif.: AltaMira Press, 1996.

Huppert, George. *After the Black Death.* Bloomington: University of Indiana Press, 1986.

———. *Les bourgeois gentilhommes.* Chicago: University of Chicago Press, 1977.

Jacob, Robert. "La Charte d'Hesdin (1243) et la vocation successorale du conjoint survivant dans les pays picard et wallon." *Tijdschrift voor Rechtsgeschiedenis* 50 (1982): 351–70.

———. *Les époux, le seigneur et la cité: Coutume et pratiques matrimoniales des bourgeois et paysans de France du Nord au Moyen Age.* Brussels: Publications des Facultés Universitaires Saint-Louis 1, 1990.

———. "Les structures patrimoniales de la conjugalité au moyen-âge dans la France du Nord: Essai d'histoire comparée des époux nobles et routiers dans les pays du groupe de coutumes 'picard-wallon.'" Ph.D. diss., Université de Paris 2, 1984.

Karlsen, Carol F. *The Devil in the Shape of a Woman.* New York: Norton, 1987.

Kelso, Ruth. *Doctrine for the Lady of the Renaissance.* Urbana: University of Illinois Press, 1956.

Kirshner, Julius. "Wives' Claims Against Insolvent Husbands in Late Medieval Italy." In *Women of the Medieval World,* edited by Julius Kirshner and Suzanne F. Wempel. Oxford: Oxford University Press, 1985.

Klapisch-Zuber, Christine. *Women, Family, and Ritual in Renaissance Italy.* Translated by Lydia Cochrane. Chicago: University of Chicago Press, 1985.

Kriedte, Peter. *Peasants, Landlords and Merchant Capitalists.* Lemington Spa, Warwickshire: Berg, 1983.

Kuehn, Thomas. "Law, Death and Heirs in the Renaissance: Repudiation of Inheritance in Florence." *Renaissance Quarterly* 65, no. 3 (Autumn 1992): 484–517.

———. *Law, Family, and Women.* Chicago: University of Chicago Press, 1991.

Lafon, Jacques. *Les époux bordelais 1450–1550: Régimes matrimoniaux et mutations sociales.* Paris: S.E.V.P.E.N., 1972.

Laslett, Peter, and Richard Wall, eds. *Household and Family in Past Time: Comparative Studies in the Size and Structure of the Domestic Group over the Last Three Centuries in England, France, Serbia, Japan and Colonial North America, with Further Materials from Western Europe.* Cambridge: Cambridge University Press, 1972.

Laurent, Henri. *Un grand commerce d'exportation au moyen âge.* Paris: Librairie E. Droz, 1935.

Le Goff, Jacques. "Histoire médiévale et histoire du droit: Un dialogue difficile." In *Storia sociale e dimensione giuridica: Strumenti d'indagine et ipotesi de lavoro; Atti dell'incontro di studio, Firenze, 26–27 aprile 1985.* Milan: Giuffre, 1986.

Leites, Edmond. "The Duty to Desire: Love, Friendship, and Sexuality in Puritan Theories of Marriage." *Journal of Social History* 15, no. 3 (Spring 1982): 383–408.

Lepointe, G. "L'évolution de la communauté entre époux dans la ville de Lille." *Revue historique de droit français et étranger,* 4th ser., 8 (1929): 524–68.

———. *La famille dans l'ancien droit.* 2d ed. Paris: Editions Domat-Montchrestien, 1947.

Le Roy Ladurie, Emmanuel. "Family Structure and Inheritance Customs in Sixteenth Century France." In *Family and Inheritance: Rural Society in Western Europe 1200–1800,* edited by Jack Goody, Joan Thirsk, and E. P. Thompson. Cambridge: Cambridge University Press, 1976.

———. *Montaillou, village occitan de 1294 à 1324.* Paris: Gallimard, 1975.

Lévi-Strauss, Claude. *The Elementary Structures of Kinship.* Translated by J. H. Bell and J. R. von Sturmer, edited by R. Needham. Boston: Beacon Press, 1969.

Lionet, P. L. *Manuel du système métrique ou livre de réduction.* Lille: Vanackers, 1820.

Little, Lester. *Religious Poverty and the Profit Economy in Medieval Europe.* Ithaca, N.Y.: Cornell University Press, 1978.

MacFarlane, Alan. *Marriage and Love in England: Modes of Reproduction, 1380–1840.* Oxford: Blackwell, 1986.

Matrician, Marian. Ph.D. diss., Rutgers University, New Brunswick, N.J. In progress.

Mauss, Marcel. *The Gift*. London: Routledge, 1990.

Maza, Sarah. "Stories in History: Cultural Narratives in Recent Works in European History." *American Historical Review* 101, no. 5 (December 1996): 1493–1515.

Meijers, E. M. "Le droit ligurien de succession." *Tijdschrift voor Rechtsgeschiedenis* 5 (1924): 16–32.

———. *Le droit ligurien de succession*. 4 vols. Haarlem: H. D. Tjeenk Willink & Zoon, 1928–36.

Mestayer, Monique. "Les contrats du mariage à Douai du XIIème au Xvème siècle, reflets du droit et de la vie d'une société urbaine." *Revue du Nord* 61, no. 241 (1979): 353–79.

———. "Les fêtes et cérémonies à Douai 1450–1550." In *La sociabilité urbaine en Europe du Nord-Ouest du XIVe au XVIIIe siècles: Actes du Colloque 5 février 1983; Mémoires de la Société d'Agriculture, Sciences et Arts de Douai*, 5th ser., vol. 8. Douai: Lefebvre-L'évêque, 1983.

———. "Le prix du blé et de l'avoine de 1329 à 1793." *Revue du Nord* 45 (1963): 157–76.

———. "Testaments douaisiens antérieurs à 1270." *Nos Patois du Nord* 7 (1962): 64–77.

Meury, Joseph, and Joël Sorre. *La Fresnais 1525–1802*. Alet, France: Alet Chamber of Commerce, 1985.

Minet, M. "Les inscriptions du registre aux bourgeois de Douai au XV siècle, 1399–1506." Master's thesis, Université Catholique de Louvain-la-Neuve, 1973.

Miskimin, Harry. *The Economy of Early Renaissance Europe, 1300–1460*. Cambridge: Cambridge University Press, 1975.

———. *The Economy of Later Renaissance Europe, 1460–1600*. Cambridge: Cambridge University Press, 1977.

Mitterauer, Michael, and Reinhard Sieder. *The European Family: Patriarchy to Partnership from the Middle Ages to the Present*. Translated by Karla Oosterveen and Manfred Horzinger. Chicago: University of Chicago Press, 1983.

Molho, Anthony. *Marriage Alliance in Late Medieval Florence*. Cambridge: Harvard University Press, 1994.

Mousnier, Roland. *Les hiérarchies sociales de 1450 à nos jours*. Paris: Presses universitaires de France, 1969.

Mundy, John, Hine. *Men and Women at Toulouse in the Age of the Cathars*. Toronto: Pontifical Institute of Mediaeval Studies, 1990.

Munro, John H. "Anglo-Flemish Competition in the International Cloth Trade, 1350–1500." In *L'Angleterre et les pays bourguignons (XIVe–XVIe siècles): Relations et comparisons (XVe–XVIe s.); Actes du 35e Rencontres du Centre Européen D'études Bourguignonnes, Oxford 1994*, 37–60. Neuchâtel: Centre Européen D'études Bourguignonnes, 1995.

———. "The Flemish 'New Draperies': The Death and Resurrection of an Old

Industry, 14th to 17th Centuries." In *The New Draperies*, edited by N. B. Harte. Oxford: Oxford University Press, 1997.

————. "Industrial Protectionism in Medieval Flanders: Urban or National?" In *The Medieval City*, edited by H. A. Miskimin, D. Herlihy, and A. L. Udovitch. New Haven: Yale University Press, 1977.

————. "Industrial Transformations in the North-West European Textile Trades, c. 1290–c. 1340: Economic Progress or Economic Crisis?" In *Before the Black Death: Studies in the "Crisis" of the Early Fourteenth Century*, edited by Bruce M. S. Campbell. Manchester: Manchester University Press, 1991.

————. "The Medieval Scarlet and the Economics of Sartorial Splendor." In *Cloth and Clothing in Medieval Europe: Essays in Memory of Professor E. M. Carus-Wilson*, edited by N. B. Harte and K. G. Ponting, no. 2 of *Passold Studies in Textile History*, 13–70. London: Heinemann Education Books, 1983.

————. "Medieval Woollens: Textiles, Textile Technology, and Industrial Organization, c. 800–1500." In *The Cambridge History of Western Textiles*. Cambridge: Cambridge University Press. In press.

————. "Medieval Woollens: The West European Woollen Industries and Their Struggles for International Markets, c. 1000–1500." In *The Cambridge History of Western Textiles*. Cambridge: Cambridge University Press. In press.

————. "Wool-Price Schedules and the Qualities of English Wools in the Later Middle Ages c. 1270–1499." *Textile History* 9 (1978): 118–69.

Nicholas, David. *Medieval Flanders*. London: Longman, 1992.

Olivier-Martin, Fr. *Histoire de la coutume de la prevoté et vicomté de Paris*. 2 vols. 1922–1930. Reprint. Paris: Editions Cujas, 1972.

Ourliac, Paul. "Histoire nouvelle et histoire du droit." *Revue historique de droit français et étranger*. 70, no. 3 (1992): 363–71.

Ourliac, Paul, and Jean-Louis Gazzaniga. *Histoire du droit privé français de l'an mil au Code civil*. Paris: A. Michel, 1985.

Ourliac, Paul, and Jehan de Malafosse. *Le droit familial*. Vol. 3 of *Histoire du droit privé*. Paris: Presses universitaires de France, 1968–1971.

Ozment, Steven. *When Fathers Ruled: Family Life in Reformation Europe*. Cambridge: Harvard University Press, 1983.

————, ed. *Magdalena and Balthasar: An Intimate Portrait of Life in 16th Century Europe*. New York: Simon and Schuster, 1986

Petot, P., and A. Vandenbossche. "Le statut de la femme dans les pays coutumier français du XIIIe au XVIIe siècle." In *La femme: Recueils de la Société de Jean Bodin pour l'histoire comparative des institutions*, vol. 12. Brussels: Editions de la librarie encyclopédique, 1962.

Pirenne, Henri. *Early Democracies in the Low Countries*. 1963. Reprint, New York: Harper and Row, 1969.

————. *Histoire de Belgique.* 4 vols. Brussels: Renaissance du Livre, 1972–75.

————. "Stages in the Social History of Capitalism." *American Historical Review* 19 (1914): 494–514.

Polanyi, Karl. *The Great Transformation.* Boston: Beacon Press, 1957.

Pollock, Sir Frederick, and Frederic William Maitland. *The History of English Law before the Time of Edward I.* 2d ed. London: Cambridge University Press, 1968.

Poudret, J. F. "La situation du conjoint survivant en pays de Vaud XIIIe–XVIe siècle." In *Mémoires de la Société pour l'histoire du droit des institutions des anciens pays bourguignons, comtois et romands,* vol. 27. Dijon: Faculté de droit des sciences économiques de Dijon, 1966.

Prevenier, Walter, and Wim Blockmans. *The Burgundian Netherlands.* Cambridge: Cambridge University Press, 1986.

Rainey, Ronald. "Dressing Down the Dressed Up: Reproving Feminine Attire in Renaissance Florence." In *Renaissance Culture and Society: Essays in Honor of Eugene F. Rice, Jr.,* edited by J. Monfasani and R. G. Musto, 217–39. New York: Italica Press, 1991.

Roper, Lyndal. *The Holy Household.* Oxford: Clarendon Press, 1989.

Rössler, Hellmuth, ed. *Deutsches Patriziät 1430–1740: Schriften zur Problematik der deutschen Führungsschichten in der Neuzeit.* Vol 3. Limburg/Lahn, Netherlands: C. A. Starke, 1968.

Rouche, M., and Pierre Demolon, eds. *Histoire de Douai.* Vol. 9 of *Collection histoire des villes du Nord/Pas-de-Calais,* edited by Y. M. Hilaire. Dunkirk: Westhoek-Editions, 1985.

Sabean, David. "Aspects of Kinship and Property in Western Europe before 1800." In *Family and Inheritance: Rural Society in Western Europe 1200–1800,* edited by Jack Goody, Joan Thirsk, and E. P. Thompson. Cambridge: Cambridge University Press, 1976.

Safley, Thomas Max. *Let No Man Put Asunder: The Control of Marriage in the German Southwest, A Comparative Study, 1550–1600.* In *Sixteenth Century Essays and Studies.* Kirksville, Mo.: Sixteenth Century Journal Publishers, Northeast Missouri State University, 1984.

Schmelzeisen, G. K. *Die Rechtsstellung der Frau in der deutschen Stadtwirtscaft.* Vol. 10 of *Arbeiten zur deutschen Rechts- und Verfassungsgeschichte.* Stuttgart: W. Kohlhammer, 1935.

Schmitt, Georg. *Die Schlüsselgewalt der Ehefrau nach deutschen Recht.* 1893.

Schneider, Jane. "Peacocks and Penguins: The Political Economy of European Cloth and Colors." *American Ethnologist* 5 (1978): 413–48.

Segalen, Martine. *Historical Anthropology of the Family.* New York: Cambridge University Press, 1986.

Seibt, Ferdinand, and Winfried Eberhard. eds., *Europa 1400: Die Krise des Spätmittelalters.* Stuttgart: Klett-Cotta, 1984.

Simons, Walter. "Begijnen en begarden in het middeleeuwse Dowaai." *Jaarboek De Franse Nederlanden* 17 (1992): 180–97.

———. "The Beguine Movement in the Southern Low Countries: A Reassessment." *Bulletin de l'Institut historique belge de Rome* 50 (1989): 63–105.

Soliday, Gerald Lymon. *A Community in Conflict: Frankfurt Society in the Seventeenth and Early Eighteenth Centuries.* Hanover, N.H.: University Press of New England, 1974.

Soly, Hugo. "The 'Betrayal' of the 16th-Century Bourgeoisie: A Myth?" *Acta historiae Neerlandicae* 8 (1979): 262–80.

Sortor, Marci. "Saint-Omer and Its Textile Trades in the Late Middle Ages: A Contribution to the Proto-Industrialization Debate." *American Historical Review* 98, no. 5. (1993): 1475–99.

Spufford, Peter. *Handbook of Medieval Exchange.* London: Royal Historical Society, 1986.

Stone, Lawrence. *The Family, Sex and Marriage in England 1500–1800.* Abridged edition. Harmondsworth, England: Penguin Books, 1985.

Tits-Dieuaide, M.-J. "Le grain et le pain dans l'administration des villes de Brabant et de Flandre au moyen-âge." In *Actes du 11e colloque international "L'initiative publique des communes en Belgique": Fondements historiques (Ancien Régime), Spa, 1–4 September 1982,* no. 65 of *Crédit Communal de Belgique collection d'histoire,* série in 8°. Brussels: Crédit Communal de Belgique, 1984.

Todd, B. "The Remarrying Widow: A Stereotype Reconsidered." In *Women in English Society, 1500–1800,* edited by M. Prior. London: Routledge, 1985.

Ulrich, Laural Thatcher. *Goodwives: Image and Reality in the Lives of Women in Northern New England, 1650–1750.* New York: Oxford University Press, 1982.

Van der Wee, Herman. "Industrial Dynamics and the Process of Urbanization and De-urbanization in the Low Countries from the Late Middle Ages to the Eighteenth Century: A Synthesis." In *The Rise and Decline of Urban Industries in Italy and the Low Countries: Late Middle Ages and Early Modern Times,* edited by Herman Van der Wee, 323–27. Leuven: Leuven University Press, 1988.

———. "Structural Changes and Specialization in the Industry of the Southern Netherlands, 1100–1600." *Economic History Review* 28 (1975): 203–21.

van Nieuwenhuysen, A. *Les finances du duc de Bourgogne, Philippe Le Hardi (1384–1404): Economie et politique.* Brussels: Editions de l'Université de Bruxelles, 1984.

———. *Les finances du duc de Bourgogne, Philippe Le Hardi (1384–1404): Le montant des ressources.* Brussels: Palais des Academies, 1990.

van Werveke, Hans. *Ambachten en erflijkheid.* Vol. 4 , no. 1 of *Mededeelingen van de Koninklijke Vlaamsche Academie voor Wetenschappen, Letteren en Schoone Kunsten van België, Klasse der Letteren.* Brussels: Erasmus, 1942.

Verhulst, Adriaan. *Histoire du paysage rural en Flandre*. Brussels: La Renaissance du livre, 1966.

———. "La laine indigène dans les anciens Pays-Bas entre le xii et le xvii siècle." *Revue historique* 14 (1972): 281–322.

von Brandt, Ashaver. "Mittelalterliche Bürgertestamente: Neuerschlossene Quellen zur Geschichte der materiellen und geistigen Kultur." In *Sitzungsberichte der Heidelberger Akademie der Wissenschaft, philosophisch-historische Klasse*, 5–32. Heidelberg: C. Winter, 1973.

Watt, Jeffrey R. *The Making of Modern Marriage: Matrimonial Control and the Rise of Sentiment in Neuchâtel, 1550–1800*. Ithaca, N.Y.: Cornell University Press, 1992.

Weber, Max. *The City*. Translated and edited by Don Martinale and Gertrud Neuwirth. New York: Free Press, 1958.

Wiesner, Merry. *Women and Gender in Early Modern Europe*. Cambridge: Cambridge University Press, 1993.

Wiltenburg, Joy. *Disorderly Women and Female Power in the Street Literature of Early Modern England and Germany*. Charlottesville: University of Virginia Press, 1992.

Yver, Jean. "Les caractères originaux du groupe de coutumes de l'oeust de la France." *Revue historique de droit français et étranger*, 4th ser., no. 30 (1952): 18–79.

———. "Les deux groupes de coutumes du Nord." *Revue du Nord* 35, no. 140 (1953): 197–220.

———. "Les deux groupes de coutumes du Nord." *Revue du Nord* 36, no. 141 (1954): 5–36.

———. *Egalité entre héritiers et exclusion des enfants dotés: Essai de géographie coutumière*. Paris: Editions Sirey, 1966.

Zupko, Ronald Edward. *French Weights and Measures before the Revolution: A Dictionary of Provincial and Local Units*. Bloomington: Indiana University Press, 1978.